D0052938

CONFESSIONS

of an

ECONOMIC

HIT MAN

"Here are the real-life details—nasty, manipulative, plain evil—of international corporate skullduggery spun into a tale rivaling the darkest espionage thriller."

—GREG PALAST, author of *The Best Democracy Money Can Buy*

JOHN PERKINS

Author of *THE SECRET OF AN AMERICAN EMPIRE*

Praise for John Perkins's
Confessions of an Economic Hit Man

"This riveting look at a world of intrigue reads like a spy novel . . . Highly recommended."
—*Library Journal*

"One of the most important nonfiction works of the year, if not the decade . . . A gripping page-turner."
—*New York Spirit*

"A bombshell. One of those rare instances in which someone deeply entrenched in our governmental/corporate imperialist structure has come forward to reveal in unequivocal terms its inner workings. A work of great insight and moral courage."
—John E. Mack, Harvard professor and
Pulitzer Prize–winning author of
A Prince of Our Disorder: The Life of T. E. Lawrence

"Perkins combines the brilliance and suspense of a Graham Greene thriller with the authority of his insider vantage point to tell a true, powerful, revealing, and bone-chilling personal story that names names, and connects the dots."
—David Korten, author of the bestselling
When Corporations Ruled the World

"Stunning and groundbreaking . . . A must-read for anyone who cares about the world."
—Lynne Twist, global activist and author of
the bestselling *The Soul of Money*

"Provocative and disturbing . . . This book succeeds as a wake-up call because the reader cannot help but assess his or her role on a personal level, thus providing an impetus for change."
—R. Paul Shaw, former lead economist and current program advisor,
Human Development Group, World Bank Institute

"A fascinating insider's view of how private multinational companies legally rob the poor of the third world, country after country."
—Josh Mailman, cofounder, the Threshold Foundation,
the Social Venture Network, and Business for Social Responsibility

"With unflinching honesty, Perkins narrates his moral awakening and struggle to break free from the corrupt system of global domination he himself helped to create. This book . . . comes from the heart. I highly recommend it."
—Michael Brownstein, author of *World on Fire*

"A thrilling story . . . The true account of a deeply dedicated and courageous man."
—Stephan Rechtschaffen, MD, cofounder, board chairperson,
and senior advisor, Omega Institute, and author of *Timeshifting*

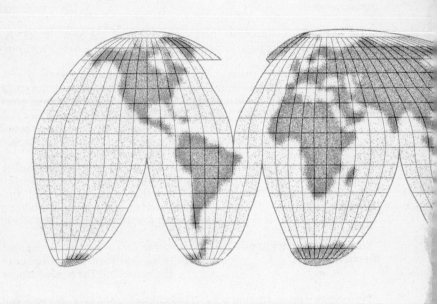

Confessions of an Economic Hit Man

John Perkins

A PLUME BOOK

PLUME
Published by Penguin Group
Penguin Group (USA) Inc., 375 Hudson Street, New York, New York 10014, U.S.A.
Penguin Group (Canada), 90 Eglinton Avenue East, Suite 700, Toronto, Ontario,
Canada M4P 2Y3 (a division of Pearson Penguin Canada Inc.)
Penguin Books Ltd., 80 Strand, London WC2R 0RL, England
Penguin Ireland, 25 St. Stephen's Green, Dublin 2, Ireland (a division of Penguin Books Ltd.)
Penguin Group (Australia), 250 Camberwell Road, Camberwell, Victoria 3124,
Australia (a division of Pearson Australia Group Pty. Ltd.)
Penguin Books India Pvt. Ltd., 11 Community Centre, Panchsheel Park,
New Delhi - 110 017, India
Penguin Group (NZ), 67 Apollo Drive, Rosedale, North Shore 0745,
Auckland, New Zealand (a division of Pearson New Zealand Ltd.)
Penguin Books (South Africa) (Pty.) Ltd., 24 Sturdee Avenue,
Rosebank, Johannesburg 2196, South Africa

Penguin Books Ltd., Registered Offices: 80 Strand, London WC2R 0RL, England

Published by Plume, a member of Penguin Group (USA) Inc. This is an authorized reprint of a
hardcover edition published by Berrett-Koehler Publishers, Inc. For information address Berrett-
Koehler Publishers, Inc., 235 Montgomery Street, Suite 650, San Francisco, CA 94104-2916.

First Plume Printing, January 2006
30 29 28 27 26 25 24 23 22 21

Copyright © John Perkins, 2004

 REGISTERED TRADEMARK—MARCA REGISTRADA

The Library of Congress has catalogued the Berrett-Koehler edition as follows:

Perkins, John 1945–
Confessions of an economic hit man / by John Perkins.
    p.   cm.
Includes bibliographical references and index.
ISBN 1-57675-301-8 (hc.)
ISBN 978-0-452-28708-2 (pbk.)
1. Perkins, John. 1945–   2. United States. National Security Agency—Biography.
3. Economists—United States—Biography.   4. Energy consultants—United States—
Biography.   5. Intelligence agents—United States—Biography.   6. Chas. T. Main, Inc.
7. World Bank—Developing countries.   8. Corporations, American—Foreign countries.
9. Corporations, American—Corrupt practices.
10. Imperialism—History—20th century.   11. Imperialism—History—21st century   I. Title.
UB271.U52P47 2004
332'.042'092—dc22   2004045353

Printed in the United States of America

To my mother and father, Ruth Moody and Jason Perkins,
who taught me about love and living and instilled
in me the courage that enabled me
to write this book.

⊕ CONTENTS

35 Piercing the Veneer 249

*Economic hit men (EHMs) are highly paid profession-
als who cheat countries around the globe out of tril-
lions of dollars. They funnel money from the World
Bank, the U.S. Agency for International Development
(USAID), and other foreign "aid" organizations into
the coffers of huge corporations and the pockets of a few
wealthy families who control the planet's natural resources. Their tools include fraudulent financial reports, rigged elections, payoffs, extortion, sex, and
murder. They play a game as old as empire, but one
that has taken on new and terrifying dimensions during this time of globalization.*

I should know; I was an EHM.

I wrote that in 1982, as the beginning of a book with the working
title, *Conscience of an Economic Hit Man*. The book was dedicated
to the presidents of two countries, men who had been my clients,
whom I respected and thought of as kindred spirits—Jaime
Roldós, president of Ecuador, and Omar Torrijos, president of
Panama. Both had just died in fiery crashes. Their deaths were not
accidental. They were assassinated because they opposed that fraternity of corporate, government, and banking heads whose goal
is global empire. We EHMs failed to bring Roldós and Torrijos
around, and the other type of hit men, the CIA-sanctioned jackals
who were always right behind us, stepped in.

I was persuaded to stop writing that book. I started it four more
times during the next twenty years. On each occasion, my decision to

begin again was influenced by current world events: the U.S. invasion of Panama in 1989, the first Gulf War, Somalia, the rise of Osama bin Laden. However, threats or bribes always convinced me to stop.

In 2003, the president of a major publishing house that is owned by a powerful international corporation read a draft of what had now become *Confessions of an Economic Hit Man*. He described it as "a riveting story that needs to be told." Then he smiled sadly, shook his head, and told me that since the executives at world headquarters might object, he could not afford to risk publishing it. He advised me to fictionalize it. "We could market you in the mold of a novelist like John Le Carré or Graham Greene."

But this is not fiction. It is the true story of my life. A more courageous publisher, one not owned by an international corporation, has agreed to help me tell it.

This story *must* be told. We live in a time of terrible crisis—and tremendous opportunity. The story of this particular economic hit man is the story of how we got to where we are and why we currently face crises that seem insurmountable. This story must be told because only by understanding our past mistakes will we be able to take advantage of future opportunities; because 9/11 happened and so did the second war in Iraq; because in addition to the three thousand people who died on September 11, 2001, at the hands of terrorists, another twenty-four thousand died from hunger and related causes. In fact, twenty-four thousand people die every single day because they are unable to obtain life-sustaining food.[1] Most important, this story must be told because today, for the first time in history, one nation has the ability, the money, and the power to change all this. It is the nation where I was born and the one I served as an EHM: the United States of America.

What finally convinced me to ignore the threats and bribes?

The short answer is that my only child, Jessica, graduated from college and went out into the world on her own. When I recently told her that I was considering publishing this book and shared my fears with her, she said, "Don't worry, dad. If they get you, I'll take over where you left off. We need to do this for the grandchildren I hope to give you someday!" That is the short answer.

The longer version relates to my dedication to the country where I was raised, to my love of the ideals expressed by our Founding Fathers, to my deep commitment to the American republic that today promises "life, liberty, and the pursuit of happiness" for all people, everywhere, and to my determination after 9/11 not to sit idly by any longer while EHMs turn that republic into a global empire. That is the skeleton version of the long answer; the flesh and blood are added in the chapters that follow.

This is a true story. I lived every minute of it. The sights, the people, the conversations, and the feelings I describe were all a part of my life. It is my personal story, and yet it happened within the larger context of world events that have shaped our history, have brought us to where we are today, and form the foundation of our children's futures. I have made every effort to present these experiences, people, and conversations accurately. Whenever I discuss historical events or re-create conversations with other people, I do so with the help of several tools: published documents; personal records and notes; recollections—my own and those of others who participated; the five manuscripts I began previously; and historical accounts by other authors, most notably recently published ones that disclose information that formerly was classified or otherwise unavailable. References are provided in the endnotes, to allow interested readers to pursue these subjects in more depth. In some cases, I combine several dialogues I had with a person into one conversation to facilitate the flow of the narrative.

My publisher asked whether we actually referred to ourselves as economic hit men. I assured him that we did, although usually only by the initials. In fact, on the day in 1971 when I began working with my teacher Claudine, she informed me, "My assignment is to mold you into an economic hit man. No one can know about your involvement—not even your wife." Then she turned serious. "Once you're in, you're in for life."

Claudine's role is a fascinating example of the manipulation that underlies the business I had entered. Beautiful and intelligent, she was highly effective; she understood my weaknesses and used them to her greatest advantage. Her job and the way she executed it exemplify the subtlety of the people behind this system.

Claudine pulled no punches when describing what I would be called upon to do. My job, she said, was "to encourage world leaders to become part of a vast network that promotes U.S. commercial interests. In the end, those leaders become ensnared in a web of debt that ensures their loyalty. We can draw on them whenever we desire—to satisfy our political, economic, or military needs. In turn, they bolster their political positions by bringing industrial parks, power plants, and airports to their people. The owners of U.S. engineering/construction companies become fabulously wealthy."

Today we see the results of this system run amok. Executives at our most respected companies hire people at near-slave wages to toil under inhuman conditions in Asian sweatshops. Oil companies wantonly pump toxins into rain forest rivers, consciously killing people, animals, and plants, and committing genocide among ancient cultures. The pharmaceutical industry denies lifesaving medicines to millions of HIV–infected Africans. Twelve million families in our own United States worry about their next meal.[2] The energy industry creates an Enron. The accounting industry creates an Andersen. The income ratio of the one-fifth of the world's population in the wealthiest countries to the one-fifth in the poorest went from 30 to 1 in 1960 to 74 to 1 in 1995.[3] The United States spends over $87 billion conducting a war in Iraq while the United Nations estimates that for less than half that amount we could provide clean water, adequate diets, sanitation services, and basic education to every person on the planet.[4]

And we wonder why terrorists attack us?

Some would blame our current problems on an organized conspiracy. I wish it were so simple. Members of a conspiracy can be rooted out and brought to justice. This system, however, is fueled by something far more dangerous than conspiracy. It is driven not by a small band of men but by a concept that has become accepted as gospel: the idea that all economic growth benefits humankind and that the greater the growth, the more widespread the benefits. This belief also has a corollary: that those people who excel at stoking the fires of economic growth should be exalted and rewarded, while those born at the fringes are available for exploitation.

The concept is, of course, erroneous. We know that in many countries economic growth benefits only a small portion of the population and may in fact result in increasingly desperate circumstances for the majority. This effect is reinforced by the corollary belief that the captains of industry who drive this system should enjoy a special status, a belief that is the root of many of our current problems and is perhaps also the reason why conspiracy theories abound. When men and women are rewarded for greed, greed becomes a corrupting motivator. When we equate the gluttonous consumption of the earth's resources with a status approaching sainthood, when we teach our children to emulate people who live unbalanced lives, and when we define huge sections of the population as subservient to an elite minority, we ask for trouble. And we get it.

In their drive to advance the global empire, corporations, banks, and governments (collectively the *corporatocracy*) use their financial and political muscle to ensure that our schools, businesses, and media support both the fallacious concept and its corollary. They have brought us to a point where our global culture is a monstrous machine that requires exponentially increasing amounts of fuel and maintenance, so much so that in the end it will have consumed everything in sight and will be left with no choice but to devour itself.

The corporatocracy is not a conspiracy, but its members do endorse common values and goals. One of corporatocracy's most important functions is to perpetuate and continually expand and strengthen the system. The lives of those who "make it," and their accoutrements—their mansions, yachts, and private jets—are presented as models to inspire us all to consume, consume, consume. Every opportunity is taken to convince us that purchasing things is our civic duty, that pillaging the earth is good for the economy and therefore serves our higher interests. People like me are paid outrageously high salaries to do the system's bidding. If we falter, a more malicious form of hit man, the jackal, steps to the plate. And if the jackal fails, then the job falls to the military.

This book is the confession of a man who, back when I was an EHM, was part of a relatively small group. People who play similar roles are more abundant now. They have more euphemistic titles, and they walk the corridors of Monsanto, General Electric, Nike, General Motors, Wal-Mart, and nearly every other major corporation in the world. In a very real sense, *Confessions of an Economic Hit Man* is their story as well as mine.

It is your story too, the story of your world and mine, of the first truly global empire. History tells us that unless we modify this story, it is guaranteed to end tragically. Empires never last. Every one of them has failed terribly. They destroy many cultures as they race toward greater domination, and then they themselves fall. No country or combination of countries can thrive in the long term by exploiting others.

This book was written so that we may take heed and remold our story. I am certain that when enough of us become aware of how we are being exploited by the economic engine that creates an insatiable appetite for the world's resources, and results in systems that foster slavery, we will no longer tolerate it. We will reassess our role in a world where a few swim in riches and the majority drown in poverty, pollution, and violence. We will commit ourselves to navigating a course toward compassion, democracy, and social justice for all.

Admitting to a problem is the first step toward finding a solution. Confessing a sin is the beginning of redemption. Let this book, then, be the start of our salvation. Let it inspire us to new levels of dedication and drive us to realize our dream of balanced and honorable societies.

Without the many people whose lives I shared and who are described in the following pages, this book would not have been written. I am grateful for the experiences and the lessons.

Beyond them, I thank the people who encouraged me to go out on a limb and tell my story: Stephan Rechtschaffen, Bill and Lynne Twist, Ann Kemp, Art Roffey, so many of the people who participated in Dream Change trips and workshops, especially my co-facilitators, Eve Bruce, Lyn Roberts-Herrick, and Mary Tendall, and my incredible wife and partner of twenty-five years, Winifred, and our daughter Jessica.

I am grateful to the many men and women who provided personal insights and information about the multinational banks, international corporations, and political innuendos of various countries, with special thanks to Michael Ben-Eli, Sabrina Bologni, Juan Gabriel Carrasco, Jamie Grant, Paul Shaw, and several others, who wish to remain anonymous but who know who they are.

Once the manuscript was written, Berrett-Koehler founder Steven Piersanti not only had the courage to take me in but also devoted endless hours as a brilliant editor, helping me to frame and reframe the book. My deepest thanks go to Steven, to Richard Perl, who introduced me to him, and also to Nova Brown, Randi Fiat, Allen Jones, Chris Lee, Jennifer Liss, Laurie Pellouchoud, and Jenny Williams, who read and critiqued the manuscript; to David Korten, who not only read and critiqued it but also made me jump through hoops to satisfy his high and excellent standards; to Paul Fedorko, my agent; to Valerie Brewster for crafting the book design; and to Todd Manza, my copy editor, a wordsmith and philosopher extraordinaire.

A special word of gratitude to Jeevan Sivasubramanian, Berrett-Koehler's managing editor, and to Ken Lupoff, Rick Wilson, María Jesús Aguiló, Pat Anderson, Marina Cook, Michael Crowley, Robin Donovan, Kristen Frantz, Tiffany Lee, Catherine Lengronne, Dianne

Platner—all the BK staff who recognize the need to raise consciousness and who work tirelessly to make this world a better place.

When Plume and the Penguin Group committed to making this book available in paperback, its staff worked diligently to create this new version, including additional material. I am eternally grateful to my editor, Emily Haynes, for taking such a strong interest from the very beginning, as well as for her patience with me and her talents as an editor and diplomat; Trena Keating, Editor in Chief; Brant Janeway, Director of Publicity; Norina Frabotta and Abigail Powers, Production Editors; Aline Akelis, Director of Subrights; Jaya Miceli, designer of the powerful new cover; and Gretchen Swartley, Marketing Coordinator. The Plume and Berrett-Koehler people coordinated beatifully and, along with Paul Fedorko, dedicated themselves to the common goal of getting this message out to more people, with a special emphasis on high school and college students.

I must thank all those men and women who worked with me at MAIN and were unaware of the roles they played in helping EHM shape the global empire; I especially thank the ones who worked for me and with whom I traveled to distant lands and shared so many precious moments. Also Ehud Sperling and his staff at Inner Traditions International, publisher of my earlier books on indigenous cultures and shamanism, and good friends who set me on this path as an author.

I am eternally grateful to the men and women who took me into their homes in the jungles, deserts, and mountains, in the cardboard shacks along the canals of Jakarta, and in the slums of countless cities around the world, who shared their food and their lives with me and who have been my greatest source of inspiration.

John Perkins
August 2004

Quito, Ecuador's capital, stretches across a volcanic valley high in the Andes, at an altitude of nine thousand feet. Residents of this city, which was founded long before Columbus arrived in the Americas, are accustomed to seeing snow on the surrounding peaks, despite the fact that they live just a few miles south of the equator.

The city of Shell, a frontier outpost and military base hacked out of Ecuador's Amazon jungle to service the oil company whose name it bears, is nearly eight thousand feet lower than Quito. A steaming city, it is inhabited mostly by soldiers, oil workers, and the indigenous people from the Shuar and Kichwa tribes who work for them as prostitutes and laborers.

To journey from one city to the other, you must travel a road that is both tortuous and breathtaking. Local people will tell you that during the trip you experience all four seasons in a single day.

Although I have driven this road many times, I never tire of the spectacular scenery. Sheer cliffs, punctuated by cascading waterfalls and brilliant bromeliads, rise up one side. On the other side, the earth drops abruptly into a deep abyss where the Pastaza River, a headwater of the Amazon, snakes its way down the Andes. The Pastaza carries water from the glaciers of Cotopaxi, one of the world's highest active volcanoes and a deity in the time of the Incas, to the Atlantic Ocean over three thousand miles away.

In 2003, I departed Quito in a Subaru Outback and headed for Shell on a mission that was like no other I had ever accepted. I was hoping to end a war I had helped create. As is the case with so many things we EHMs must take responsibility for, it is a war that is virtually unknown anywhere outside the country where it is fought. I was on my way to meet with the Shuars, the Kichwas, and their neighbors the Achuars, the Zaparos, and the Shiwiars—tribes determined to prevent our oil companies from destroying their homes, families, and lands, even if it means they must die in the process. For them, this is a war about the survival of their children and cultures, while for us it is about power, money, and natural resources. It is one part of the struggle for world domination and the dream of a few greedy men, global empire.[1]

That is what we EHMs do best: we build a global empire. We are an elite group of men and women who utilize international financial organizations to foment conditions that make other nations subservient to the corporatocracy running our biggest corporations, our government, and our banks. Like our counterparts in the Mafia, EHMs provide favors. These take the form of loans to develop infrastructure—electric generating plants, highways, ports, airports, or industrial parks. A condition of such loans is that engineering and construction companies from our own country must build all these projects. In essence, most of the money never leaves the United States; it is simply transferred from banking offices in Washington to engineering offices in New York, Houston, or San Francisco.

Despite the fact that the money is returned almost immediately to corporations that are members of the corporatocracy (the creditor), the recipient country is required to pay it all back, principal plus interest. If an EHM is completely successful, the loans are so large that the debtor is forced to default on its payments after a few years. When this happens, then like the Mafia we demand our pound of flesh. This often includes one or more of the following: control over United Nations votes, the installation of military bases, or access to precious resources such as oil or the Panama Canal. Of course, the debtor still owes us the money—and another country is added to our global empire.

Driving from Quito toward Shell on this sunny day in 2003, I thought back thirty-five years to the first time I arrived in this part of the world. I had read that although Ecuador is only about the size of Nevada, it has more than thirty active volcanoes, over 15 percent of the world's bird species, and thousands of as-yet-unclassified plants, and that it is a land of diverse cultures where nearly as many people speak ancient indigenous languages as speak Spanish. I found it fascinating and certainly exotic; yet, the words that kept coming to mind back then were *pure, untouched,* and *innocent.*

Much has changed in thirty-five years.

At the time of my first visit in 1968, Texaco had only just discovered petroleum in Ecuador's Amazon region. Today, oil accounts for nearly half the country's exports. A trans-Andean pipeline built shortly after my first visit has since leaked over a half million barrels of oil into the fragile rain forest —more than twice the amount spilled by the Exxon *Valdez.*[2] Today, a new $1.3 billion, three hundred–mile pipeline constructed by an EHM–organized consortium promises to make Ecuador one of the world's top ten suppliers of oil to the United States.[3] Vast areas of rain forest have fallen, macaws and jaguars have all but vanished, three Ecuadorian indigenous cultures have been driven to the verge of collapse, and pristine rivers have been transformed into flaming cesspools.

During this same period, the indigenous cultures began fighting back. For instance, on May 7, 2003, a group of American lawyers representing more than thirty thousand indigenous Ecuadorian people filed a $1 billion lawsuit against ChevronTexaco Corp. The suit asserts that between 1971 and 1992 the oil giant dumped into open holes and rivers over four million gallons per day of toxic wastewater contaminated with oil, heavy metals, and carcinogens, and that the company left behind nearly 350 uncovered waste pits that continue to kill both people and animals.[4]

Outside the window of my Outback, great clouds of mist rolled in from the forests and up the Pastaza's canyons. Sweat soaked my shirt, and my stomach began to churn, but not just from the intense tropical heat and the serpentine twists in the road. Knowing the part I had played in destroying this beautiful country was once again taking its toll. Because of my fellow EHMs and me, Ecuador is in far worse shape today than she was before we introduced her to the miracles of modern economics, banking, and engineering. Since 1970, during this period known euphemistically as the Oil Boom, the official poverty level grew from 50 to 70 percent, under- or unemployment increased from 15 to 70 percent, and public debt increased from $240 million to $16 billion. Meanwhile, the share of national resources allocated to the poorest segments of the population declined from 20 to 6 percent.[5]

Unfortunately, Ecuador is not the exception. Nearly every country we EHMs have brought under the global empire's umbrella has suffered a similar fate.[6] Third world debt has grown to more than $2.5 trillion, and the cost of servicing it—over $375 billion per year as of 2004—is more than all third world spending on health and education, and twenty times what developing countries receive annually in foreign aid. Over half the people in the world survive on less than two dollars per day, which is roughly the same amount they received in the early 1970s. Meanwhile, the top 1 percent of third world households accounts for 70 to 90 percent of all private financial wealth and real estate ownership in their country; the actual percentage depends on the specific country.[7]

The Subaru slowed as it meandered through the streets of the beautiful resort town of Baños, famous for the hot baths created by underground volcanic rivers that flow from the highly active Mount Tungurahgua. Children ran along beside us, waving and trying to sell us gum and cookies. Then we left Baños behind. The spectacular scenery ended abruptly as the Subaru sped out of paradise and into a modern vision of Dante's *Inferno*.

A gigantic monster reared up from the river, a mammoth gray wall. Its dripping concrete was totally out of place, completely unnatural and incompatible with the landscape. Of course, seeing it there should not have surprised me. I knew all along that it would be waiting in ambush. I had encountered it many times before and in the past had praised it as a symbol of EHM accomplishments. Even so, it made my skin crawl.

That hideous, incongruous wall is a dam that blocks the rushing Pastaza River, diverts its waters through huge tunnels bored into the mountain, and converts the energy to electricity. This is the 156-megawatt Agoyan hydroelectric project. It fuels the industries that make a handful of Ecuadorian families wealthy, and it has been the source of untold suffering for the farmers and indigenous people who live along the river. This hydroelectric plant is just one of many projects developed through my efforts and those of other EHMs. Such projects are the reason Ecuador is now a member of the global empire, and the reason why the Shuars and Kichwas and their neighbors threaten war against our oil companies.

Because of EHM projects, Ecuador is awash in foreign debt and must devote an inordinate share of its national budget to paying this off, instead of using its capital to help the millions of its citizens officially classified as dangerously impoverished. The only way Ecuador can buy down its foreign obligations is by selling its rain forests to the oil companies. Indeed, one of the reasons the EHMs set their sights on Ecuador in the first place was because the sea of oil beneath its Amazon region is believed to rival the oil fields of the Middle East.[8] The global empire demands its pound of flesh in the form of oil concessions.

These demands became especially urgent after September 11, 2001, when Washington feared that Middle Eastern supplies might cease. On top of that, Venezuela, our third-largest oil supplier, had recently elected a populist president, Hugo Chávez, who took a strong stand against what he referred to as U.S. imperialism; he threatened to cut off oil sales to the United States. The EHMs had failed in Iraq and Venezuela, but we had succeeded in Ecuador; now we would milk it for all it is worth.

Ecuador is typical of countries around the world that EHMs have brought into the economic-political fold. For every $100 of crude taken out of the Ecuadorian rain forests, the oil companies receive $75. Of the remaining $25, three-quarters must go to paying off the foreign debt. Most of the remainder covers military and other government expenses—which leaves about $2.50 for health, education, and programs aimed at helping the poor.[9] Thus, out of every $100 worth of oil torn from the Amazon, less than $3 goes to the people who need the money most, those whose lives have been so adversely impacted by the dams, the drilling, and the pipelines, and who are dying from lack of edible food and potable water.

All of those people—millions in Ecuador, billions around the planet—are potential terrorists. Not because they believe in communism or anarchism or are intrinsically evil, but simply because they are desperate. Looking at this dam, I wondered—as I have so often in so many places around the world—when these people would take action, like the Americans against England in the 1770s or Latin Americans against Spain in the early 1800s.

The subtlety of this modern empire building puts the Roman centurions, the Spanish conquistadors, and the eighteenth- and nineteenth-century European colonial powers to shame. We EHMs are crafty; we learned from history. Today we do not carry swords. We do not wear armor or clothes that set us apart. In countries like Ecuador, Nigeria, and Indonesia, we dress like local schoolteachers and shop owners. In Washington and Paris, we look like government bureaucrats and bankers. We appear humble, normal. We visit project sites and stroll through impoverished villages. We profess altruism, talk with local papers about the wonderful humanitarian things we are doing. We cover the conference tables of government committees with our spreadsheets and financial projections, and we lecture at the Harvard Business School about the miracles of macroeconomics. We are on the record, in the open. Or so we portray ourselves and so are we accepted. It is how the system works. We seldom resort to anything illegal because the system itself is built on subterfuge, and the system is by definition legitimate.

However—and this is a very large caveat—if we fail, an even more sinister breed steps in, ones we EHMs refer to as the jackals, men who trace their heritage directly to those earlier empires. The jackals are always there, lurking in the shadows. When they emerge, heads of state are overthrown or die in violent "accidents."[10] And if by chance the jackals fail, as they failed in Afghanistan and Iraq, then the old models resurface. When the jackals fail, young Americans are sent in to kill and to die.

As I passed the monster, that hulking mammoth wall of gray concrete rising from the river, I was very conscious of the sweat that soaked my clothes and of the tightening in my intestines. I headed on down into the jungle to meet with the indigenous people who are determined to fight to the last man in order to stop this empire I helped create, and I was overwhelmed with feelings of guilt.

How, I asked myself, did a nice kid from rural New Hampshire ever get into such a dirty business?

PART I: 1963–1971

CHAPTER 1

An Economic Hit Man Is Born

It began innocently enough.

I was an only child, born into the middle class in 1945. Both my parents came from three centuries of New England Yankee stock; their strict, moralistic, staunchly Republican attitudes reflected generations of puritanical ancestors. They were the first in their families to attend college—on scholarships. My mother became a high school Latin teacher. My father joined World War II as a Navy lieutenant and was in charge of the armed guard gun crew on a highly flammable merchant marine tanker in the Atlantic. When I was born, in Hanover, New Hampshire, he was recuperating from a broken hip in a Texas hospital. I did not see him until I was a year old.

He took a job teaching languages at Tilton School, a boys' boarding school in rural New Hampshire. The campus stood high on a hill, proudly—some would say arrogantly—towering over the town of the same name. This exclusive institution limited its enrollment to about fifty students in each grade level, nine through twelve. The students were mostly the scions of wealthy families from Buenos Aires, Caracas, Boston, and New York.

My family was cash starved; however, we most certainly did not see ourselves as poor. Although the school's teachers received very little salary, all our needs were provided free: food, housing, heat, water, and the workers who mowed our lawn and shoveled our snow. Beginning on my fourth birthday, I ate in the prep school dining room, shagged balls for the soccer teams my dad coached, and handed out towels in the locker room.

It is an understatement to say that the teachers and their wives felt superior to the locals. I used to hear my parents joking about being the lords of the manor, ruling over the lowly peasants—the townies. I knew it was more than a joke.

My elementary and middle school friends belonged to that peasant class; they were very poor. Their parents were dirt farmers, lumberjacks, and mill workers. They resented "the preppies on the hill," and in turn, my father and mother discouraged me from socializing with the townie girls, who they called "tarts" and "sluts." I had shared schoolbooks and crayons with these girls since first grade, and over the years, I fell in love with three of them: Ann, Priscilla, and Judy. I had a hard time understanding my parents' perspective; however, I deferred to their wishes.

Every year we spent the three months of my dad's summer vacation at a lake cottage built by my grandfather in 1921. It was surrounded by forests, and at night we could hear owls and mountain lions. We had no neighbors; I was the only child within walking distance. In the early years, I passed the days by pretending that the trees were knights of the Round Table and damsels in distress named Ann, Priscilla, or Judy (depending on the year). My passion was, I had no doubt, as strong as that of Lancelot for Guinevere—and even more secretive.

At fourteen, I received free tuition to Tilton School. With my parents' prodding, I rejected everything to do with the town and never saw my old friends again. When my new classmates went home to their mansions and penthouses for vacation, I remained alone on the hill. Their girlfriends were debutantes; I had no girlfriends. All the girls I knew were "sluts"; I had cast them off, and they had forgotten me. I was alone—and terribly frustrated.

My parents were masters at manipulation; they assured me that I was privileged to have such an opportunity and that some day I would be grateful. I would find the perfect wife, one suited to our high moral standards. Inside, though, I seethed. I craved female companionship—sex; the idea of a slut was most alluring.

However, rather than rebelling, I repressed my rage and expressed my frustration by excelling. I was an honor student, captain of two varsity teams, editor of the school newspaper. I was determined to show up my rich classmates and to leave Tilton behind forever. During my senior year, I was awarded a full athletic scholarship to Brown and an academic scholarship to Middlebury. I chose Brown, mainly because I preferred being an athlete—and because it was located in a city. My mother had graduated from Middlebury and my father had received his master's degree there, so even though Brown was in the Ivy League, they preferred Middlebury.

"What if you break your leg?" my father asked. "Better to take the academic scholarship." I buckled.

Middlebury was, in my perception, merely an inflated version of Tilton—albeit in rural Vermont instead of rural New Hampshire. True, it was coed, but I was poor and most everyone else was wealthy, and I had not attended school with a female in four years. I lacked confidence, felt outclassed, was miserable. I pleaded with my dad to let me drop out or take a year off. I wanted to move to Boston and learn about life and women. He would not hear of it. "How can I pretend to prepare other parents' kids for college if my own won't stay in one?" he asked.

I have come to understand that life is composed of a series of coincidences. How we react to these—how we exercise what some refer to as *free will*—is everything; the choices we make within the boundaries of the twists of fate determine who we are. Two major coincidences that shaped my life occurred at Middlebury. One came in the form of an Iranian, the son of a general who was a personal adviser to the shah; the other was a beautiful young woman named Ann, like my childhood sweetheart.

The first, whom I will call Farhad, had played professional soccer in Rome. He was endowed with an athletic physique, curly black hair, soft walnut eyes, and a background and charisma that made him irresistible to women. He was my opposite in many ways. I worked hard to win his friendship, and he taught me many things that would serve me well in the years to come. I also met Ann. Although she was seriously dating a young man who attended another college, she took me under her wing. Our platonic relationship was the first truly loving one I had ever experienced.

Farhad encouraged me to drink, party, and ignore my parents. I consciously chose to stop studying. I decided I would break my academic leg to get even with my father. My grades plummeted; I lost my scholarship. Halfway through my sophomore year, I elected to drop out. My father threatened to disown me; Farhad egged me on. I stormed into the dean's office and quit school. It was a pivotal moment in my life.

Farhad and I celebrated my last night in town together at a local bar. A drunken farmer, a giant of a man, accused me of flirting with his wife, picked me up off my feet, and hurled me against a wall. Farhad stepped between us, drew a knife, and slashed the farmer open at the cheek. Then he dragged me across the room and shoved me through a window, out onto a ledge high above Otter Creek. We jumped and made our way along the river and back to our dorm.

The next morning, when interrogated by the campus police, I lied and refused to admit any knowledge of the incident. Nevertheless, Farhad was expelled. We both moved to Boston and shared an apartment there. I landed a job at Hearst's *Record American/Sunday Advertiser* newspapers, as a personal assistant to the editor in chief of the *Sunday Advertiser*.

Later that year, 1965, several of my friends at the newspaper were drafted. To avoid a similar fate, I entered Boston University's College of Business Administration. By then, Ann had broken up with her old boyfriend, and she often traveled down from Middlebury to visit. I welcomed her attention. She graduated in 1967, while I still had another year to complete at BU. She adamantly refused to move in with me until we were married. Although I joked about being blackmailed, and in fact did resent what I saw as a continuation of my parents' archaic and prudish set of moral standards, I enjoyed our times together and I wanted more. We married.

Ann's father, a brilliant engineer, had masterminded the navigational system for an important class of missile and was rewarded with a high-level position in the Department of the Navy. His best friend, a man Ann called Uncle Frank (not his real name), was employed as an executive at the highest echelons of the National Security Agency (NSA), the country's least-known—and by most accounts largest—spy organization.

Shortly after our marriage, the military summoned me for my physical. I passed and therefore faced the prospect of Vietnam upon graduation. The idea of fighting in Southeast Asia tore me apart emotionally, though war has always fascinated me. I was raised on tales about my colonial ancestors—who include Thomas Paine and Ethan Allen—and I had visited all the New England and upstate New York battle sites of both the French and Indian and the Revolutionary wars. I read every historical novel I could find. In fact, when Army Special Forces units first entered Southeast Asia, I was eager to sign up. But as the media exposed the atrocities and the inconsistencies of U.S. policy, I experienced a change of heart. I found myself wondering whose side Paine would have taken. I was sure he would have joined our Vietcong enemies.

Uncle Frank came to my rescue. He informed me that an NSA job made one eligible for draft deferment, and he arranged for a series of meetings at his agency, including a day of grueling polygraph-monitored interviews. I was told that these tests would determine whether I was suitable material for NSA recruitment and training, and if I was, would provide a profile of my strengths and weaknesses, which would be used to map out my career. Given my attitude toward the Vietnam War, I was convinced I would fail the tests.

Under examination, I admitted that as a loyal American I opposed the war, and I was surprised when the interviewers did not pursue this subject. Instead, they focused on my upbringing, my attitudes toward my parents, the emotions generated by the fact I grew up as a poor puritan among so many wealthy, hedonistic preppies. They also explored my frustration about the lack of women, sex, and money in my life, and the fantasy world that had evolved as a result. I was amazed by the attention they gave to my relationship with Farhad and by their interest in my willingness to lie to the campus police to protect him.

At first I assumed all these things that seemed so negative to me marked me as an NSA reject, but the interviews continued, suggesting otherwise. It was not until several years later that I realized that from an NSA viewpoint these negatives actually are positive. Their assessment had less to do with issues of loyalty to my country than with the frustrations of my life. Anger at my parents, an obsession with women, and my ambition to live the good life gave them a hook; I was seducible. My determination to excel in school and in sports, my ultimate rebellion against my father, my ability to get along with foreigners, and my willingness to lie to the police were exactly the types of attributes they sought. I also discovered, later, that Farhad's father worked for the U.S. intelligence community in Iran; my friendship with Farhad was therefore a definite plus.

A few weeks after the NSA testing, I was offered a job to start training in the art of spying, to begin after I received my degree from BU several months later. However, before I had officially accepted this offer, I impulsively attended a seminar given at BU by a Peace Corps recruiter. A major selling point was that, like the NSA, Peace Corps jobs made one eligible for draft deferments.

The decision to sit in on that seminar was one of those coincidences that seemed insignificant at the time but turned out to have life-changing implications. The recruiter described several places in the world that especially needed volunteers. One of these was the Amazon rain forest where, he pointed out, indigenous people lived very much as natives of North America had until the arrival of Europeans.

I had always dreamed of living like the Abnakis who inhabited New Hampshire when my ancestors first settled there. I knew I had Abnaki blood in my veins, and I wanted to learn the type of forest lore they understood so well. I approached the recruiter after his talk and asked about the possibility of being assigned to the Amazon. He assured me there was a great need for volunteers in that region and that my chances would be excellent. I called Uncle Frank.

To my surprise, Uncle Frank encouraged me to consider the Peace Corps. He confided that after the fall of Hanoi—which in those days was deemed a certainty by men in his position—the Amazon would become a hot spot.

"Loaded with oil," he said. "We'll need good agents there— people who understand the natives." He assured me that the Peace Corps would be an excellent training ground, and he urged me to become proficient in Spanish as well as in local indigenous dialects. "You might," he chuckled, "end up working for a private company instead of the government."

I did not understand what he meant by that at the time. I was being upgraded from spy to EHM, although I had never heard the term and would not for a few more years. I had no idea that there were hundreds of men and women scattered around the world, working for consulting firms and other private companies, people who never received a penny of salary from any government agency and yet were serving the interests of empire. Nor could I have guessed that a new type, with more euphemistic titles, would number in the thousands by the end of the millennium, and that I would play a significant role in shaping this growing army.

Ann and I applied to the Peace Corps and requested an assignment in the Amazon. When our acceptance notification arrived, my first reaction was one of extreme disappointment. The letter stated that we would be sent to Ecuador.

Oh no, I thought. I requested the Amazon, not Africa.

I went to an atlas and looked up Ecuador. I was dismayed when I could not find it anywhere on the African continent. In the index, though, I discovered that it is indeed located in Latin America, and I saw on the map that the river systems flowing off its Andean glaciers form the headwaters to the mighty Amazon. Further reading assured me that Ecuador's jungles were some of the world's most diverse and formidable, and that the indigenous people still lived much as they had for millennia. We accepted.

Ann and I completed Peace Corps training in Southern California and headed for Ecuador in September 1968. We lived in the Amazon with the Shuar whose lifestyle did indeed resemble that of precolonial North American natives; we also worked in the Andes with descendants of the Incas. It was a side of the world I never dreamed still existed. Until then, the only Latin Americans I had met were the wealthy preppies at the school where my father taught. I found myself sympathizing with these indigenous people who subsisted on hunting and farming. I felt an odd sort of kinship with them. Somehow, they reminded me of the townies I had left behind.

One day a man in a business suit, Einar Greve, landed at the airstrip in our community. He was a vice president at Chas. T. Main, Inc. (MAIN), an international consulting firm that kept a very low profile and that was in charge of studies to determine whether the World Bank should lend Ecuador and its neighboring countries billions of dollars to build hydroelectric dams and other infrastructure projects. Einar also was a colonel in the U.S. Army Reserve.

He started talking with me about the benefits of working for a company like MAIN. When I mentioned that I had been accepted by the NSA before joining the Peace Corps, and that I was considering going back to them, he informed me that he sometimes acted as an NSA liaison; he gave me a look that made me suspect that part of his assignment was to evaluate my capabilities. I now believe that he was updating my profile, and especially sizing up my abilities to survive in environments most North Americans would find hostile.

We spent a couple of days together in Ecuador, and afterward communicated by mail. He asked me to send him reports assessing Ecuador's economic prospects. I had a small portable typewriter, loved to write, and was quite happy to comply with this request. Over a period of about a year, I sent Einar at least fifteen long letters. In these letters, I speculated on Ecuador's economic and political future, and I appraised the growing frustration among the indigenous communities as they struggled to confront oil companies, international development agencies, and other attempts to draw them into the modern world.

When my Peace Corps tour was over, Einar invited me to a job interview at MAIN headquarters in Boston. During our private meeting, he emphasized that MAIN's primary business was engineering but that his biggest client, the World Bank, recently had begun insisting that he keep economists on staff to produce the critical economic forecasts used to determine the feasibility and magnitude of engineering projects. He confided that he had previously hired three highly qualified economists with impeccable credentials—two with master's degrees and one with a PhD. They had failed miserably.

"None of them," Einar said, "can handle the idea of producing economic forecasts in countries where reliable statistics aren't available." He went on to tell me that, in addition, all of them had found it impossible to fulfill the terms of their contracts, which required them to travel to remote places in countries like Ecuador, Indonesia, Iran, and Egypt, to interview local leaders, and to provide personal assessments about the prospects for economic development in those regions. One had suffered a nervous breakdown in an isolated Panamanian village; he was escorted by Panamanian police to the airport and put on a plane back to the United States.

"The letters you sent me indicate that you don't mind sticking your neck out, even when hard data isn't available. And given your living conditions in Ecuador, I'm confident you can survive almost anywhere." He told me that he already had fired one of those economists and was prepared to do the same with the other two, if I accepted the job.

So it was that in January 1971 I was offered a position as an economist with MAIN. I had turned twenty-six—the magical age when the draft board no longer wanted me. I consulted with Ann's family; they encouraged me to take the job, and I assumed this reflected Uncle Frank's attitude as well. I recalled him mentioning the possibility I would end up working for a private firm. Nothing was ever stated openly, but I had no doubt that my employment at MAIN was a consequence of the arrangements Uncle Frank had made three years earlier, in addition to my experiences in Ecuador and my willingness to write about that country's economic and political situation.

My head reeled for several weeks, and I had a very swollen ego. I had earned only a bachelor's degree from BU, which did not seem to warrant a position as an economist with such a lofty consulting company. I knew that many of my BU classmates who had been rejected by the draft and had gone on to earn MBAs and other graduate degrees would be overcome with jealousy. I visualized myself as a dashing secret agent, heading off to exotic lands, lounging beside hotel swimming pools, surrounded by gorgeous bikini-clad women, martini in hand.

Although this was merely fantasy, I would discover that it held elements of truth. Einar had hired me as an economist, but I was soon to learn that my real job went far beyond that, and that it was in fact closer to James Bond's than I ever could have guessed.

CHAPTER 2

"In for Life"

In legal parlance, MAIN would be called a closely held corporation; roughly 5 percent of its two thousand employees owned the company. These were referred to as partners or associates, and their position was coveted. Not only did the partners have power over everyone else, but also they made the big bucks. Discretion was their hallmark; they dealt with heads of state and other chief executive officers who expect their consultants, like their attorneys and psychotherapists, to honor a strict code of absolute confidentiality. Talking with the press was taboo. It simply was not tolerated. As a consequence, hardly anyone outside MAIN had ever heard of us, although many were familiar with our competitors, such as Arthur D. Little, Stone & Webster, Brown & Root, Halliburton, and Bechtel.

I use the term *competitors* loosely, because in fact MAIN was in a league by itself. The majority of our professional staff was engineers, yet we owned no equipment and never constructed so much as a storage shed. Many MAINers were ex-military; however, we did not contract with the Department of Defense or with any of the military services. Our stock-in-trade was something so different from the norm that during my first months there even I could not figure out what we did. I knew only that my first real assignment would be in Indonesia, and that I would be part of an eleven-man team sent to create a master energy plan for the island of Java.

I also knew that Einar and others who discussed the job with me were eager to convince me that Java's economy would boom, and that if I wanted to distinguish myself as a good forecaster (and to therefore be offered promotions), I would produce projections that demonstrated as much.

"Right off the chart," Einar liked to say. He would glide his fingers through the air and up over his head. "An economy that will soar like a bird!"

Einar took frequent trips that usually lasted only two to three days. No one talked much about them or seemed to know where he had gone. When he was in the office, he often invited me to sit with him for a few minutes over coffee. He asked about Ann, our new apartment, and the cat we had brought with us from Ecuador. I grew bolder as I came to know him better, and I tried to learn more about him and what I would be expected to do in my job. But I never received answers that satisfied me; he was a master at turning conversations around. On one such occasion, he gave me a peculiar look.

"You needn't worry," he said. "We have high expectations for you. I was in Washington recently . . ." His voice trailed off and he smiled inscrutably. "In any case, you know we have a big project in Kuwait. It'll be a while before you leave for Indonesia. I think you should use some of your time to read up on Kuwait. The Boston Public Library is a great resource, and we can get you passes to the MIT and Harvard libraries."

After that, I spent many hours in those libraries, especially in the BPL, which was located a few blocks away from the office and very close to my Back Bay apartment. I became familiar with Kuwait as well as with many books on economic statistics, published by the United Nations, the International Monetary Fund (IMF), and the World Bank. I knew that I would be expected to produce econometric models for Indonesia and Java, and I decided that I might as well get started by doing one for Kuwait.

However, my BS in business administration had not prepared me as an econometrician, so I spent a lot of time trying to figure out how to go about it. I went so far as to enroll in a couple of courses on the subject. In the process, I discovered that statistics can be manipulated to produce a large array of conclusions, including those substantiating the predilections of the analyst.

MAIN was a macho corporation. There were only four women who held professional positions in 1971. However, there were perhaps two hundred women divided between the cadres of personal secretaries—every vice president and department manager had one—and the steno pool, which served the rest of us. I had become accustomed to this gender bias, and I was therefore especially astounded by what happened one day in the BPL's reference section.

An attractive brunette woman came up and sat in a chair across the table from me. In her dark green business suit, she looked very sophisticated. I judged her to be several years my senior, but I tried to focus on not noticing her, on acting indifferent. After a few minutes, without a word, she slid an open book in my direction. It contained a table with information I had been searching for about Kuwait—and a card with her name, Claudine Martin, and her title, Special Consultant to Chas. T. Main, Inc. I looked up into her soft green eyes, and she extended her hand.

"I've been asked to help in your training," she said. I could not believe this was happening to me.

Beginning the next day, we met in Claudine's Beacon Street apartment, a few blocks from MAIN's Prudential Center headquarters. During our first hour together, she explained that my position was an unusual one and that we needed to keep everything highly confidential. She told me that no one had given me specifics about my job because no one was authorized to—except her. Then she informed me that her assignment was to mold me into an economic hit man.

The very name awakened old cloak-and-dagger dreams. I was embarrassed by the nervous laughter I heard coming from me. She smiled and assured me that humor was one of the reasons they used the term. "Who would take it seriously?" she asked.

I confessed ignorance about the role of economic hit men.

"You're not alone," she laughed. "We're a rare breed, in a dirty business. No one can know about your involvement—not even your wife." Then she turned serious. "I'll be very frank with you, teach you all I can during the next weeks. Then you'll have to choose. Your decision is final. Once you're in, you're in for life." After that, she seldom used the full name; we were simply EHMs.

I know now what I did not then—that Claudine took full advantage of the personality weaknesses the NSA profile had disclosed about me. I do not know who supplied her with the information—Einar, the NSA, MAIN's personnel department, or someone else—only that she used it masterfully. Her approach, a combination of physical seduction and verbal manipulation, was tailored specifically for me, and yet it fit within the standard operating procedures I have since seen used by a variety of businesses when the stakes are high and the pressure to close lucrative deals is great. She knew from the start that I would not jeopardize my marriage by disclosing our clandestine activities. And she was brutally frank when it came to describing the shadowy side of things that would be expected of me.

I have no idea who paid her salary, although I have no reason to suspect it was not, as her business card implied, MAIN. At the time, I was too naive, intimidated, and bedazzled to ask the questions that today seem so obvious.

Claudine told me that there were two primary objectives of my work. First, I was to justify huge international loans that would funnel money back to MAIN and other U.S. companies (such as

Bechtel, Halliburton, Stone & Webster, and Brown & Root) through massive engineering and construction projects. Second, I would work to bankrupt the countries that received those loans (after they had paid MAIN and the other U.S. contractors, of course) so that they would be forever beholden to their creditors, and so they would present easy targets when we needed favors, including military bases, UN votes, or access to oil and other natural resources.

My job, she said, was to forecast the effects of investing billions of dollars in a country. Specifically, I would produce studies that projected economic growth twenty to twenty-five years into the future and that evaluated the impacts of a variety of projects. For example, if a decision was made to lend a country $1 billion to persuade its leaders not to align with the Soviet Union, I would compare the benefits of investing that money in power plants with the benefits of investing in a new national railroad network or a telecommunications system. Or I might be told that the country was being offered the opportunity to receive a modern electric utility system, and it would be up to me to demonstrate that such a system would result in sufficient economic growth to justify the loan. The critical factor, in every case, was gross national product. The project that resulted in the highest average annual growth of GNP won. If only one project was under consideration, I would need to demonstrate that developing it would bring superior benefits to the GNP.

The unspoken aspect of every one of these projects was that they were intended to create large profits for the contractors, and to make a handful of wealthy and influential families in the receiving countries very happy, while assuring the long-term financial dependence and therefore the political loyalty of governments around the world. The larger the loan, the better. The fact that the debt burden placed on a country would deprive its poorest citizens of health, education, and other social services for decades to come was not taken into consideration.

Claudine and I openly discussed the deceptive nature of GNP. For instance, the growth of GNP may result even when it profits only one person, such as an individual who owns a utility company, and even if the majority of the population is burdened with debt. The rich get richer and the poor grow poorer. Yet, from a statistical standpoint, this is recorded as economic progress.

Like U.S. citizens in general, most MAIN employees believed we were doing countries favors when we built power plants, highways, and ports. Our schools and our press have taught us to perceive all of our actions as altruistic. Over the years, I've repeatedly heard comments like, "If they're going to burn the U.S. flag and demonstrate against our embassy, why don't we just get out of their damn country and let them wallow in their own poverty?"

People who say such things often hold diplomas certifying that they are well educated. However, these people have no clue that the main reason we establish embassies around the world is to serve our own interests, which during the last half of the twentieth century meant turning the American republic into a global empire. Despite credentials, such people are as uneducated as those eighteenth-century colonists who believed that the Indians fighting to defend their lands were servants of the devil.

Within several months, I would leave for the island of Java in the country of Indonesia, described at that time as the most heavily populated piece of real estate on the planet. Indonesia also happened to be an oil-rich Muslim nation and a hotbed of communist activity.

"It's the next domino after Vietnam," is the way Claudine put it. "We must win the Indonesians over. If they join the Communist bloc, well . . ." She drew a finger across her throat and then smiled sweetly. "Let's just say you need to come up with a very optimistic forecast of the economy, how it will mushroom after all the new power plants and distribution lines are built. That will allow US-AID and the international banks to justify the loans. You'll be well rewarded, of course, and can move on to other projects in exotic places. The world is your shopping cart." She went on to warn me that my role would be tough. "Experts at the banks will come after you. It's their job to punch holes in your forecasts—that's what they're paid to do. Making you look bad makes them look good."

One day I reminded Claudine that the MAIN team being sent to Java included ten other men. I asked if they all were receiving the same type of training as me. She assured me they were not.

"They're engineers," she said. "They design power plants, transmission and distribution lines, and seaports and roads to bring in the fuel. You're the one who predicts the future. Your forecasts determine the magnitude of the systems they design—and the size of the loans. You see, you're the key."

Every time I walked away from Claudine's apartment, I wondered whether I was doing the right thing. Somewhere in my heart, I suspected I was not. But the frustrations of my past haunted me. MAIN seemed to offer everything my life had lacked, and yet I kept asking myself if Tom Paine would have approved. In the end, I convinced myself that by learning more, by experiencing it, I could better expose it later—the old "working from the inside" justification.

When I shared this idea with Claudine, she gave me a perplexed look. "Don't be ridiculous. Once you're in, you can never get out. You must decide for yourself, before you get in any deeper." I understood her, and what she said frightened me. After I left, I strolled down Commonwealth Avenue, turned onto Dartmouth Street, and assured myself that I was the exception.

One afternoon some months later, Claudine and I sat in a window settee watching the snow fall on Beacon Street. "We're a small, exclusive club," she said. "We're paid—well paid—to cheat countries around the globe out of billions of dollars. A large part of your job is to encourage world leaders to become part of a vast network that promotes U.S. commercial interests. In the end, those leaders become ensnared in a web of debt that ensures their loyalty. We can draw on them whenever we desire—to satisfy our political, economic, or military needs. In turn, these leaders bolster their political positions by bringing industrial parks, power plants, and airports to their people. Meanwhile, the owners of U.S. engineering and construction companies become very wealthy."

That afternoon, in the idyllic setting of Claudine's apartment, relaxing in the window while snow swirled around outside, I learned the history of the profession I was about to enter. Claudine described how throughout most of history, empires were built largely through military force or the threat of it. But with the end of World War II, the emergence of the Soviet Union, and the specter of nuclear holocaust, the military solution became just too risky.

The decisive moment occurred in 1951, when Iran rebelled against a British oil company that was exploiting Iranian natural resources and its people. The company was the forerunner of British Petroleum, today's BP. In response, the highly popular, democratically elected Iranian prime minister (and *TIME* magazine's Man of the Year in 1951), Mohammad Mossadegh, nationalized all Iranian petroleum assets. An outraged England sought the help of her World War II ally, the United States. However, both countries feared that military retaliation would provoke the Soviet Union into taking action on behalf of Iran.

Instead of sending in the Marines, therefore, Washington dispatched CIA agent Kermit Roosevelt (Theodore's grandson). He performed brilliantly, winning people over through payoffs and threats. He then enlisted them to organize a series of street riots and violent demonstrations, which created the impression that Mossadegh was both unpopular and inept. In the end, Mossadegh went down, and he spent the rest of his life under house arrest. The pro-American Mohammad Reza Shah became the unchallenged dictator. Kermit Roosevelt had set the stage for a new profession, the one whose ranks I was joining.[1]

Roosevelt's gambit reshaped Middle Eastern history even as it rendered obsolete all the old strategies for empire building. It also coincided with the beginning of experiments in "limited non-nuclear military actions," which ultimately resulted in U.S. humiliations in Korea and Vietnam. By 1968, the year I interviewed with the NSA, it had become clear that if the United States wanted to realize its dream of global empire (as envisioned by men like presidents Johnson and Nixon), it would have to employ strategies modeled on Roosevelt's Iranian example. This was the only way to beat the Soviets without the threat of nuclear war.

There was one problem, however. Kermit Roosevelt was a CIA employee. Had he been caught, the consequences would have been dire. He had orchestrated the first U.S. operation to overthrow a foreign government, and it was likely that many more would follow, but it was important to find an approach that would not directly implicate Washington.

Fortunately for the strategists, the 1960s also witnessed another type of revolution: the empowerment of international corporations and of multinational organizations such as the World Bank and the IMF. The latter were financed primarily by the United States and our sister empire builders in Europe. A symbiotic relationship developed between governments, corporations, and multinational organizations.

By the time I enrolled in BU's business school, a solution to the Roosevelt-as-CIA-agent problem had already been worked out. U.S. intelligence agencies—including the NSA—would identify prospective EHMs, who could then be hired by international corporations. These EHMs would never be paid by the government; instead, they would draw their salaries from the private sector. As a result, their dirty work, if exposed, would be chalked up to corporate greed rather than to government policy. In addition, the corporations that hired them, although paid by government agencies and their multinational banking counterparts (with taxpayer money), would be insulated from congressional oversight and public scrutiny, shielded by a growing body of legal initiatives, including trademark, international trade, and Freedom of Information laws.[2]

"So you see," Claudine concluded, "we are just the next generation in a proud tradition that began back when you were in first grade."

CHAPTER 3

Indonesia: Lessons for an EHM

In addition to learning about my new career, I also spent time reading books about Indonesia. "The more you know about a country before you get there, the easier your job will be," Claudine had advised. I took her words to heart.

When Columbus set sail in 1492, he was trying to reach Indonesia, known at the time as the Spice Islands. Throughout the colonial era, it was considered a treasure worth far more than the Americas. Java, with its rich fabrics, fabled spices, and opulent kingdoms, was both the crown jewel and the scene of violent clashes between Spanish, Dutch, Portuguese, and British adventurers. The Netherlands emerged triumphant in 1750, but even though the Dutch controlled Java, it took them more than 150 years to subdue the outer islands.

When the Japanese invaded Indonesia during World War II, Dutch forces offered little resistance. As a result, Indonesians, especially the Javanese, suffered terribly. Following the Japanese surrender, a charismatic leader named Sukarno emerged to declare independence. Four years of fighting finally ended on December 27, 1949, when the Netherlands lowered its flag and returned sovereignty to a people who had known nothing but struggle and domination for more than three centuries. Sukarno became the new republic's first president.

Ruling Indonesia, however, proved to be a greater challenge than defeating the Dutch. Far from homogeneous, the archipelago of about 17,500 islands was a boiling pot of tribalism, divergent cultures, dozens of languages and dialects, and ethnic groups who nursed centuries-old animosities. Conflicts were frequent and brutal, and Sukarno clamped down. He suspended parliament in 1960 and was named president-for-life in 1963. He formed close alliances with Communist governments around the world, in exchange for military equipment and training. He sent Russian-armed Indonesian troops into neighboring Malaysia in an attempt to spread communism throughout Southeast Asia and win the approval of the world's Socialist leaders.

Opposition built, and a coup was launched in 1965. Sukarno escaped assassination only through the quick wits of his mistress. Many of his top military officers and his closest associates were less lucky. The events were reminiscent of those in Iran in 1953. In the end, the Communist Party was held responsible—especially those factions aligned with China. In the army-initiated massacres that followed, an estimated three hundred thousand to five hundred thousand people were killed. The head of the military, General Suharto, took over as president in 1968.[1]

By 1971, the United States' determination to seduce Indonesia away from communism was heightened because the outcome of the Vietnam War was looking very uncertain. President Nixon had begun a series of troop withdrawals in the summer of 1969, and U.S. strategy was taking on a more global perspective. The strategy focused on preventing a domino effect of one country after another falling under Communist rule, and it focused on a couple of countries; Indonesia was the key. MAIN's electrification project was part of a comprehensive plan to ensure American dominance in Southeast Asia.

The premise of U.S. foreign policy was that Suharto would serve Washington in a manner similar to the shah of Iran. The United States also hoped the nation would serve as a model for other countries in the region. Washington based part of its strategy on the assumption that gains made in Indonesia might have positive repercussions throughout the Islamic world, particularly in the explosive Middle East. And if that were not incentive enough, Indonesia had oil. No one was certain about the magnitude or quality of its reserves, but oil company seismologists were exuberant over the possibilities.

As I pored over the books at the BPL, my excitement grew. I began to imagine the adventures ahead. In working for MAIN, I would be trading the rugged Peace Corps lifestyle for a much more luxurious and glamorous one. My time with Claudine already represented the realization of one of my fantasies; it seemed too good to be true. I felt at least partially vindicated for serving the sentence at that all-boys' prep school.

Something else was also happening in my life: Ann and I were not getting along. I think she must have sensed that I was leading two lives. I justified it as the logical result of the resentment I felt toward her for forcing us to get married in the first place. Never mind that she had nurtured and supported me through the challenges of our Peace Corps assignment in Ecuador; I still saw her as a continuation of my pattern of giving in to my parents' whims. Of course, as I look back on it, I'm sure my relationship with Claudine was a major factor. I could not tell Ann about this, but she sensed it. In any case, we decided to move into separate apartments.

One day in 1971, about a week before my scheduled departure for Indonesia, I arrived at Claudine's place to find the small dining room table set with an assortment of cheeses and breads, and there was a fine bottle of Bordeaux. She toasted me.

"You've made it." She smiled, but somehow it seemed less than sincere. "You're now one of us."

We chatted casually for half an hour or so; then, as we were finishing off the wine, she gave me a look unlike any I had seen before. "Never admit to anyone about our meetings," she said in a stern voice. "I won't forgive you if you do, ever, and I'll deny I ever met you." She glared at me—perhaps the only time I felt threatened by her—and then gave a cold laugh. "Talking about us would make life dangerous for you."

I was stunned. I felt terrible. But later, as I walked alone back to the Prudential Center, I had to admit to the cleverness of the scheme. The fact is that all our time together had been spent in her apartment. There was not a trace of evidence about our relationship, and no one at MAIN was implicated in any way. There was also part of me that appreciated her honesty; she had not deceived me the way my parents had about Tilton and Middlebury.

CHAPTER 4

Saving a Country from Communism

I had a romanticized vision of Indonesia, the country where I was to live for the next three months. Some of the books I read featured photographs of beautiful women in brightly colored sarongs, exotic Balinese dancers, shamans blowing fire, and warriors paddling long dugout canoes in emerald waters at the foot of smoking volcanoes. Particularly striking was a series on the magnificent black-sailed galleons of the infamous Bugi pirates, who still sailed the seas of the archipelago, and who had so terrorized early European sailors that they returned home to warn their children, "Behave yourselves, or the Bugimen will get you." Oh, how those pictures stirred my soul.

The history and legends of that country represent a cornucopia of larger-than-life figures: wrathful gods; Komodo dragons; tribal sultans; and ancient tales that long before the birth of Christ had traveled across Asian mountains, through Persian deserts, and over the Mediterranean to embed themselves in the deepest realms of our collective psyche. The very names of its fabled islands—Java, Sumatra, Borneo, Sulawesi—seduced the mind. Here was a land of mysticism, myth, and erotic beauty; an elusive treasure sought but never found by Columbus; a princess wooed yet never possessed by Spain, by Holland, by Portugal, by Japan; a fantasy and a dream.

My expectations were high, and I suppose they mirrored those of the great explorers. Like Columbus, though, I should have known to temper my fantasies. Perhaps I could have guessed that the beacon shines on a destiny that is not always the one we envision. Indonesia offered treasures, but it was not the chest of panaceas I had come to expect. In fact, my first days in Indonesia's steamy capital, Jakarta, in the summer of 1971, were shocking.

The beauty was certainly present. Gorgeous women sporting colorful sarongs. Lush gardens ablaze with tropical flowers. Exotic Balinese dancers. Bicycle cabs with fanciful, rainbow-colored scenes painted on the sides of the high seats, where passengers reclined in front of the pedaling drivers. Dutch Colonial mansions and turreted mosques. But there was also an ugly, tragic side to the city. Lepers holding out bloodied stumps instead of hands. Young girls offering their bodies for a few coins. Once-splendid Dutch canals turned into cesspools. Cardboard hovels where entire families lived along the trash-lined banks of black rivers. Blaring horns and choking fumes. The beautiful and the ugly, the elegant and the vulgar, the spiritual and the profane. This was Jakarta, where the enticing scent of cloves and orchid blossoms battled the miasma of open sewers for dominance.

I had seen poverty before. Some of my New Hampshire classmates lived in cold-water tarpaper shacks and arrived at school wearing thin jackets and frayed tennis shoes on subzero winter days, their unwashed bodies reeking of old sweat and manure. I had lived in mud shacks with Andean peasants whose diet consisted almost entirely of dried corn and potatoes, and where it sometimes seemed that a newborn was as likely to die as to experience a birthday. I had seen poverty, but nothing to prepare me for Jakarta.

Our team, of course, was quartered in the country's fanciest hotel, the Hotel InterContinental Indonesia. Owned by Pan American Airways, like the rest of the InterContinental chain scattered around the globe, it catered to the whims of wealthy foreigners, especially oil executives and their families. On the evening of our first day, our project manager Charlie Illingworth hosted a dinner for us in the elegant restaurant on the top floor.

Charlie was a connoisseur of war; he devoted most of his free time to reading history books and historical novels about great military leaders and battles. He was the epitome of the pro–Vietnam War armchair soldier. As usual, this night he was wearing khaki slacks and a short-sleeved khaki shirt with military-style epaulettes.

After welcoming us, he lit up a cigar. "To the good life," he sighed, raising a glass of champagne.

We joined him. "To the good life." Our glasses clinked.

Cigar smoke swirling around him, Charlie glanced about the room. "We will be well pampered here," he said, nodding his head appreciatively. "The Indonesians will take very good care of us. As will the U.S. Embassy people. But let's not forget that we have a mission to accomplish." He looked down at a handful of note cards. "Yes, we're here to develop a master plan for the electrification of Java—the most populated land in the world. But that's just the tip of the iceberg."

His expression turned serious; he reminded me of George C. Scott playing General Patton, one of Charlie's heroes. "We are here to accomplish nothing short of saving this country from the clutches of communism. As you know, Indonesia has a long and tragic history. Now, at a time when it is poised to launch itself into the twentieth century, it is tested once again. Our responsibility is to make sure that Indonesia doesn't follow in the footsteps of its northern neighbors, Vietnam, Cambodia, and Laos. An integrated electrical system is a key element. That, more than any other single factor (with the possible exception of oil), will assure that capitalism and democracy rule.

"Speaking of oil," he said. He took another puff on his cigar and flipped past a couple of the note cards. "We all know how dependent our own country is on oil. Indonesia can be a powerful ally to us in that regard. So, as you develop this master plan, please do everything you can to make sure that the oil industry and all the others that serve it—ports, pipelines, construction companies—get whatever they are likely to need in the way of electricity for the entire duration of this twenty-five-year plan."

He raised his eyes from his note cards and looked directly at me. "Better to err on the high side than to underestimate. You don't want the blood of Indonesian children—or our own—on your hands. You don't want them to live under the hammer and sickle or the Red flag of China!"

As I lay in my bed that night, high above the city, secure in the luxury of a first-class suite, an image of Claudine came to me. Her discourses on foreign debt haunted me. I tried to comfort myself by recalling lessons learned in my macroeconomics courses at business school. After all, I told myself, I am here to help Indonesia rise out of a medieval economy and take its place in the modern industrial world. But I knew that in the morning I would look out my window, across the opulence of the hotel's gardens and swimming pools, and see the hovels that fanned out for miles beyond. I would know that babies were dying out there for lack of food and potable water, and that infants and adults alike were suffering from horrible diseases and living in terrible conditions.

Tossing and turning in my bed, I found it impossible to deny that Charlie and everyone else on our team were here for selfish reasons. We were promoting U.S. foreign policy and corporate interests. We were driven by greed rather than by any desire to make life better for the vast majority of Indonesians. A word came to mind: corporatocracy. I was not sure whether I had heard it before or had just invented it, but it seemed to describe perfectly the new elite who had made up their minds to attempt to rule the planet.

This was a close-knit fraternity of a few men with shared goals, and the fraternity's members moved easily and often between corporate boards and government positions. It struck me that the current president of the World Bank, Robert McNamara, was a perfect example. He had moved from a position as president of Ford Motor Company, to secretary of defense under presidents Kennedy and Johnson, and now occupied the top post at the world's most powerful financial institution.

I also realized that my college professors had not understood the true nature of macroeconomics: that in many cases helping an economy grow only makes those few people who sit atop the pyramid even richer, while it does nothing for those at the bottom except to push them even lower. Indeed, promoting capitalism often results in a system that resembles medieval feudal societies. If any of my professors knew this, they had not admitted it—probably because big corporations, and the men who run them, fund colleges. Exposing the truth would undoubtedly cost those professors their jobs—just as such revelations could cost me mine.

These thoughts continued to disturb my sleep every night that I spent at the Hotel InterContinental Indonesia. In the end, my primary defense was a highly personal one: I had fought my way out of that New Hampshire town, the prep school, and the draft. Through a combination of coincidences and hard work, I had earned a place in the good life. I also took comfort in the fact that I was doing the right thing in the eyes of my culture. I was on my way to becoming a successful and respected economist. I was doing what business school had prepared me for. I was helping implement a development model that was sanctioned by the best minds at the world's top think tanks.

Nonetheless, in the middle of the night I often had to console myself with a promise that someday I would expose the truth. Then I would read myself to sleep with Louis L'Amour novels about gunfighters in the Old West.

CHAPTER 5

Selling My Soul

Our eleven-man team spent six days in Jakarta registering at the U.S. Embassy, meeting various officials, organizing ourselves, and relaxing around the pool. The number of Americans who lived at the Hotel InterContinental amazed me. I took great pleasure in watching the beautiful young women—wives of U.S. oil and construction company executives—who passed their days at the pool and their evenings in the half dozen posh restaurants in and around the hotel.

Then Charlie moved our team to the mountain city of Bandung. The climate was milder, the poverty less obvious, and the distractions fewer. We were given a government guesthouse known as the Wisma, complete with a manager, a cook, a gardener, and a staff of servants. Built during the Dutch Colonial period, the Wisma was a haven. Its spacious veranda faced tea plantations that flowed across rolling hills and up the slopes of Java's volcanic mountains. In addition to housing, we were provided with eleven Toyota off-road vehicles, each with a driver and translator. Finally, we were presented with memberships to the exclusive Bandung Golf and Racket Club, and we were housed in a suite of offices at the local headquarters of Perusahaan Umum Listrik Negara (PLN), the government-owned electric utility company.

For me, the first several days in Bandung involved a series of meetings with Charlie and Howard Parker. Howard was in his seventies and was the retired chief load forecaster for the New England Electric System. Now he was responsible for forecasting the amount of energy and generating capacity (the load) the island of Java would need over the next twenty-five years, as well as for breaking this down into city and regional forecasts. Since electric demand is highly correlated with economic growth, his forecasts depended on my economic projections. The rest of our team would develop the master plan around these forecasts, locating and designing power plants, transmission and distribution lines, and fuel transportation systems in a manner that would satisfy our projections as efficiently as possible. During our meetings, Charlie continually emphasized the importance of my job, and he badgered me about the need to be very optimistic in my forecasts. Claudine had been right; I was the key to the entire master plan.

"The first few weeks here," Charlie explained, "are about data collection."

He, Howard, and I were seated in big rattan chairs in Charlie's plush private office. The walls were decorated with batik tapestries depicting epic tales from the ancient Hindu texts of the Ramayana. Charlie puffed on a fat cigar.

"The engineers will put together a detailed picture of the current electric system, port capacities, roads, railroads, all those sorts of things." He pointed his cigar at me. "You gotta act fast. By the end of month one, Howard'll need to get a pretty good idea about the full extent of the economic miracles that'll happen when we get the new grid online. By the end of the second month, he'll need more details—broken down into regions. The last month will be about filling in the gaps. That'll be critical. All of us will put our heads together then. So, before we leave we gotta be absolutely certain we have all the information we'll need. Home for Thanksgiving, that's my motto. There's no coming back."

Howard appeared to be an amiable, grandfatherly type, but he was actually a bitter old man who felt cheated by life. He had never reached the pinnacle of the New England Electric System and he deeply resented it. "Passed over," he told me repeatedly, "because I refused to buy the company line." He had been forced into retirement and then, unable to tolerate staying at home with his wife, had accepted a consulting job with MAIN. This was his second assignment, and I had been warned by both Einar and Charlie to watch out for him. They described him with words like *stubborn, mean,* and *vindictive.*

As it turned out, Howard was one of my wisest teachers, although not one I was ready to accept at the time. He had never received the type of training Claudine had given me. I suppose they considered him too old, or perhaps too stubborn. Or maybe they figured he was only in it for the short run, until they could lure in a more pliable full-timer like me. In any case, from their standpoint, he turned out to be a problem. Howard clearly saw the situation and the role they wanted him to play, and he was determined not to be a pawn. All the adjectives Einar and Charlie had used to describe him were appropriate, but at least some of his stubbornness grew out of his personal commitment not to be their servant. I doubt he had ever heard the term economic hit man, but he knew they intended to use him to promote a form of imperialism he could not accept.

He took me aside after one of our meetings with Charlie. He wore a hearing aid and fiddled with the little box under his shirt that controlled its volume.

"This is between you and me," Howard said in a hushed voice. We were standing at the window in the office we shared, looking out at the stagnant canal that wound past the PLN building. A young woman was bathing in its foul waters, attempting to retain some semblance of modesty by loosely draping a sarong around her otherwise naked body. "They'll try to convince you that this economy is going to skyrocket," he said. "Charlie's ruthless. Don't let him get to you."

His words gave me a sinking feeling, but also a desire to convince him that Charlie was right; after all, my career depended on pleasing my MAIN bosses.

"Surely this economy will boom," I said, my eyes drawn to the woman in the canal. "Just look at what's happening."

"So there you are," he muttered, apparently unaware of the scene in front of us. "You've already bought their line, have you?"

A movement up the canal caught my attention. An elderly man had descended the bank, dropped his pants, and squatted at the edge of the water to answer nature's call. The young woman saw him but was undeterred; she continued bathing. I turned away from the window and looked directly at Howard.

"I've been around," I said. "I may be young, but I just got back from three years in South America. I've seen what can happen when oil is discovered. Things change fast."

"Oh, I've been around too," he said mockingly. "A great many years. I'll tell you something, young man. I don't give a damn for your oil discoveries and all that. I forecasted electric loads all my life—during the Depression, World War II, times of bust and boom. I've seen what Route 128's so-called Massachusetts Miracle did for Boston. And I can say for sure that no electric load ever grew by more than 7 to 9 percent a year for any sustained period. And that's in the best of times. Six percent is more reasonable."

I stared at him. Part of me suspected he was right, but I felt defensive. I knew I had to convince him, because my own conscience cried out for justification.

"Howard, this isn't Boston. This is a country where, until now, no one could even get electricity. Things are different here."

He turned on his heel and waved his hand as though he could brush me away.

"Go ahead," he snarled. "Sell out. I don't give a damn what you come up with." He jerked his chair from behind his desk and fell into it. "I'll make my electricity forecast based on what I believe, not some pie-in-the-sky economic study." He picked up his pencil and started to scribble on a pad of paper.

It was a challenge I could not ignore. I went and stood in front of his desk.

"You'll look pretty stupid if I come up with what everyone expects—a boom to rival the California gold rush—and you forecast electricity growth at a rate comparable to Boston in the 1960s."

He slammed the pencil down and glared at me. "Unconscionable! That's what it is. You—all of you—" he waved his arms at the offices beyond our walls, "you've sold your souls to the devil. You're in it for the money. Now," he feigned a smile and reached under his shirt, "I'm turning off my hearing aid and going back to work."

It shook me to the core. I stomped out of the room and headed for Charlie's office. Halfway there, I stopped, uncertain about what I intended to accomplish. Instead, I turned and walked down the stairs, out the door, into the afternoon sunlight. The young woman was climbing out of the canal, her sarong wrapped tightly about her body. The elderly man had disappeared. Several boys played in the canal, splashing and shouting at each other. An older woman was standing knee-deep in the water, brushing her teeth; another was scrubbing clothes.

A huge lump grew in my throat. I sat down on a slab of broken concrete, trying to disregard the pungent odor from the canal. I fought hard to hold back the tears; I needed to figure out why I felt so miserable.

You're in it for the money. I heard Howard's words, over and over. He had struck a raw nerve.

The little boys continued to splash each other, their gleeful voices filling the air. I wondered what I could do. What would it take to make me carefree like them? The question tormented me as I sat there watching them cavort in their blissful innocence, apparently unaware of the risk they took by playing in that fetid water. An elderly, hunchbacked man with a gnarled cane hobbled along the bank above the canal. He stopped and watched the boys, and his face broke into a toothless grin.

Perhaps I could confide in Howard; maybe together we would arrive at a solution. I immediately felt a sense of relief. I picked up a little stone and threw it into the canal. As the ripples faded, however, so did my euphoria. I knew I could do no such thing. Howard was old and bitter. He had already passed up opportunities to advance his own career. Surely, he would not buckle now. I was young, just starting out, and certainly did not want to end up like him.

Staring into the water of that putrid canal, I once again saw images of the New Hampshire prep school on the hill, where I had spent vacations alone while the other boys went off to debutante balls. Slowly the sorry fact settled in. Once again, there was no one I could talk to.

That night I lay in bed, thinking for a long time about the people in my life—Howard, Charlie, Claudine, Ann, Einar, Uncle Frank—wondering what my life would be like if I had never met them. Where would I be living? Not Indonesia, that was for sure. I wondered also about my future, about where I was headed. I pondered the decision confronting me. Charlie had made it clear that he expected Howard and me to come up with growth rates of at least 17 percent per annum. What kind of forecast would I produce?

Suddenly a thought came to me that soothed my soul. Why had it not occurred to me before? The decision was not mine at all. Howard had said that he would do what he considered right, regardless of my conclusions. I could please my bosses with a high economic forecast and he would make his own decision; my work would have no effect on the master plan. People kept emphasizing the importance of my role, but they were wrong. A great burden had been lifted. I fell into a deep sleep.

A few days later, Howard was taken ill with a severe amoebic attack. We rushed him to a Catholic missionary hospital. The doctors prescribed medication and strongly recommended that he return immediately to the United States. Howard assured us that he already had all the data he needed and could easily complete the load forecast from Boston. His parting words to me were a reiteration of his earlier warning.

"No need to cook the numbers," he said. "I'll not be part of that scam, no matter what you say about the miracles of economic growth!"

PART II: 1971–1975

CHAPTER 6

My Role as Inquisitor

Our contracts with the Indonesian government, the Asian Development Bank, and USAID required that someone on our team visit all the major population centers in the area covered by the master plan. I was designated to fulfill this condition. As Charlie put it, "You survived the Amazon; you know how to handle bugs, snakes, and bad water."

Along with a driver and translator, I visited many beautiful places and stayed in some pretty dismal lodgings. I met with local business and political leaders and listened to their opinions about the prospects for economic growth. However, I found most of them reluctant to share information with me. They seemed intimidated by my presence. Typically, they told me that I would have to check with their bosses, with government agencies, or with corporate headquarters in Jakarta. I sometimes suspected some sort of conspiracy was directed at me.

These trips were usually short, not more than two or three days. In between, I returned to the Wisma in Bandung. The woman who managed it had a son a few years younger than me. His name was Rasmon, but to everyone except his mother he was

Rasy. A student of economics at a local university, he immediately took an interest in my work. In fact, I suspected that at some point he would approach me for a job. He also began to teach me Bahasa Indonesia.

Creating an easy-to-learn language had been President Sukarno's highest priority after Indonesia won its independence from Holland. Over 350 languages and dialects are spoken throughout the archipelago,[1] and Sukarno realized that his country needed a common vocabulary in order to unite people from the many islands and cultures. He recruited an international team of linguists, and Bahasa Indonesia was the highly successful result. Based on Malay, it avoids many of the tense changes, irregular verbs, and other complications that characterize most languages. By the early 1970s, the majority of Indonesians spoke it, although they continued to rely on Javanese and other local dialects within their own communities. Rasy was a great teacher with a wonderful sense of humor, and compared to learning Shuar or even Spanish, Bahasa was easy.

Rasy owned a motor scooter and took it upon himself to introduce me to his city and people. "I'll show you a side of Indonesia you haven't seen," he promised one evening, and urged me to hop on behind him.

We passed shadow-puppet shows, musicians playing traditional instruments, fire-blowers, jugglers, and street vendors selling every imaginable ware, from contraband American cassettes to rare indigenous artifacts. Finally, we ended up at a tiny coffeehouse populated by young men and women whose clothes, hats, and hairstyles would have been right in fashion at a Beatles concert in the late 1960s; however, everyone was distinctly Indonesian. Rasy introduced me to a group seated around a table and we sat down.

They all spoke English, with varying degrees of fluency, but they appreciated and encouraged my attempts at Bahasa. They talked about this openly and asked me why Americans never learned their language. I had no answer. Nor could I explain why I was the only American or European in this part of the city, even though you could always find plenty of us at the Golf and Racket Club, the posh restaurants, the movie theaters, and the upscale supermarkets.

It was a night I shall always remember. Rasy and his friends treated me as one of their own. I enjoyed a sense of euphoria from being there, sharing their city, food, and music, smelling the clove cigarettes and other aromas that were part of their lives, joking and laughing with them. It was like the Peace Corps all over again, and I found myself wondering why I had thought that I wanted to travel first class and separate myself from people like this. As the night wore on, they became increasingly interested in learning my thoughts about their country and about the war my country was fighting in Vietnam. Every one of them was horrified by what they referred to as "the illegal invasion," and they were relieved to discover I shared their feelings.

By the time Rasy and I returned to the guesthouse it was late and the place was dark. I thanked him profusely for inviting me into his world; he thanked me for opening up to his friends. We promised to do it again, hugged, and headed off to our respective rooms.

That experience with Rasy whetted my appetite for spending more time away from the MAIN team. The next morning, I had a meeting with Charlie and told him I was becoming frustrated trying to obtain information from local people. In addition, most of the statistics I needed for developing economic forecasts could only be found at government offices in Jakarta. Charlie and I agreed that I would need to spend one to two weeks in Jakarta.

He expressed sympathy for me, having to abandon Bandung for the steaming metropolis, and I professed to detest the idea. Secretly, however, I was excited by the opportunity to have some time to myself, to explore Jakarta and to live at the elegant Hotel InterContinental Indonesia. Once in Jakarta, however, I discovered that I now viewed life from a different perspective. The night spent with Rasy and the young Indonesians, as well as my travels around the country, had changed me. I found that I saw my fellow Americans in a different light. The young wives seemed not quite so beautiful. The chain-link fence around the pool and the steel bars outside the windows on the lower floors, which I had barely noticed before, now took on an ominous appearance. The food in the hotel's elegant restaurants seemed insipid.

I noticed something else too. During my meetings with political and business leaders, I became aware of subtleties in the way they treated me. I had not perceived it before, but now I saw that many of them resented my presence. For example, when they introduced me to each other, they often used Bahasa terms that according to my dictionary translated to *inquisitor* and *interrogator*. I purposely neglected disclosing my knowledge of their language—even my translator knew only that I could recite a few stock phrases—and I purchased a good Bahasa/English dictionary, which I often used after leaving them.

Were these addresses just coincidences of language? Misinterpretations in my dictionary? I tried to convince myself they were. Yet, the more time I spent with these men, the more convinced I became that I was an intruder, that an order to cooperate had come down from someone, and that they had little choice but to comply. I had no idea whether a government official, a banker, a general, or the U.S. Embassy had sent the order. All I knew was that although they invited me into their offices, offered me tea, politely answered my questions, and in every overt manner seemed to welcome my presence, beneath the surface there was a shadow of resignation and rancor.

It made me wonder, too, about their answers to my questions and about the validity of their data. For instance, I could never just walk into an office with my translator and meet with someone; we first had to set up an appointment. In itself, this would not have seemed so strange, except that doing so was outrageously time consuming. Since the phones seldom worked, we had to drive through the traffic-choked streets, which were laid out in such a contorted manner that it could take an hour to reach a building only blocks away. Once there, we were asked to fill out several forms. Eventually, a male secretary would appear. Politely—always with the courteous smile for which the Javanese are famous—he would question me about the types of information I desired, and then he would establish a time for the meeting.

Without exception, the scheduled appointment was at least several days away, and when the meeting finally occurred I was handed a folder of prepared materials. The industry owners gave me five- and ten-year plans, the bankers had charts and graphs, and the government officials provided lists of projects that were in the process of leaving the drawing boards to become engines of economic growth. Everything these captains of commerce and government provided, and all they said during the interviews, indicated that Java was poised for perhaps the biggest boom any economy had ever enjoyed. No one—not a single person—ever questioned this premise or gave me any negative information.

As I headed back to Bandung, though, I found myself wondering about all these experiences; something was deeply disturbing. It occurred to me that everything I was doing in Indonesia was more like a game than reality. It was as though we were playing a game of poker. We kept our cards hidden. We could not trust each other or count on the reliability of the information we shared. Yet, this game was deadly serious, and its outcome would impact millions of lives for decades to come.

CHAPTER 7

Civilization on Trial

"I'm taking you to a *dalang*," Rasy beamed. "You know, the famous Indonesian puppet masters." He was obviously pleased to have me back in Bandung. "There's a very important one in town tonight."

He drove me on his scooter through parts of his city I did not know existed, through sections filled with traditional Javanese *kampong* houses, which looked like a poor person's version of tiny tile-roofed temples. Gone were the stately Dutch Colonial mansions and office buildings I had grown to expect. The people were obviously poor, yet they bore themselves with great pride. They wore threadbare but clean batik sarongs, brightly colored blouses, and wide-brimmed straw hats. Everywhere we went we were greeted with smiles and laughter. When we stopped, children rushed up to touch me and feel the fabric of my jeans. One little girl stuck a fragrant frangipani blossom in my hair.

We parked the scooter near a sidewalk theater where several hundred people were gathered, some standing, others sitting in portable chairs. The night was clear and beautiful. Although we were in the heart of the oldest section of Bandung, there were no streetlights, so the stars sparkled over our heads. The air was filled with the aromas of wood fires, peanuts, and cloves.

Rasy disappeared into the crowd and soon returned with many of the young people I had met at the coffeehouse. They offered me hot tea, little cakes, and *sate*, tiny bits of meat cooked in peanut oil. I must have hesitated before accepting the latter, because one of the women pointed at a small fire. "Very fresh meat," she laughed. "Just cooked."

Then the music started—the hauntingly magical sounds of the *gamalong*, an instrument that conjures images of temple bells.

"The dalang plays all the music by himself," Rasy whispered. "He also works all the puppets and speaks their voices, several languages. We'll translate for you."

It was a remarkable performance, combining traditional legends with current events. I would later learn that the dalang is a shaman who does his work in trance. He had over a hundred puppets and he spoke for each in a different voice. It was a night I will never forget, and one that has influenced the rest of my life.

After completing a classic selection from the ancient texts of the Ramayana, the dalang produced a puppet of Richard Nixon, complete with the distinctive long nose and sagging jowls. The U.S. president was dressed like Uncle Sam, in a stars-and-stripes top hat and tails. He was accompanied by another puppet, which wore a three-piece pin-striped suit. The second puppet carried in one hand a bucket decorated with dollar signs. He used his free hand to wave an American flag over Nixon's head in the manner of a slave fanning a master.

A map of the Middle and Far East appeared behind the two, the various countries hanging from hooks in their respective positions. Nixon immediately approached the map, lifted Vietnam off its hook, and thrust it to his mouth. He shouted something that was translated as, "Bitter! Rubbish. We don't need any more of this!" Then he tossed it into the bucket and proceeded to do the same with other countries.

I was surprised, however, to see that his next selections did not include the domino nations of Southeast Asia. Rather, they were all Middle Eastern countries—Palestine, Kuwait, Saudi Arabia, Iraq, Syria, and Iran. After that, he turned to Pakistan and Afghanistan. Each time, the Nixon doll screamed out some epithet before dropping the country into his bucket, and in every instance, his vituperative words were anti-Islamic: "Muslim dogs," "Mohammed's monsters," and "Islamic devils."

The crowd became very excited, the tension mounting with each new addition to the bucket. They seemed torn between fits of laughter, shock, and rage. At times, I sensed they took offense at the puppeteer's language. I also felt intimidated; I stood out in this crowd, taller than the rest, and I worried that they might direct their anger at me. Then Nixon said something that made my scalp tingle when Rasy translated it.

"Give this one to the World Bank. See what it can do to make us some money off Indonesia." He lifted Indonesia from the map and moved to drop it into the bucket, but just at that moment another puppet leaped out of the shadows. This puppet represented an Indonesian man, dressed in batik shirt and khaki slacks, and he wore a sign with his name clearly printed on it.

"A popular Bandung politician," Rasy explained.

This puppet literally flew between Nixon and Bucket Man and held up his hand.

"Stop!" he shouted. "Indonesia is sovereign."

The crowd burst into applause. Then Bucket Man lifted his flag and thrust it like a spear into the Indonesian, who staggered and died a most dramatic death. The audience members booed, hooted, screamed, and shook their fists. Nixon and Bucket Man stood there, looking out at us. They bowed and left the stage.

"I think I should go," I said to Rasy.

He placed a hand protectively around my shoulder. "It's okay," he said. "They have nothing against you personally." I wasn't so sure.

Later we all retired to the coffeehouse. Rasy and the others assured me that they had not been informed ahead of time about the Nixon–World Bank skit. "You never know what to expect from that puppeteer," one of the young men observed.

I wondered aloud whether this had been staged in my honor. Someone laughed and said I had a very big ego. "Typical of Americans," he added, patting my back congenially.

"Indonesians are very conscious of politics," the man in the chair beside me said. "Don't Americans go to shows like this?"

A beautiful woman, an English major at the university, sat across the table from me. "But you do work for the World Bank, don't you?" she asked.

I told her that my current assignment was for the Asian Development Bank and the United States Agency for International Development.

"Aren't they really all the same?" She didn't wait for an answer. "Isn't it like the play tonight showed? Doesn't your government look at Indonesia and other countries as though we are just a bunch of . . ." She searched for the word.

"Grapes," one of her friends coached.

"Exactly. A bunch of grapes. You can pick and choose. Keep England. Eat China. And throw away Indonesia."

"After you've taken all our oil," another woman added.

I tried to defend myself but was not at all up to the task. I wanted to take pride in the fact that I had come to this part of town and had stayed to watch the entire anti-U.S. performance, which I might have construed as a personal assault. I wanted them to see the courage of what I had done, to know that I was the only member of my team who bothered to learn Bahasa or had any desire to take in their culture, and to point out that I was the sole foreigner attending this production. But I decided it would be more prudent not to mention any of this. Instead, I tried to refocus the conversation. I asked them why they thought the dalang had singled out Muslim countries, except for Vietnam.

The beautiful English major laughed at this. "Because that's the plan."

"Vietnam is just a holding action," one of the men interjected, "like Holland was for the Nazis. A stepping-stone."

"The real target," the woman continued, "is the Muslim world."

I could not let this go unanswered. "Surely," I protested, "you can't believe that the United States is anti-Islamic."

"Oh no?" she asked. "Since when? You need to read one of your own historians—a Brit named Toynbee. Back in the fifties he predicted that the real war in the next century would not be between Communists and capitalists, but between Christians and Muslims."

"Arnold Toynbee said that?" I was stunned.

"Yes. Read *Civilization on Trial* and *The World and the West*."

"But why should there be such animosity between Muslims and Christians?" I asked.

Looks were exchanged around the table. They appeared to find it hard to believe that I could ask such a foolish question.

"Because," she said slowly, as though addressing someone slow-witted or hard of hearing, "the West—especially its leader, the U.S.—is determined to take control of all the world, to become the greatest empire in history. It has already gotten very close to succeeding. The Soviet Union currently stands in its way, but the Soviets will not endure. Toynbee could see that. They have no religion, no faith, no substance behind their ideology. History demonstrates that faith—soul, a belief in higher powers—is essential. We Muslims have it. We have it more than anyone else in the world, even more than the Christians. So we wait. We grow strong."

"We will take our time," one of the men chimed in, "and then like a snake we will strike."

"What a horrible thought!" I could barely contain myself. "What can we do to change this?"

The English major looked me directly in the eyes. "Stop being so greedy," she said, "and so selfish. Realize that there is more to the world than your big houses and fancy stores. People are starving and you worry about oil for your cars. Babies are dying of thirst and you search the fashion magazines for the latest styles. Nations like ours are drowning in poverty, but your people don't even hear our cries for help. You shut your ears to the voices of those who try to tell you these things. You label them radicals or Communists. You must open your hearts to the poor and down-trodden, instead of driving them further into poverty and servitude. There's not much time left. If you don't change, you're doomed."

Several days later the popular Bandung politician, whose puppet stood up to Nixon and was impaled by Bucket Man, was struck and killed by a hit-and-run driver.

CHAPTER 8

Jesus, Seen Differently

The memory of that dalang stuck with me. So did the words of the beautiful English major. That night in Bandung catapulted me to a new level of thinking and feeling. While I had not exactly ignored the implications of what we were doing in Indonesia, my reactions had been ruled by emotions, and I usually had been able to calm my feelings by calling on reason, on the example of history, and on the biological imperative. I had justified our involvement as part of the human condition, convincing myself that Einar, Charlie, and the rest of us were simply acting as men always have: taking care of ourselves and our families.

My discussion with those young Indonesians, however, forced me to see another aspect of the issue. Through their eyes, I realized that a selfish approach to foreign policy does not serve or protect future generations anywhere. It is myopic, like the annual reports of the corporations and the election strategies of the politicians who formulate that foreign policy.

As it turned out, the data I needed for my economic forecasts required frequent visits to Jakarta. I took advantage of my time alone there to ponder these matters and to write about them in a journal. I wandered the streets of that city, handed money to beggars, and attempted to engage lepers, prostitutes, and street urchins in conversation.

Meanwhile, I pondered the nature of foreign aid, and I considered the legitimate role that developed countries (DCs, in World Bank jargon) might play in helping alleviate poverty and misery in less-developed countries (LDCs). I began to wonder when foreign aid is genuine and when it is only greedy and self-serving. Indeed, I began to question whether such aid is ever altruistic, and if not, whether that could be changed. I was certain that countries like my own should take decisive action to help the sick and starving of the world, but I was equally certain that this was seldom—if ever—the prime motivation for our intervention.

I kept coming back to one main question: if the objective of foreign aid is imperialism, is that so wrong? I often found myself envying people like Charlie who believed so strongly in our system that they wanted to force it on the rest of the world. I doubted whether limited resources would allow the whole world to live the opulent life of the United States, when even the United States had millions of citizens living in poverty. In addition, it wasn't entirely clear to me that people in other nations actually want to live like us. Our own statistics about violence, depression, drug abuse, divorce, and crime indicated that although ours was one of the wealthiest societies in history, it may also be one of the least happy societies. Why would we want others to emulate us?

Perhaps Claudine had warned me of all this. I was no longer sure what it was she had been trying to tell me. In any case, intellectual arguments aside, it had now become painfully clear that my days of innocence were gone. I wrote in my journal:

> Is anyone in the U.S. innocent? Although those at the very pinnacle of the economic pyramid gain the most, millions of us depend—either directly or indirectly— on the exploitation of the LDCs for our livelihoods.

The resources and cheap labor that feed nearly all our businesses come from places like Indonesia, and very little ever makes its way back. The loans of foreign aid ensure that today's children and their grandchildren will be held hostage. They will have to allow our corporations to ravage their natural resources and will have to forego education, health, and other social services merely to pay us back. The fact that our own companies already received most of this money to build the power plants, airports, and industrial parks does not factor into this formula. Does the excuse that most Americans are unaware of this constitute innocence? Uninformed and intentionally misinformed, yes—but innocent?

Of course, I had to face the fact that I was now numbered among those who actively misinform.

The concept of a worldwide holy war was a disturbing one, but the longer I contemplated it, the more convinced I became of its possibility. It seemed to me, however, that if this jihad were to occur it would be less about Muslims versus Christians than it would be about LDCs versus DCs, perhaps with Muslims at the forefront. We in the DCs were the users of resources; those in the LDCs were the suppliers. It was the colonial mercantile system all over again, set up to make it easy for those with power and limited natural resources to exploit those with resources but no power.

I did not have a copy of Toynbee with me, but I knew enough history to understand that suppliers who are exploited long enough will rebel. I only had to return to the American Revolution and Tom Paine for a model. I recalled that Britain justified its taxes by claiming that England was providing aid to the colonies in the form of military protection against the French and the Indians. The colonists had a very different interpretation.

What Paine offered to his countrymen in the brilliant *Common Sense* was the soul that my young Indonesian friends had referred to—an idea, a faith in the justice of a higher power, and a religion of freedom and equality that was diametrically opposed to the British monarchy and its elitist class systems. What Muslims offered was similar: faith in a higher power and a belief that developed countries have no right to subjugate and exploit the rest of the world. Like colonial minutemen, Muslims were threatening to fight for their rights, and like the British in the 1770s, we classified such actions as terrorism. History appeared to be repeating itself.

I wondered what sort of a world we might have if the United States and its allies diverted all the monies expended in colonial wars—like the one in Vietnam—to eradicating world hunger or to making education and basic health care available to all people, including our own. I wondered how future generations would be affected if we committed to alleviating the sources of misery and to protecting watersheds, forests, and other natural areas that ensure clean water, air, and the things that feed our spirits as well as our bodies. I could not believe that our Founding Fathers had envisioned the right to life, liberty, and the pursuit of happiness to exist only for Americans, so why were we now implementing strategies that promoted the imperialist values they had fought against?

On my last night in Indonesia, I awoke from a dream, sat up in bed, and switched on the light. I had the feeling that someone was in the room with me. I peered around at the familiar Hotel Inter-Continental furniture, the batik tapestries, and the framed shadow puppets hanging on the walls. Then the dream came back.

I had seen Christ standing in front of me. He seemed like the same Jesus I had talked with every night when, as a young boy, I shared my thoughts with him after saying my formal prayers. Except that the Jesus of my childhood was fair-skinned and blond, while this one had curly black hair and a dark complexion. He bent down and heaved something up to his shoulder. I expected a cross. Instead, I saw the axle of a car with the attached wheel rim protruding above his head, forming a metallic halo. Grease dripped like blood down his forehead. He straightened, peered into my eyes, and said, "If I were to come now, you would see me differently." I asked him why. "Because," he answered, "the world has changed."

The clock told me it was nearly daylight. I knew I could not go back to sleep, so I dressed, took the elevator to the empty lobby, and wandered into the gardens around the swimming pool. The moon was bright; the sweet smell of orchids filled the air. I sat down in a lounge chair and wondered what I was doing here, why the coincidences of my life had taken me along this path, why Indonesia. I knew my life had changed, but I had no idea how drastically.

Ann and I met in Paris on my way home, to attempt reconciliation. Even during this French vacation, however, we continued to quarrel. Although there were many special and beautiful moments, I think we both came to the realization that our long history of anger and resentment was too large an obstacle. Besides, there was so much I could not tell her. The only person I could share such things with was Claudine, and I thought about her constantly. Ann and I landed at Boston's Logan Airport and took a taxi to our separate apartments in the Back Bay.

CHAPTER 9

Opportunity of a Lifetime

The true test of Indonesia awaited me at MAIN. I went to the Prudential Center headquarters first thing in the morning, and while I was standing with dozens of other employees at the elevator I learned that Mac Hall, MAIN's enigmatic, octogenarian chairman and CEO, had promoted Einar to president of the Portland, Oregon office. As a result, I now officially reported to Bruno Zambotti.

Nicknamed "the silver fox" because of the color of his hair and his uncanny ability to outmaneuver everyone who challenged him, Bruno had the dapper good looks of Cary Grant. He was eloquent, and he held both an engineering degree and an MBA. He understood econometrics and was vice president in charge of MAIN's electrical power division and of most of our international projects. He also was the obvious choice to take over as president of the corporation when his mentor, the aging Jake Dauber, retired. Like most MAIN employees, I was awed and terrified by Bruno Zambotti.

Just before lunch, I was summoned to Bruno's office. Following a cordial discussion about Indonesia, he said something that made me jump to the edge of my seat.

"I'm firing Howard Parker. We don't need to go into the details, except to say that he's lost touch with reality." His smile was disconcertingly pleasant as he tapped his finger against a sheaf of papers on his desk. "Eight percent a year. That's his load forecast. Can you believe it? In a country with the potential of Indonesia!"

His smile faded and he looked me squarely in the eye. "Charlie Illingworth tells me that your economic forecast is right on target and will justify load growth of between 17 and 20 percent. Is that right?"

I assured him it was.

He stood up and offered me his hand. "Congratulations. You've just been promoted."

Perhaps I should have gone out and celebrated at a fancy restaurant with other MAIN employees—or even by myself. However, my mind was on Claudine. I was dying to tell her about my promotion and all my experiences in Indonesia. She had warned me not to call her from abroad, and I had not. Now I was dismayed to find that her phone was disconnected, with no forwarding number. I went looking for her.

A young couple had moved into her apartment. It was lunchtime but I believe I roused them from their bed; obviously annoyed, they professed to know nothing about Claudine. I paid a visit to the real estate agency, pretending to be a cousin. Their files indicated they had never rented to anyone with her name; the previous lease had been issued to a man who would remain anonymous by his request. Back at the Prudential Center, MAIN's employment office also claimed to have no record of her. They admitted only to a "special consultants" file that was not available for my scrutiny.

By late afternoon, I was exhausted and emotionally drained. On top of everything else, a bad case of jet lag had set in. Returning to my empty apartment, I felt desperately lonely and abandoned. My promotion seemed meaningless or, even worse, to be a badge of my willingness to sell out. I threw myself onto the bed, overwhelmed with despair. I had been used by Claudine and then discarded. Determined not to give in to my anguish, I shut down my emotions. I lay there on my bed staring at the bare walls for what seemed like hours.

Finally, I managed to pull myself together. I got up, swallowed a beer, and smashed the empty bottle against a table. Then I stared out the window. Looking down a distant street, I thought I saw her walking toward me. I started for the door and then returned to the window for another look. The woman had come closer. I could see that she was attractive, and that her walk was reminiscent of Claudine's, but it was not Claudine. My heart sank, and my feelings changed from anger and loathing to fear.

An image flashed before me of Claudine flailing, falling in a rain of bullets, assassinated. I shook it off, took a couple Valium, and drank myself to sleep.

The next morning, a call from MAIN's personnel department woke me from my stupor. Its chief, Paul Mormino, assured me he understood my need for rest, but he urged me to come in that afternoon.

"Good news," he said. "The best thing for catching up with yourself."

I obeyed the summons and learned that Bruno had been more than true to his word. I had not only been promoted to Howard's old job; I had been given the title of Chief Economist and a raise. It did cheer me up a bit.

I took the afternoon off and wandered down along the Charles River with a quart of beer. As I sat there, watching the sailboats and nursing combined jet lag and vicious hangover, I convinced myself that Claudine had done her job and had moved on to her next assignment. She had always emphasized the need for secrecy. She would call me. Mormino had been right. My jet lag—and my anxiety—dissipated.

During the next weeks, I tried to put all thoughts of Claudine aside. I focused on writing my report on the Indonesian economy and on revising Howard's load forecasts. I came up with the type of study my bosses wanted to see: a growth in electric demand averaging 19 percent per annum for twelve years after the new system was completed, tapering down to 17 percent for eight more years, and then holding at 15 percent for the remainder of the twenty-five-year projection.

I presented my conclusions at formal meetings with the international lending agencies. Their teams of experts questioned me extensively and mercilessly. By then, my emotions had turned into a sort of grim determination, not unlike those that had driven me to excel rather than to rebel during my prep school days. Nonetheless, Claudine's memory always hovered close. When a sassy young economist out to make a name for himself at the Asian Development Bank grilled me relentlessly for an entire afternoon, I recalled the advice Claudine had given me as we sat in her Beacon Street apartment those many months before.

"Who can see twenty-five years into the future?" she had asked. "Your guess is as good as theirs. Confidence is everything."

I convinced myself I was an expert, reminding myself that I had experienced more of life in developing countries than many of the men—some of them twice my age—who now sat in judgment of my work. I had lived in the Amazon and had traveled to parts of Java no one else wanted to visit. I had taken a couple of intensive courses aimed at teaching executives the finer points of econometrics, and I told myself that I was part of the new breed of statistically oriented, econometric-worshipping whiz kids that appealed to Robert McNamara, the buttoned-down president of the World Bank, former president of Ford Motor Company, and John Kennedy's secretary of defense. Here was a man who had built his reputation on numbers, on probability theory, on mathematical models, and—I suspected—on the bravado of a very large ego.

I tried to emulate both McNamara and my boss, Bruno. I adopted manners of speech that imitated the former, and I took to walking with the swagger of the latter, attaché case swinging at my side. Looking back, I have to wonder at my gall. In truth, my expertise was extremely limited, but what I lacked in training and knowledge I made up for in audacity.

And it worked. Eventually the team of experts stamped my reports with their seals of approval.

During the ensuing months, I attended meetings in Tehran, Caracas, Guatemala City, London, Vienna, and Washington, DC. I met famous personalities, including the shah of Iran, the former presidents of several countries, and Robert McNamara himself. Like prep school, it was a world of men. I was amazed at how my new title and the accounts of my recent successes before the international lending agencies affected other people's attitudes toward me.

At first, all the attention went to my head. I began to think of myself as a Merlin who could wave his wand over a country, causing it suddenly to light up, industries sprouting like flowers. Then I became disillusioned. I questioned my own motives and those of all the people I worked with. It seemed that a glorified title or a PhD did little to help a person understand the plight of a leper living beside a cesspool in Jakarta, and I doubted that a knack for manipulating statistics enabled a person to see into the future. The better I came to know those who made the decisions that shape the world, the more skeptical I became about their abilities and their goals. Looking at the faces around the meeting room tables, I found myself struggling very hard to restrain my anger.

Eventually, however, this perspective also changed. I came to understand that most of those men believed they were doing the right thing. Like Charlie, they were convinced that communism and terrorism were evil forces—rather than the predictable reactions to decisions they and their predecessors had made—and that they had a duty to their country, to their offspring, and to God to convert the world to capitalism. They also clung to the principle of survival of the fittest; if they happened to enjoy the good fortune to have been born into a privileged class instead of inside a cardboard shack, then they saw it as an obligation to pass this heritage on to their progeny.

I vacillated between viewing such people as an actual conspiracy and simply seeing them as a tight-knit fraternity bent on dominating the world. Nonetheless, over time I began to liken them to the plantation owners of the pre–Civil War South. They were men drawn together in a loose association by common beliefs and shared self-interest, rather than an exclusive group meeting in clandestine hideaways with focused and sinister intent. The plantation autocrats had grown up with servants and slaves, had been educated to believe that it was their right and even their duty to take care of the "heathens" and to convert them to the owners' religion and way of life. Even if slavery repulsed them philosophically, they could, like Thomas Jefferson, justify it as a necessity, the collapse of which would result in social and economic chaos. The leaders of the modern oligarchies, what I now thought of as the corporatocracy, seemed to fit the same mold.

I also began to wonder who benefits from war and the mass production of weapons, from the damming of rivers and the destruction of indigenous environments and cultures. I began to look at who benefits when hundreds of thousands of people die from insufficient food, polluted water, or curable diseases. Slowly, I came to realize that in the long run no one benefits, but in the short term those at the top of the pyramid—my bosses and me—appear to benefit, at least materially.

This raised several other questions: Why does this situation persist? Why has it endured for so long? Does the answer lie simply in the old adage that "might is right," that those with the power perpetuate the system?

It seemed insufficient to say that power alone allows this situation to persist. While the proposition that might makes right explained a great deal, I felt there must be a more compelling force at work here. I recalled an economics professor from my business school days, a man from northern India, who lectured about limited resources, about man's need to grow continually, and about the principle of slave labor. According to this professor, all successful capitalist systems involve hierarchies with rigid chains of command, including a handful at the very top who control descending orders of subordinates, and a massive army of workers at the bottom, who in relative economic terms truly can be classified as slaves. Ultimately, then, I became convinced that we encourage this system because the corporatocracy has convinced us that God has given us the right to place a few of our people at the very top of this capitalist pyramid and to export our system to the entire world.

Of course, we are not the first to do this. The list of practitioners stretches back to the ancient empires of North Africa, the Middle East, and Asia, and works its way up through Persia, Greece, Rome, the Christian Crusades, and all the European empire builders of the post-Columbian era. This imperialist drive has been and continues to be the cause of most wars, pollution, starvation, species extinctions, and genocides. And it has always taken a serious toll on the conscience and well-being of the citizens of those empires, contributing to social malaise and resulting in a situation where the wealthiest cultures in human history are plagued with the highest rates of suicide, drug abuse, and violence.

I thought extensively on these questions, but I avoided considering the nature of my own role in all of this. I tried to think of myself not as an EHM but as a chief economist. It sounded so very legitimate, and if I needed any confirmation, I could look at my pay stubs: all were from MAIN, a private corporation. I didn't earn a penny from the NSA or any government agency. And so I became convinced. Almost.

One afternoon Bruno called me into his office. He walked behind my chair and patted me on the shoulder. "You've done an excellent job," he purred. "To show our appreciation, we're giving you the opportunity of a lifetime, something few men ever receive, even at twice your age."

CHAPTER 10

Panama's President and Hero

I landed at Panama's Tucumen International Airport late one April night in 1972, during a tropical deluge. As was common in those days, I shared a taxi with several other executives, and because I spoke Spanish, I ended up in the front seat beside the driver. I stared blankly out the taxi's windshield. Through the rain, the headlights illuminated a billboard portrait of a handsome man with a prominent brow and flashing eyes. One side of his wide-brimmed hat was hooked rakishly up. I recognized him as the hero of modern Panama, Omar Torrijos.

I had prepared for this trip in my customary fashion, by visiting the reference section of the Boston Public Library. I knew that one of the reasons for Torrijos's popularity among his people was that he was a firm defender of both Panama's right of self-rule and of its claims to sovereignty over the Panama Canal. He was determined that the country under his leadership would avoid the pitfalls of its ignominious history.

Panama was part of Colombia when the French engineer Ferdinand de Lesseps, who directed construction of the Suez Canal, decided to build a canal through the Central American isthmus, to connect the Atlantic and Pacific oceans. Beginning in 1881, the French undertook a mammoth effort that met with one catastrophe after another. Finally, in 1889, the project ended in financial disaster—but it had inspired a dream in Theodore Roosevelt. During the first years of the twentieth century, the United States demanded that Colombia sign a treaty turning the isthmus over to a North American consortium. Colombia refused.

In 1903, President Roosevelt sent in the U.S. warship *Nashville*. U.S. soldiers landed, seized and killed a popular local militia commander, and declared Panama an independent nation. A puppet government was installed and the first Canal Treaty was signed; it established an American zone on both sides of the future waterway, legalized U.S. military intervention, and gave Washington virtual control over this newly formed "independent" nation.

Interestingly, the treaty was signed by U.S. Secretary of State Hay and a French engineer, Philippe Bunau-Varilla, who had been part of the original team, but it was not signed by a single Panamanian. In essence, Panama was forced to leave Colombia in order to serve the United States, in a deal struck by an American and a Frenchman—in retrospect, a prophetic beginning.[1]

For more than half a century, Panama was ruled by an oligarchy of wealthy families with strong connections to Washington. They were right-wing dictators who took whatever measures they deemed necessary to ensure that their country promoted U.S. interests. In the manner of most of the Latin American dictators who allied themselves with Washington, Panama's rulers interpreted U.S. interests to mean putting down any populist movement that smacked of socialism. They also supported the CIA and NSA in anti-Communist activities throughout the hemisphere, and they helped big American businesses like Rockefeller's Standard Oil and United Fruit Company. These governments apparently did not feel that U.S. interests were promoted by improving the lives of people who lived in dire poverty or served as virtual slaves to the big plantations and corporations.

Panama's ruling families were well rewarded for their support; U.S. military forces intervened on their behalf a dozen times between the declaration of Panamanian independence and 1968. However, that year, while I was still a Peace Corps volunteer in Ecuador, the course of Panamanian history suddenly changed. A coup overthrew Arnulfo Arias, the latest in the parade of dictators, and Omar Torrijos emerged as the head of state, although he had not actively participated in the coup.[2]

Torrijos was highly regarded by the Panamanian middle and lower classes. He himself had grown up in the rural city of Santiago, where his parents taught school. He had risen quickly through the ranks of the National Guard, Panama's primary military unit and an institution that during the 1960s gained increasing support among the poor. Torrijos earned a reputation for listening to the dispossessed. He walked the streets of their shantytowns, held meetings in slums politicians didn't dare to enter, helped the unemployed find jobs, and often donated his own limited financial resources to families stricken by illness or tragedy.[3]

His love of life and his compassion for people reached even beyond Panama's borders. Torrijos was committed to turning his nation into a haven for fugitives from persecution, a place that would offer asylum to refugees from both sides of the political fence, from leftist opponents of Chile's Pinochet to right-wing anti-Castro guerrillas. Many people saw him as an agent of peace, a perception that earned him praise throughout the hemisphere. He also developed a reputation as a leader who was dedicated to resolving differences among the various factions that were tearing apart so many Latin American countries: Honduras, Guatemala, El Salvador, Nicaragua, Cuba, Colombia, Peru, Argentina, Chile, and Paraguay. His small nation of two million people served as a model of social reform and an inspiration for world leaders as diverse as the labor organizers who plotted the dismemberment of the Soviet Union and Islamic militants like Muammar Gadhafi of Libya.[4]

My first night in Panama, stopped at the traffic light, peering past the noisy windshield wipers, I was moved by this man smiling down at me from the billboard—handsome, charismatic, and courageous. I knew from my hours at the BPL that he stood behind his beliefs. For the first time in its history, Panama was not a puppet of Washington or of anyone else. Torrijos never succumbed to the temptations offered by Moscow or Beijing; he believed in social reform and in helping those born into poverty, but he did not advocate communism. Unlike Castro, Torrijos was determined to win freedom from the United States without forging alliances with the United States' enemies.

I had stumbled across an article in some obscure journal in the BPL racks that praised Torrijos as a man who would alter the history of the Americas, reversing a long-term trend toward U.S. domination. The author cited as his starting point Manifest Destiny—the doctrine, popular with many Americans during the 1840s, that the conquest of North America was divinely ordained; that God, not men, had ordered the destruction of Indians, forests, and buffalo, the draining of swamps and the channeling of rivers, and the development of an economy that depends on the continuing exploitation of labor and natural resources.

The article got me to thinking about my country's attitude toward the world. The Monroe Doctrine, originally enunciated by President James Monroe in 1823, was used to take Manifest Destiny a step further when, in the 1850s and 1860s, it was used to assert that the United States had special rights all over the hemisphere, including the right to invade any nation in Central or South America that refused to back U.S. policies. Teddy Roosevelt invoked the Monroe Doctrine to justify U.S. intervention in the Dominican Republic, in Venezuela, and during the "liberation" of Panama from Colombia. A string of subsequent U.S. presidents—most notably Taft, Wilson, and Franklin Roosevelt—relied on it to expand Washington's Pan-American activities through the end of World War II. Finally, during the latter half of the twentieth century, the United States used the Communist threat to justify expansion of this concept to countries around the globe, including Vietnam and Indonesia.[5]

Now, it seemed, one man was standing in Washington's way. I knew that he was not the first—leaders like Castro and Allende had gone before him—but Torrijos alone was doing it outside the realm of Communist ideology and without claiming that his movement was a revolution. He was simply saying that Panama had its own rights—to sovereignty over its people, its lands, and a waterway that bisected it—and that these rights were as valid and as divinely bestowed as any enjoyed by the United States.

Torrijos also objected to the School of the Americas and to the U.S. Southern Command's tropical warfare training center, both located in the Canal Zone. For years, the United States armed forces had invited Latin American dictators and presidents to send their sons and military leaders to these facilities—the largest and best equipped outside North America. There, they learned interrogation and covert operational skills as well as military tactics that they would use to fight communism and to protect their own assets and those of the oil companies and other private corporations. They also had opportunities to bond with the United States' top brass.

These facilities were hated by Latin Americans—except for the few wealthy ones who benefited from them. They were known to provide schooling for right-wing death squads and the torturers who had turned so many nations into totalitarian regimes. Torrijos made it clear that he did not want training centers located in Panama—and that he considered the Canal Zone to be included within his borders.[6]

Seeing the handsome general on the billboard, and reading the caption beneath his face—"Omar's ideal is freedom; the missile is not invented that can kill an ideal!"—I felt a shiver run down my spine. I had a premonition that the story of Panama in the twentieth century was far from over, and that Torrijos was in for a difficult and perhaps even tragic time.

The tropical storm battered against the windshield, the traffic light turned green, and the driver honked his horn at the car ahead of us. I thought about my own position. I had been sent to Panama to close the deal on what would become MAIN's first truly comprehensive master development plan. This plan would create a justification for World Bank, Inter-American Development Bank, and USAID investment of billions of dollars in the energy, transportation, and agricultural sectors of this tiny and very crucial country. It was, of course, a subterfuge, a means of making Panama forever indebted and thereby returning it to its puppet status.

As the taxi started to move through the night, a paroxysm of guilt flashed through me, but I suppressed it. What did I care? I had taken the plunge in Java, sold my soul, and now I could create my opportunity of a lifetime. I could become rich, famous, and powerful in one blow.

CHAPTER 11

Pirates in the Canal Zone

The next day, the Panamanian government sent a man to show me around. His name was Fidel, and I was immediately drawn to him. He was tall and slim and took an obvious pride in his country. His great-great-grandfather had fought beside Bolívar to win independence from Spain. I told him I was related to Tom Paine, and was thrilled to learn that Fidel had read *Common Sense* in Spanish. He spoke English, but when he discovered I was fluent in the language of his country, he was overcome with emotion.

"Many of your people live here for years and never bother to learn it," he said.

Fidel took me on a drive through an impressively prosperous sector of his city, which he called the New Panama. As we passed modern glass-and-steel skyscrapers, he explained that Panama had more international banks than any other country south of the Rio Grande.

"We're often called the Switzerland of the Americas," he said. "We ask very few questions of our clients."

Late in the afternoon, with the sun sliding toward the Pacific, we headed out on an avenue that followed the contours of the bay.

A long line of ships was anchored there. I asked Fidel whether there was a problem with the canal.

"It's always like this," he replied with a laugh. "Lines of them, waiting their turn. Half the traffic is coming from or going to Japan. More even than the United States."

I confessed that this was news to me.

"I'm not surprised," he said. "North Americans don't know much about the rest of the world."

We stopped at a beautiful park in which bougainvillea crept over ancient ruins. A sign proclaimed that this was a fort built to protect the city against marauding English pirates. A family was setting up for an evening picnic: a father, mother, son and daughter, and an elderly man who I assumed was the children's grandfather. I felt a sudden longing for the tranquility that seemed to embrace these five people. As we passed them, the couple smiled, waved, and greeted us in English. I asked if they were tourists, and they laughed. The man came over to us.

"I'm third generation in the Canal Zone," he explained proudly. "My granddad came three years after it was created. He drove one of the mules, the tractors that hauled ships through the locks." He pointed at the elderly man, who was preoccupied helping the children set the picnic table. "My dad was an engineer and I've followed in his footsteps."

The woman had returned to helping her father-in-law and children. Beyond them, the sun dipped into the blue water. It was a scene of idyllic beauty, reminiscent of a Monet painting. I asked the man if they were U.S. citizens.

He looked at me incredulously. "Of course. The Canal Zone is U.S. territory." The boy ran up to tell his father that dinner was ready.

"Will your son be the fourth generation?"

The man brought his hands together in a sign of prayer and raised them toward the sky.

"I pray to the good Lord every day that he may have that opportunity. Living in the Zone is a wonderful life." Then he lowered his hands and stared directly at Fidel. "I just hope we can hold on to her for another fifty years. That despot Torrijos is making a lot of waves. A dangerous man."

A sudden urge gripped me, and I said to him, in Spanish, "*Adios*. I hope you and your family have a good time here, and learn lots about Panama's culture."

He gave me a disgusted look. "I don't speak their language," he said. Then he turned abruptly and headed toward his family and the picnic.

Fidel stepped close to me, placed an arm around my shoulders, and squeezed tightly. "Thank you," he said.

Back in the city, Fidel drove us through an area he described as a slum.

"Not our worst," he said. "But you'll get the flavor."

Wooden shacks and ditches filled with standing water lined the street, the frail homes suggesting dilapidated boats scuttled in a cesspool. The smell of rot and sewage filled our car as children with distended bellies ran alongside. When we slowed, they congregated at my side, calling me *uncle* and begging for money. It reminded me of Jakarta.

Graffiti covered many of the walls. There were a few of the usual hearts with couples' names scrawled inside, but most of the graffiti were slogans expressing hatred of the United States: "Go home, gringo," "Stop shitting in our canal," "Uncle Sam, slave master," and "Tell Nixon that Panama is not Vietnam." The one that chilled my heart the most, however, read, "Death for freedom is the way to Christ." Scattered among these were posters of Omar Torrijos.

"Now the other side," Fidel said. "I've got official papers and you're a U.S. citizen, so we can go." Beneath a magenta sky, he drove us into the Canal Zone. As prepared as I thought I was, it was not enough. I could hardly believe the opulence of the place—huge white buildings, manicured lawns, plush homes, golf courses, stores, and theaters.

"The facts," he said. "Everything in here is U.S. property. All the businesses—the supermarkets, barbershops, beauty salons, restaurants, all of them—are exempt from Panamanian laws and taxes. There are seven 18-hole golf courses, U.S. post offices scattered conveniently around, U.S. courts of law and schools. It truly is a country within a country."

"What an affront!"

Fidel peered at me as though making a quick assessment. "Yes," he agreed. "That's a pretty good word for it. Over there," he pointed back toward the city, "income per capita is less than one thousand dollars a year, and unemployment rates are 30 percent. Of course, in the little shantytown we just visited, no one makes close to one thousand dollars, and hardly anyone has a job."

"What's being done?"

He turned and gave me a look that seemed to change from anger to sadness.

"What *can* we do?" He shook his head. "I don't know, but I'll say this: Torrijos is trying. I think it may be the death of him, but he sure as hell is giving it all he's got. He's a man who'll go down fighting for his people."

As we headed out of the Canal Zone, Fidel smiled. "You like to dance?" Without waiting for me to reply, he said, "Let's get some dinner, and then I'll show you yet another side of Panama."

CHAPTER 12

Soldiers and Prostitutes

After a juicy steak and a cold beer, we left the restaurant and drove down a dark street. Fidel advised me never to walk in this area. "When you come here, take a cab right to the front door." He pointed. "Just there, beyond the fence, is the Canal Zone."

He drove on until we arrived at a vacant lot filled with cars. He found an empty spot and parked. An old man hobbled up to us. Fidel got out and patted him on the back. Then he ran his hand lovingly across the fender of his car.

"Take good care of her. She's my lady." He handed the man a bill.

We took a short footpath out of the parking lot and suddenly found ourselves on a street flooded with flashing neon lights. Two boys raced past, pointing sticks at each other and making the sounds of men shooting guns. One slammed into Fidel's legs, his head reaching barely as high as Fidel's thigh. The little boy stopped and stood back.

"I'm sorry, sir," he gasped in Spanish.

Fidel placed both his hands on the boy's shoulders. "No harm done, my man," he said. "But tell me, what were you and your friend shooting at?"

The other boy came up to us. He placed his arm protectively around the first. "My brother," he explained. "We're sorry."

"It's okay," Fidel chuckled gently. "He didn't hurt me. I just asked him what you guys were shooting at. I think I used to play the same game."

The brothers glanced at each other. The older one smiled. "He's the gringo general at the Canal Zone. He tried to rape our mother and I'm sending him packing, back to where he belongs."

Fidel stole a look at me. "Where does he belong?"

"At home, in the United States."

"Does your mother work here?"

"Over there." Both boys pointed proudly at a neon light down the street. "Bartender."

"Go on then." Fidel handed them each a coin. "But be careful. Stay in the lights."

"Oh yes, sir. Thank you." They raced off.

As we walked on, Fidel explained that Panamanian women were prohibited by law from prostitution. "They can tend bar and dance, but cannot sell their bodies. That's left to the imports."

We stepped inside the bar and were blasted with a popular American song. My eyes and ears took a moment to adjust. A couple of burly U.S. soldiers stood near the door; bands around their uniformed arms identified them as MPs.

Fidel led me along a bar, and then I saw the stage. Three young women were dancing there, entirely naked except for their heads. One wore a sailor's cap, another a green beret, and the third a cowboy hat. They had spectacular figures and were laughing. They seemed to be playing a game with one another, as though dancing in a competition. The music, the way they danced, the stage—it could have been a disco in Boston, except that they were naked.

We pushed our way through a group of young English-speaking men. Although they wore T-shirts and blue jeans, their crew cuts gave them away as soldiers from the Canal Zone's military base. Fidel tapped a waitress on the shoulder. She turned, let out a scream of delight, and threw her arms around him. The group of young men watched this intently, glancing at one another with disapproval. I wondered if they thought Manifest Destiny included this Panamanian woman. The waitress led us to a corner. From somewhere, she produced a small table and two chairs.

As we settled in, Fidel exchanged greetings in Spanish with two men at a table beside ours. Unlike the soldiers, they wore printed short-sleeved shirts and creased slacks. The waitress returned with a couple of Balboa beers, and Fidel patted her on the rump as she turned to leave. She smiled and threw him a kiss. I glanced around and was relieved to discover that the young men at the bar were no longer watching us; they were focused on the dancers.

The majority of the patrons were English-speaking soldiers, but there were others, like the two beside us, who obviously were Panamanians. They stood out because their hair would not have passed inspection, and because they did not wear T-shirts and jeans. A few of them sat at tables, others leaned against the walls. They seemed to be highly alert, like border collies guarding flocks of sheep.

Women roamed the tables. They moved constantly, sitting on laps, shouting to the waitresses, dancing, swirling, singing, taking turns on the stage. They wore tight skirts, T-shirts, jeans, clinging dresses, high heels. One was dressed in a Victorian gown and veil. Another wore only a bikini. It was obvious that only the most beautiful could survive here. I marveled at the numbers who made their way to Panama and wondered at the desperation that had driven them to this.

"All from other countries?" I shouted to Fidel above the music.

He nodded. "Except . . ." He pointed at the waitresses. "They're Panamanian."

"What countries?"

"Honduras, El Salvador, Nicaragua, and Guatemala."

"Neighbors."

"Not entirely. Costa Rica and Colombia are our closest neighbors."

The waitress who had led us to this table came and sat on Fidel's knee. He gently rubbed her back.

"Clarissa," he said, "please tell my North American friend why they left their countries." He nodded his head in the direction of the stage. Three new girls were accepting the hats from the others, who jumped down and started dressing. The music switched to salsa, and as the newcomers danced, they shed their clothes to the rhythm.

Clarissa held out her right hand. "I'm pleased to meet you," she said. Then she stood up and reached for our empty bottles. "In answer to Fidel's question, these girls come here to escape brutality. I'll bring a couple more Balboas."

After she left, I turned to Fidel. "Come on," I said. "They're here for U.S. dollars."

"True. But why so many from the countries where fascist dictators rule?"

I glanced back at the stage. The three of them were giggling and throwing the sailor's cap around like a ball. I looked Fidel in the eye. "You're not kidding, are you?"

"No," he said seriously, "I wish I were. Most of these girls have lost their families—fathers, brothers, husbands, boyfriends. They grew up with torture and death. Dancing and prostitution don't seem all that bad to them. They can make a lot of money here, then start fresh somewhere, buy a little shop, open a café —"

He was interrupted by a commotion near the bar. I saw a waitress swing her fist at one of the soldiers, who caught her hand and began to twist her wrist. She screamed and fell to her knee. He laughed and shouted to his buddies. They all laughed. She tried to hit him with her free hand. He twisted harder. Her face contorted with pain.

The MPs remained by the door, watching calmly. Fidel jumped to his feet and started toward the bar. One of the men at the table next to ours held out a hand to stop him. *"Tranquilo, hermano,"* he said. "Be calm, brother. Enrique has control."

A tall, slim Panamanian came out of the shadows near the stage. He moved like a cat and was upon the soldier in an instant. One hand encircled the man's throat while the other doused him in the face with a glass of water. The waitress slipped away. Several of the Panamanians who had been lounging against the walls formed a protective semicircle around the tall bouncer. He lifted the soldier against the bar and said something I couldn't hear. Then he raised his voice and spoke slowly in English, loudly enough for everyone in the still room to hear over the music.

"The waitresses are off-limits to you guys, and you don't touch the others until after you pay them."

The two MPs finally swung into action. They approached the cluster of Panamanians. "We'll take it from here, Enrique," they said.

The bouncer lowered the soldier to the floor and gave his neck a final squeeze, forcing the other's head back and eliciting a cry of pain.

"Do you understand me?" There was a feeble groan. "Good." He pushed the soldier at the two MPs. "Get him out of here."

Conversations with the General

The invitation was completely unexpected. One morning during that same 1972 visit, I was sitting in an office I had been given at the Instituto de Recursos Hidraulicos y Electrificación, Panama's government-owned electric utility company. I was poring over a sheet of statistics when a man knocked gently on the frame of my open door. I invited him in, pleased with any excuse to take my attention off the numbers. He announced himself as the general's chauffeur and said he had come to take me to one of the general's bungalows.

An hour later, I was sitting across the table from General Omar Torrijos. He was dressed casually, in typical Panamanian style: khaki slacks and a short-sleeved shirt buttoned down the front, light blue with a delicate green pattern. He was tall, fit, and handsome. He seemed amazingly relaxed for a man with his responsibilities. A lock of dark hair fell over his prominent forehead.

He asked about my recent travels to Indonesia, Guatemala, and Iran. The three countries fascinated him, but he seemed especially intrigued with Iran's king, Shah Mohammad Reza Pahlavi. The shah had come to power in 1941, after the British and Soviets overthrew his father, whom they accused of collaborating with Hitler.[1]

"Can you imagine," Torrijos asked, "being part of a plot to dethrone your own father?"

Panama's head of state knew a good deal about the history of this far-off land. We talked about how the tables were turned on the shah in 1951, and how his own premier, Mohammad Mossadegh, forced him into exile. Torrijos knew, as did most of the world, that it had been the CIA that labeled the premier a Communist and that stepped in to restore the shah to power. However, he did not know—or at least did not mention—the parts Claudine had shared with me, about Kermit Roosevelt's brilliant maneuvers and the fact that this had been the beginning of a new era in imperialism, the match that had ignited the global empire conflagration.

"After the shah was reinstated," Torrijos continued, "he launched a series of revolutionary programs aimed at developing the industrial sector and bringing Iran into the modern era."

I asked him how he happened to know so much about Iran.

"I make it my point," he said. "I don't think too highly of the shah's politics—his willingness to overthrow his own father and become a CIA puppet—but it looks as though he's doing good things for his country. Perhaps I can learn something from him. If he survives."

"You think he won't?"

"He has powerful enemies."

"And some of the world's best bodyguards."

Torrijos gave me a sardonic look. "His secret police, SAVAK, have the reputation of being ruthless thugs. That doesn't win many friends. He won't last much longer." He paused, then rolled his eyes. "Bodyguards? I have a few myself." He waved at the door. "You think they'll save my life if your country decides to get rid of me?"

I asked whether he truly saw that as a possibility.

He raised his eyebrows in a manner that made me feel foolish for asking such a question. "We have the Canal. That's a lot bigger than Arbenz and United Fruit."

I had researched Guatemala, and I understood Torrijos's meaning. United Fruit Company had been that country's political equivalent of Panama's canal. Founded in the late 1800s, United Fruit soon grew into one of the most powerful forces in Central America. During the early 1950s, reform candidate Jacobo Arbenz was elected president of Guatemala in an election hailed all over the hemisphere as a model of the democratic process. At the time, less than 3 percent of Guatemalans owned 70 percent of the land. Arbenz promised to help the poor dig their way out of starvation, and after his election he implemented a comprehensive land reform program.

"The poor and middle classes throughout Latin America applauded Arbenz," Torrijos said. "Personally, he was one of my heroes. But we also held our breath. We knew that United Fruit opposed these measures, since they were one of the largest and most oppressive landholders in Guatemala. They also owned big plantations in Colombia, Costa Rica, Cuba, Jamaica, Nicaragua, Santo Domingo, and here in Panama. They couldn't afford to let Arbenz give the rest of us ideas."

I knew the rest: United Fruit had launched a major public relations campaign in the United States, aimed at convincing the American public and congress that Arbenz was part of a Russian plot and that Guatemala was a Soviet satellite. In 1954, the CIA orchestrated a coup. American pilots bombed Guatemala City and the democratically elected Arbenz was overthrown, replaced by Colonel Carlos Castillo Armas, a ruthless right-wing dictator.

The new government owed everything to United Fruit. By way of thanks, the government reversed the land reform process, abolished taxes on the interest and dividends paid to foreign investors, eliminated the secret ballot, and jailed thousands of its critics. Anyone who dared to speak out against Castillo was persecuted. Historians trace the violence and terrorism that plagued Guatemala for most of the rest of the century to the not-so-secret alliance between United Fruit, the CIA, and the Guatemalan army under its colonel dictator.[2]

"Arbenz was assassinated," Torrijos continued. "Political and character assassination." He paused and frowned. "How could your people swallow that CIA rubbish? I won't go so easily. The military here are my people. Political assassination won't do." He smiled.

"The CIA itself will have to kill me!"

We sat in silence for a few moments, each lost in his own thoughts. Torrijos was the first to speak. He leaned forward and lowered his voice. "And now I'm up against Bechtel."

This startled me. Bechtel was the world's most powerful engineering firm and a frequent collaborator on projects with MAIN. In the case of Panama's master plan, I had assumed that they were one of our major competitors.

"What do you mean?"

"We've been considering building a new canal, a sea-level one, without locks. It can handle bigger ships. The Japanese may be interested in financing it."

"They're the Canal's biggest clients."

"Exactly. Of course, if they provide the money, they will do the construction."

It struck me. "Bechtel will be out in the cold."

"The biggest construction job in recent history." He paused. "Bechtel's loaded with Nixon, Ford, and Bush cronies." (Bush, as U.S. ambassador to the UN, and Ford, as House Minority Leader and Chairman of the Republican National Convention, were well-known to Torrijos as Republican powerbrokers.) "I've been told that the Bechtel family pulls the strings of the Republican Party."

This conversation left me feeling very uncomfortable. I was one of the people who perpetuated the system he so despised, and I was certain he knew it. My job of convincing him to accept international loans in exchange for hiring U.S. engineering and construction firms appeared to have hit a mammoth wall. I decided to confront him head-on.

"General," I asked, "why did you invite me here?"

He glanced at his watch and smiled. "Yes, time now to get down to our own business. Panama needs your help. I need your help."

I was stunned. "My help? What can I do for you?"

"We will take back the Canal. But that's not enough." He relaxed into his chair. "We must also serve as a model. We must show that we care about our poor and we must demonstrate beyond any doubt that our determination to win our independence is not dictated by Russia, China, or Cuba. We must prove to the world that Panama is a reasonable country, that we stand not *against* the United States but *for* the rights of the poor."

He crossed one leg over the other. "In order to do that we need to build up an economic base that is like none in this hemisphere. Electricity, yes—but electricity that reaches the poorest of our poor and is subsidized. The same for transportation and communications. And especially for agriculture. Doing that will take money—your money, the World Bank and the Inter-American Development Bank."

Once again, he leaned forward. His eyes held mine. "I understand that your company wants more work and usually gets it by inflating the size of projects—wider highways, bigger power plants, deeper harbors. This time is different, though. Give me what's best for my people, and I'll give you all the work you want."

What he proposed was totally unexpected, and it both shocked and excited me. It certainly defied all I had learned at MAIN. Surely, he knew that the foreign aid game was a sham—he had to know. It existed to make him rich and to shackle his country with debt. It was there so Panama would be forever obligated to the United States and the corporatocracy. It was there to keep Latin America on the path of Manifest Destiny and forever subservient to Washington and Wall Street. I was certain that he knew that the system was based on the assumption that all men in power are corruptible, and that his decision not to use it for his personal benefit would be seen as a threat, a new form of domino that might start a chain reaction and eventually topple the entire system.

I looked across the coffee table at this man who certainly understood that because of the Canal he enjoyed a very special and unique power, and that it placed him in a particularly precarious position. He had to be careful. He already had established himself as a leader among LDC leaders. If he, like his hero Arbenz, was determined to take a stand, the world would be watching. How would the system react? More specifically, how would the U.S. government react? Latin American history was littered with dead heroes.

I also knew I was looking at a man who challenged all the justifications I had formulated for my own actions. This man certainly had his share of personal flaws, but he was no pirate, no Henry Morgan or Francis Drake—those swashbuckling adventurers who used letters of marque from English kings as a cloak to legitimatize piracy. The picture on the billboard had not been your typical political deception. "Omar's ideal is freedom; the missile is not invented that can kill an ideal!" Hadn't Tom Paine penned something similar?

It made me wonder, though. Perhaps ideals do not die, but what about the men behind them? Che, Arbenz, Allende; the latter was the only one still alive, but for how long? And it raised another question: how would I respond if Torrijos were thrust into the role of martyr?

By the time I left him we both understood that MAIN would get the contract for the master plan, and that I would see to it that we did Torrijos's bidding.

CHAPTER 14

Entering a New and Sinister Period in Economic History

As chief economist, I not only was in charge of a department at MAIN and responsible for the studies we carried out around the globe, but I also was expected to be conversant with current economic trends and theories. The early 1970s were a time of major shifts in international economics.

During the 1960s, a group of countries had formed OPEC, the cartel of oil-producing nations, largely in response to the power of the big refining companies. Iran was also a major factor. Even though the shah owed his position and possibly his life to the United States' clandestine intervention during the Mossadegh struggle—or perhaps because of that fact—the shah was acutely aware that the tables could be turned on him at any time. The heads of state of other petroleum-rich nations shared this awareness and the paranoia that accompanied it. They also knew that the major international oil companies, known as "The Seven Sisters," were collaborating to hold down petroleum prices—and thus the revenues they paid to the producing countries—as a means of reaping their own windfall profits. OPEC was organized in order to strike back.

This all came to a head in the early 1970s, when OPEC brought the industrial giants to their knees. A series of concerted actions, ending with a 1973 oil embargo symbolized by long lines at U.S. gas stations, threatened to bring on an economic catastrophe rivaling the Great Depression. It was a systemic shock to the developed world economy, and of a magnitude that few people could begin to comprehend.

The oil crisis could not have come at a worse time for the United States. It was a confused nation, full of fear and self-doubt, reeling from a humiliating war in Vietnam and a president who was about to resign. Nixon's problems were not limited to Southeast Asia and Watergate. He had stepped up to the plate during an era that, in retrospect, would be understood as the threshold of a new epoch in world politics and economics. In those days, it seemed that the "little guys," including the OPEC countries, were getting the upper hand.

I was fascinated by world events. My bread was buttered by the corporatocracy, yet some secret side of me enjoyed watching my masters being put in their places. I suppose it assuaged my guilt a bit. I saw the shadow of Thomas Paine standing on the sidelines, cheering OPEC on.

None of us could have been aware of the full impact of the embargo at the time it was happening. We certainly had our theories, but we could not understand what has since become clear. In hindsight, we know that economic growth rates after the oil crisis were about half those prevailing in the 1950s and 1960s, and that they have taken place against much greater inflationary pressure. The growth that did occur was structurally different and did not create nearly as many jobs, so unemployment soared. To top it all off, the international monetary system took a blow; the network of fixed exchange rates, which had prevailed since the end of World War II, essentially collapsed.

During that time, I frequently got together with friends to discuss these matters over lunch or over beers after work. Some of these people worked for me—my staff included very smart men and women, mostly young, who for the most part were free-thinkers, at least by conventional standards. Others were executives at Boston think tanks or professors at local colleges, and one was an assistant to a state congressman. These were informal meetings, sometimes attended by as few as two of us, while others might include a dozen participants. The sessions were always lively and raucous.

When I look back at those discussions, I am embarrassed by the sense of superiority I often felt. I knew things I could not share. My friends sometimes flaunted their credentials—connections on Beacon Hill or in Washington, professorships and PhDs—and I would answer this in my role as chief economist of a major consulting firm, who traveled around the world first class. Yet, I could not discuss my private meetings with men like Torrijos, or the things I knew about the ways we were manipulating countries on every continent. It was both a source of inner arrogance and a frustration.

When we talked about the power of the little guys, I had to exercise a great deal of restraint. I knew what none of them could possibly know, that the corporatocracy, its band of EHMs, and the jackals waiting in the background would never allow the little guys to gain control. I only had to draw upon the examples of Arbenz and Mossadegh—and more recently, upon the 1973 CIA overthrow of Chile's democratically elected president, Salvador Allende. In fact, I understood that the stranglehold of global empire was growing stronger, despite OPEC—or, as I suspected at the time but did not confirm until later, with OPEC's help.

Our conversations often focused on the similarities between the early 1970s and the 1930s. The latter represented a major watershed in the international economy and in the way it was studied, analyzed, and perceived. That decade opened the door to Keynesian economics and to the idea that government should play a major role in managing markets and providing services such as health, unemployment compensation, and other forms of welfare. We were moving away from old assumptions that markets were self-regulating and that the state's intervention should be minimal.

The Depression resulted in the New Deal and in policies that promoted economic regulation, governmental financial manipulation, and the extensive application of fiscal policy. In addition, both the Depression and World War II led to the creation of organizations like the World Bank, the IMF, and the General Agreement on Tariffs and Trade (GATT). The 1960s was a pivotal decade in this period and in the shift from neoclassic to Keynesian economics. It happened under the Kennedy and Johnson administrations, and perhaps the most important single influence was one man, Robert McNamara.

McNamara was a frequent visitor to our discussion groups—in absentia, of course. We all knew about his meteoric rise to fame, from manager of planning and financial analysis at Ford Motor Company in 1949 to Ford's president in 1960, the first company head selected from outside the Ford family. Shortly after that, Kennedy appointed him secretary of defense.

McNamara became a strong advocate of a Keynesian approach to government, using mathematical models and statistical approaches to determine troop levels, allocation of funds, and other strategies in Vietnam. His advocacy of "aggressive leadership" became a hallmark not only of government managers but also of corporate executives. It formed the basis of a new philosophical approach to teaching management at the nation's top business schools, and it ultimately led to a new breed of CEOs who would spearhead the rush to global empire.[1]

As we sat around the table discussing world events, we were especially fascinated by McNamara's role as president of the World Bank, a job he accepted soon after leaving his post as secretary of defense. Most of my friends focused on the fact that he symbolized what was popularly known as the military-industrial complex. He had held the top position in a major corporation, in a government cabinet, and now at the most powerful bank in the world. Such an apparent breach in the separation of powers horrified many of them; I may have been the only one among us who was not in the least surprised.

I see now that Robert McNamara's greatest and most sinister contribution to history was to jockey the World Bank into becoming an agent of global empire on a scale never before witnessed. He also set a precedent. His ability to bridge the gaps between the primary components of the corporatocracy would be fine-tuned by his successors. For instance, George Shultz was secretary of the treasury and chairman of the Council on Economic Policy under Nixon, served as Bechtel president, and then became secretary of state under Reagan. Caspar Weinberger was a Bechtel vice president and general counsel, and later the secretary of defense under Reagan. Richard Helms was Johnson's CIA director and then became ambassador to Iran under Nixon. Richard Cheney served as secretary of defense under George H. W. Bush, as Halliburton president, and as U.S. vice president to George W. Bush. Even a president of the United States, George H. W. Bush, began as founder of Zapata Petroleum Corp, served as U.S. ambassador to the U.N. under presidents Nixon and Ford, and was Ford's CIA director.

Looking back, I am struck by the innocence of those days. In many respects, we were still caught up in the old approaches to empire building. Kermit Roosevelt had shown us a better way when he overthrew an Iranian democrat and replaced him with a despotic king. We EHMs were accomplishing many of our objectives in places like Indonesia and Ecuador, and yet Vietnam was a stunning example of how easily we could slip back into old patterns.

It would take the leading member of OPEC, Saudi Arabia, to change that.

CHAPTER 15

The Saudi Arabian
Money-laundering Affair

In 1974, a diplomat from Saudi Arabia showed me photos of Riyadh, the capital of his country. Included in these photos was a herd of goats rummaging among piles of refuse outside a government building. When I asked the diplomat about them, his response shocked me. He told me that they were the city's main garbage disposal system.

"No self-respecting Saudi would ever collect trash," he said. "We leave it to the beasts."

Goats! In the capital of the world's greatest oil kingdom. It seemed unbelievable.

At the time, I was one of a group of consultants just beginning to try to piece together a solution to the oil crisis. Those goats led me to an understanding of how that solution might evolve, especially given the country's pattern of development over the previous three centuries.

Saudi Arabia's history is full of violence and religious fanaticism. In the eighteenth century, Mohammed ibn Saud, a local warlord, joined forces with fundamentalists from the ultraconservative Wahhabi sect. It was a powerful union, and during the next two hundred years the Saud family and their Wahhabi allies conquered most of the Arabian Peninsula, including Islam's holiest sites, Mecca and Medina.

Saudi society reflected the puritanical idealism of its founders, and a strict interpretation of Koranic beliefs was enforced. Religious police ensured adherence to the mandate to pray five times a day. Women were required to cover themselves from head to toe. Punishment for criminals was severe; public executions and stonings were common. During my first visit to Riyadh, I was amazed when my driver told me I could leave my camera, briefcase, and even my wallet in plain sight inside our car, parked near the open market, without locking it.

"No one," he said, "would think of stealing here. Thieves have their hands cut off."

Later that day, he asked me if I would like to visit so-called Chop Chop Square and watch a beheading. Wahhabism's adherence to what we would consider extreme puritanism made the streets safe from thieves—and demanded the harshest form of corporal punishment for those who violated the laws. I declined the invitation.

The Saudi view of religion as an important element of politics and economics contributed to the oil embargo that shook the Western world. On October 6, 1973 (Yom Kippur, the holiest of Jewish holidays), Egypt and Syria launched simultaneous attacks on Israel. It was the beginning of the October War—the fourth and most destructive of the Arab-Israeli wars, and the one that would have the greatest impact on the world. Egypt's President Sadat pressured Saudi Arabia's King Faisal to retaliate against the United States' complicity with Israel by employing what Sadat referred to as "the oil weapon." On October 16, Iran and the five Arab Gulf states, including Saudi Arabia, announced a 70 percent increase in the posted price of oil.

Meeting in Kuwait City, Arab oil ministers pondered further options. The Iraqi representative was vehemently in favor of tar-

geting the United States. He called on the other delegates to na-
tionalize American businesses in the Arab world, to impose a total
oil embargo on the United States and on all other nations
friendly to Israel, and to withdraw Arab funds from every American bank. He pointed out that Arab bank accounts were substantial and that this action could result in a panic not unlike that of
1929.

Other Arab ministers were reluctant to agree to such a radical
plan, but on October 17 they did decide to move forward with a
more limited embargo, which would begin with a 5 percent cut in
production and then impose an additional 5 percent reduction
every month until their political objectives were met. They
agreed that the United States should be punished for its pro-
Israeli stance and should therefore have the most severe embargo
levied against it. Several of the countries attending the meeting
announced that they would implement cutbacks of 10 percent,
rather than 5 percent.

On October 19, President Nixon asked Congress for $2.2 bil-
lion in aid to Israel. The next day, Saudi Arabia and other Arab
producers imposed a total embargo on oil shipments to the
United States.[1]

The oil embargo ended on March 18, 1974. Its duration was
short, its impact immense. The selling price of Saudi oil leaped
from $1.39 a barrel on January 1, 1970, to $8.32 on January 1,
1974.[2] Politicians and future administrations would never forget
the lessons learned during the early- to mid-1970s. In the long
run, the trauma of those few months served to strengthen the corporatocracy; its three pillars—big corporations, international
banks, and government—bonded as never before. That bond
would endure.

The embargo also resulted in significant attitude and policy
changes. It convinced Wall Street and Washington that such an
embargo could never again be tolerated. Protecting our oil supplies had always been a priority; after 1973, it became an obses-

sion. The embargo elevated Saudi Arabia's status as a player in world politics and forced Washington to recognize the kingdom's strategic importance to our own economy. Furthermore, it encouraged U.S. corporatocracy leaders to search desperately for methods to funnel petrodollars back to America, and to ponder the fact that the Saudi government lacked the administrative and institutional frameworks to properly manage its mushrooming wealth.

For Saudi Arabia, the additional oil income resulting from the price hikes was a mixed blessing. It filled the national coffers with billions of dollars; however, it also served to undermine some of the strict religious beliefs of the Wahhabis. Wealthy Saudis traveled around the world. They attended schools and universities in Europe and the United States. They bought fancy cars and furnished their houses with Western-style goods. Conservative religious beliefs were replaced by a new form of materialism—and it was this materialism that presented a solution to fears of future oil crises.

Almost immediately after the embargo ended, Washington began negotiating with the Saudis, offering them technical support, military hardware and training, and an opportunity to bring their nation into the twentieth century, in exchange for petrodollars and, most important, assurances that there would never again be another oil embargo. The negotiations resulted in the creation of a most extraordinary organization, the United States–Saudi Arabian Joint Economic Commission. Known as JECOR, it embodied an innovative concept that was the opposite of traditional foreign aid programs: it relied on Saudi money to hire American firms to build up Saudi Arabia.

Although overall management and fiscal responsibility were delegated to the U.S. Department of the Treasury, this commission was independent to the extreme. Ultimately, it would spend billions of dollars over a period of more than twenty-five years, with virtually no congressional oversight. Because no U.S. funding was involved, Congress had no authority in the matter, despite Treasury's role. After studying JECOR extensively, David Holden and Richard Johns conclude, "It was the most far-reaching agreement of its kind ever concluded by the U.S. with a developing country. It had the potential to entrench the U.S. deeply in the Kingdom, fortifying the concept of mutual interdependence."[3]

The Department of the Treasury brought MAIN in at an early stage to serve as an adviser. I was summoned and told that my job would be critical, and that everything I did and learned should be considered highly confidential. From my vantage point, it seemed like a clandestine operation. At the time, I was led to believe that MAIN was the lead consultant in that process; I subsequently came to realize that we were one of several consultants whose expertise was sought.

Since everything was done in the greatest secrecy, I was not privy to Treasury's discussions with other consultants, and I therefore cannot be certain about the importance of my role in this precedent-setting deal. I do know that the arrangement established new standards for EHMs and that it launched innovative alternatives to the traditional approaches for advancing the interests of empire. I also know that most of the scenarios that evolved from my studies were ultimately implemented, that MAIN was rewarded with one of the first major—and extremely profitable—contracts in Saudi Arabia, and that I received a large bonus that year.

My job was to develop forecasts of what might happen in Saudi Arabia if vast amounts of money were invested in its infrastructure, and to map out scenarios for spending that money. In short, I was asked to apply as much creativity as I could to justifying the infusion of hundreds of millions of dollars into the Saudi Arabian economy, under conditions that would include U.S. engineering and construction companies. I was told to do this on my own, not to rely on my staff, and I was sequestered in a small conference room several floors above the one where my department was located. I was warned that my job was both a matter of national security and potentially very lucrative for MAIN.

I understood, of course, that the primary objective here was not the usual—to burden this country with debts it could never repay—but rather to find ways that would assure that a large portion of petrodollars found their way back to the United States. In the process, Saudi Arabia would be drawn in, its economy would become increasingly intertwined with and dependent upon ours, and presumably it would grow more Westernized and therefore more sympathetic with and integrated into our system.

Once I got started, I realized that the goats wandering the streets of Riyadh were the symbolic key; they were a sore point among Saudis jet-setting around the world. Those goats begged to be replaced by something more appropriate for this desert kingdom that craved entry into the modern world. I also knew that OPEC economists were stressing the need for oil-rich countries to obtain more value-added products from their petroleum. Rather than simply exporting crude oil, the economists were urging these countries to develop industries of their own, to use this oil to produce petroleum-based products they could sell to the rest of the world at a higher price than that brought by the crude itself.

This twin realization opened the door to a strategy I felt certain would be a win-win situation for everyone. The goats, of course, were merely an entry point. Oil revenues could be employed to hire U.S. companies to replace the goats with the world's most modern garbage collection and disposal system, and the Saudis could take great pride in this state-of-the-art technology.

I came to think of the goats as one side of an equation that could be applied to most of the kingdom's economic sectors, a formula for success in the eyes of the royal family, the U.S. Department of the Treasury, and my bosses at MAIN. Under this formula, money would be earmarked to create an industrial sector focused on transforming raw petroleum into finished products for export. Large petrochemical complexes would rise from the desert, and around them, huge industrial parks. Naturally, such a plan would also require the construction of thousands of megawatts of electrical generating capacity, transmission and distribution lines, highways, pipelines, communications networks, and transportation systems, including new airports, improved seaports, a vast array of service industries, and the infrastructure essential to keep all these cogs turning.

We all had high expectations that this plan would evolve into a model of how things should be done in the rest of the world. Globe-trotting Saudis would sing our praises; they would invite leaders from many countries to come to Saudi Arabia and witness the miracles we had accomplished; those leaders would then call on us to help them devise similar plans for their countries and—in most cases, for countries outside the ring of OPEC—would arrange World Bank or other debt-ridden methods for financing them. The global empire would be well served.

As I worked through these ideas, I thought of the goats, and the words of my driver often echoed in my ears: "No self-respecting Saudi would ever collect trash." I had heard that refrain repeatedly, in many different contexts. It was obvious that the Saudis had no intention of putting their own people to work at menial tasks, whether as laborers in industrial facilities or in the actual construction of any of the projects. In the first place, there were too few of them. In addition, the royal House of Saud had indicated a commitment to providing its citizens with a level of education and a lifestyle that were inconsistent with those of manual laborers. The Saudis might manage others, but they had no desire or motivation to become factory and construction workers. Therefore, it would be necessary to import a labor force from other countries—countries where labor was cheap and where people needed work. If possible, the labor should come from other Middle Eastern or Islamic countries, such as Egypt, Palestine, Pakistan, and Yemen.

This prospect created an even greater new stratagem for development opportunities. Mammoth housing complexes would have to be constructed for these laborers, as would shopping malls, hospitals, fire and police department facilities, water and sewage treatment plants, electrical, communications, and transportation networks—in fact, the end result would be to create modern cities where once only deserts had existed. Here, too, was the opportunity to explore emerging technologies in, for example, desalinization plants, microwave systems, health care complexes, and computer technologies.

Saudi Arabia was a planner's dream come true, and also a fantasy realized for anyone associated with the engineering and construction business. It presented an economic opportunity unrivaled by any other in history: an underdeveloped country with virtually unlimited financial resources and a desire to enter the modern age in a big way, very quickly.

I must admit that I enjoyed this job immensely. There was no solid data available in Saudi Arabia, in the Boston Public Library, or anywhere else that justified the use of econometric models in this context. In fact, the magnitude of the job—the total and immediate transformation of an entire nation on a scale never before witnessed—meant that even had historical data existed, it would have been irrelevant.

Nor was anyone expecting this type of quantitative analysis, at least not at this stage of the game. I simply put my imagination to work and wrote reports that envisioned a glorious future for the kingdom. I had rule-of-thumb numbers I could use to estimate such things as the approximate cost to produce a megawatt of electricity, a mile of road, or adequate water, sewage, housing, food, and public services for one laborer. I was not supposed to refine these estimates or to draw final conclusions. My job was simply to describe a series of plans (more accurately, perhaps, "visions") of what might be possible, and to arrive at rough estimates of the costs associated with them.

I always kept in mind the true objectives: maximizing payouts to U.S. firms and making Saudi Arabia increasingly dependent on the United States. It did not take long to realize how closely the two went together; almost all the newly developed projects would require continual upgrading and servicing, and they were so highly technical as to assure that the companies that originally developed them would have to maintain and modernize them. In fact, as I moved forward with my work, I began to assemble two lists for each of the projects I envisioned: one for the types of design-and-construction contracts we could expect, and another for long-term service and management agreements. MAIN, Bechtel, Brown & Root, Halliburton, Stone & Webster, and many other U.S. engineers and contractors would profit handsomely for decades to come.

Beyond the purely economic, there was another twist that would render Saudi Arabia dependent on us, though in a very different way. The modernization of this oil-rich kingdom would trigger adverse reactions. For instance, conservative Muslims would be furious; Israel and other neighboring countries would feel threatened. The economic development of this nation was likely to spawn the growth of another industry: protecting the Arabian Peninsula. Private companies specializing in such activities, as well as the U.S. military and defense industry, could expect generous contracts—and, once again, long-term service and management agreements. Their presence would require another phase of engineering and construction projects, including airports, missile sites, personnel bases, and all of the infrastructure associated with such facilities.

I sent my reports in sealed envelopes through interoffice mail, addressed to "Treasury Department Project Manager." I occasionally met with a couple of other members of our team—vice presidents at MAIN and my superiors. Since we had no official name for this project, which was still in the research and development phase and was not yet part of JECOR, we referred to it only—and with hushed voices—as SAMA. Ostensibly, this stood for Saudi Arabian Money-laundering Affair, but it was also a tongue-in-cheek play on words; the kingdom's central bank was called the Saudi Arabian Monetary Agency, or SAMA.

Sometimes a Treasury representative would join us. I asked few questions during these meetings. Mainly, I just described my work, responded to their comments, and agreed to try to do whatever was asked of me. The vice presidents and Treasury representatives were especially impressed with my ideas about the long-term service and management agreements. It prodded one of the vice presidents to coin a phrase we often used after that, referring to the kingdom as "the cow we can milk until the sun sets on our retirement." For me, that phrase always conjured images of goats rather than cows.

It was during those meetings that I came to realize that several of our competitors were involved in similar tasks, and that in the end we all expected to be awarded lucrative contracts as a result of our efforts. I assumed that MAIN and the other firms were footing the bill for this preliminary work, taking a short-term risk in order to throw our hats into the ring. This assumption was reinforced by the fact that the number I charged my time to on our daily personal time sheets appeared to be a general and administrative overhead account. Such an approach was typical of the research and development/proposal preparation phase of most projects. In this case, the initial investment certainly far exceeded the norm, but those vice presidents seemed extremely confident about the payback.

Despite the knowledge that our competitors were also involved, we all assumed that there was enough work to go around. I also had been in the business long enough to believe that the rewards bestowed would reflect the level of Treasury's acceptance of the work we had done, and that those consultants who came up with the approaches that were finally implemented would receive the choicest contracts. I took it as a personal challenge to create scenarios that would make it to the design-and-construct stage. My star was already rising rapidly at MAIN. Being a key player in SAMA would guarantee its acceleration, if we were successful.

During our meetings, we also openly discussed the likelihood that SAMA and the entire JECOR operation would set new precedents. It represented an innovative approach to creating lucrative work in countries that did not need to incur debts through the international banks. Iran and Iraq came immediately to mind as two additional examples of such countries. Moreover, given human nature, we felt that the leaders of such countries would likely be motivated to try to emulate Saudi Arabia. There seemed little doubt that the 1973 oil embargo—which had initially appeared to be so negative—would end up offering many unexpected gifts to the engineering and construction business, and would help to further pave the road to global empire.

I worked on that visionary phase for about eight months— although never for more than several intense days at a time— sequestered in my private conference room or in my apartment overlooking Boston Common. My staff all had other assignments and pretty much took care of themselves, although I checked in on them periodically. Over time, the secrecy around our work declined. More people became aware that something big involving Saudi Arabia was going on. Excitement swelled, rumors swirled. The vice presidents and Treasury representatives grew more open—in part, I believe, because they themselves became privy to more information as details about the ingenious scheme emerged.

Under this evolving plan, Washington wanted the Saudis to guarantee to maintain oil supplies and prices at levels that could fluctuate but that would always remain acceptable to the United States and our allies. If other countries such as Iran, Iraq, Indonesia, or Venezuela threatened embargoes, Saudi Arabia, with its vast petroleum supplies, would step in to fill the gap; simply the knowledge that they might do so would, in the long run, discourage other countries from even considering an embargo. In exchange for this guarantee, Washington would offer the House of Saud an amazingly attractive deal: a commitment to provide total and unequivocal U.S. political and—if necessary—military support, thereby ensuring their continued existence as the rulers of their country.

It was a deal the House of Saud could hardly refuse, given its geographic location, lack of military might, and general vulnerability to neighbors like Iran, Syria, Iraq, and Israel. Naturally, therefore, Washington used its advantage to impose one other critical condition, a condition that redefined the role of EHMs in the world and served as a model we would later attempt to apply in other countries, most notably in Iraq. In retrospect, I sometimes find it difficult to understand how Saudi Arabia could have accepted this condition. Certainly, most of the rest of the Arab world, OPEC, and other Islamic countries were appalled when they discovered the terms of the deal and the manner in which the royal house capitulated to Washington's demands.

The condition was that Saudi Arabia would use its petrodollars to purchase U.S. government securities; in turn, the interest earned by these securities would be spent by the U.S. Department of the Treasury in ways that enabled Saudi Arabia to emerge from a medieval society into the modern, industrialized world. In other words, the interest compounding on billions of dollars of the kingdom's oil income would be used to pay U.S. companies to fulfill the vision I (and presumably some of my competitors) had come up with, to convert Saudi Arabia into a modern industrial power. Our own U.S. Department of the Treasury would hire us, at Saudi expense, to build infrastructure projects and even entire cities throughout the Arabian Peninsula.

Although the Saudis reserved the right to provide input regarding the general nature of these projects, the reality was that an elite corps of foreigners (mostly infidels, in the eyes of Muslims) would determine the future appearance and economic makeup of the Arabian Peninsula. And this would occur in a kingdom founded on conservative Wahhabi principles and run according to those principles for several centuries. It seemed a huge leap of faith on their part, yet under the circumstances, and due to the political and military pressures undoubtedly brought to bear by Washington, I suspected the Saud family felt they had few alternatives.

From our perspective, the prospects for immense profits seemed limitless. It was a sweetheart deal with potential to set an amazing precedent. And to make the deal even sweeter, no one had to obtain congressional approval—a process loathed by corporations, particularly privately owned ones like Bechtel and MAIN, which prefer not to open their books or share their secrets with anyone. Thomas W. Lippman, an adjunct scholar at the Middle East Institute and a former journalist, eloquently summarizes the salient points of this deal:

> The Saudis, rolling in cash, would deliver hundreds of millions of dollars to Treasury, which held on to the funds until they were needed to pay vendors or employees. This system assured that the Saudi money would be recycled back into the American economy . . . It also ensured that the commission's managers could undertake whatever projects they and the Saudis agreed were useful without having to justify them to Congress.[4]

Establishing the parameters for this historic undertaking took less time than anyone could have imagined. After that, however, we had to figure out a way to implement it. To set the process in motion, someone at the highest level of government was dispatched to Saudi Arabia—an extremely confidential mission. I never knew for sure, but I believe the envoy was Henry Kissinger.

Whoever the envoy was, his first job was to remind the royal family about what had happened in neighboring Iran when

Mossadegh tried to oust British petroleum interests. Next, he would outline a plan that would be too attractive for them to turn down, in effect conveying to the Saudis that they had few alternatives. I have no doubt that they were left with the distinct impression that they could either accept our offer and thus gain assurances that we would support and protect them as rulers, or they could refuse—and go the way of Mossadegh. When the envoy returned to Washington, he brought with him the message that the Saudis would like to comply.

There was just one slight obstacle. We would have to convince key players in the Saudi government. This, we were informed, was a family matter. Saudi Arabia was not a democracy, and yet it seemed that within the House of Saud there was a need for consensus.

In 1975, I was assigned to one of those key players. I always thought of him as Prince W., although I never determined that he was actually a crown prince. My job was to persuade him that the Saudi Arabia Money-laundering Affair would benefit his country as well as him personally.

This was not as easy as it appeared at first. Prince W. professed himself a good Wahhabi and insisted that he did not want to see his country follow in the footsteps of Western commercialism. He also claimed that he understood the insidious nature of what we were proposing. We had, he said, the same objectives as the crusaders a millennium earlier: the Christianization of the Arab world. In fact, he was partially right about this. In my opinion, the difference between the crusaders and us was a matter of degree. Europe's medieval Catholics claimed their goal was to save Muslims from purgatory; we claimed that we wanted to help the Saudis modernize. In truth, I believe the crusaders, like the corporatocracy, were primarily seeking to expand their empire.

Religious beliefs aside, Prince W. had one weakness—for beautiful blondes. It seems almost ludicrous to mention what has now become an unfair stereotype, and I should mention that Prince W.

was the only man among many Saudis I have known who had this proclivity, or at least the only one who was willing to let me see it. Yet, it played a role in structuring this historic deal, and it demonstrates how far I would go to complete my mission.

CHAPTER 16

Pimping, and Financing Osama bin Laden

From the start, Prince W. let me know that whenever he came to visit me in Boston he expected to be entertained by a woman of his liking, and that he expected her to perform more functions than those of a simple escort. But he most definitely did not want a professional call girl, someone he or his family members might bump into on the street or at a cocktail party. My meetings with Prince W. were held in secret, which made it easier for me to comply with his wishes.

"Sally" was a beautiful blue-eyed blonde woman who lived in the Boston area. Her husband, a United Airlines pilot who traveled a great deal both on and off the job, made little attempt to hide his infidelities. Sally had a cavalier attitude about her husband's activities. She appreciated his salary, the plush Boston condo, and the benefits a pilot's spouse enjoyed in those days. A decade earlier, she had been a hippie who had become accustomed to promiscuous sex, and she found the idea of a secret source of income attractive. She agreed to give Prince W. a try, on one condition: she insisted that the future of their relationship depended entirely upon his behavior and attitude toward her.

Fortunately for me, each met the other's criteria.

The Prince W.–Sally Affair, a subchapter of the Saudi Arabia Money-laundering Affair, created its own set of problems for me. MAIN strictly prohibited its partners from doing anything illicit. From a legal standpoint, I was procuring sex—pimping—an illegal activity in Massachusetts, and so the main problem was figuring out how to pay for Sally's services. Luckily, the accounting department allowed me great liberties with my expense account. I was a good tipper, and I managed to persuade waiters in some of the most posh restaurants in Boston to provide me with blank receipts; it was an era when people, not computers, filled out receipts.

Prince W. grew bolder as time went by. Eventually, he wanted me to arrange for Sally to come and live in his private cottage in Saudi Arabia. This was not an unheard-of request in those days; there was an active trade in young women between certain European countries and the Middle East. These women were given contracts for some specified period of time, and when the contract expired they went home to very substantial bank accounts. Robert Baer, a case officer in the CIA's directorate of operations for twenty years, and a specialist in the Middle East, sums it up: "In the early 1970s, when the petrodollars started flooding in, enterprising Lebanese began smuggling hookers into the kingdom for the princes . . . Since no one in the royal family knows how to balance a checkbook, the Lebanese became fabulously wealthy."[1]

I was familiar with this situation and even knew people who could arrange such contracts. However, for me, there were two major obstacles: Sally and the payment. I was certain Sally was not about to leave Boston and move to a desert mansion in the Middle East. It was also pretty obvious that no collection of blank restaurant receipts would cover this expense.

Prince W. took care of the latter concern by assuring me that he expected to pay for his new mistress himself; I was only required to make the arrangements. It also gave me great relief when he went on to confide that the Saudi Arabian Sally did not have to be the exact same person as the one who had kept him company in the United States. I made calls to several friends who had Lebanese contacts in London and Amsterdam. Within a couple of weeks, a surrogate Sally signed a contract.

Prince W. was a complex person. Sally satisfied a corporeal desire, and my ability to help the prince in this regard earned me his trust. However, it by no means convinced him that SAMA was a strategy he wanted to recommend for his country. I had to work very hard to win my case. I spent many hours showing him statistics and helping him analyze studies we had undertaken for other countries, including the econometric models I had developed for Kuwait while training with Claudine, during those first few months before heading to Indonesia. Eventually he relented.

I am not familiar with the details of what went on between my fellow EHMs and the other key Saudi players. All I know is that the entire package was finally approved by the royal family. MAIN was rewarded for its part with one of the first highly lucrative contracts, administered by the U.S. Department of the Treasury. We were commissioned to make a complete survey of the country's disorganized and outmoded electrical system and to design a new one that would meet standards equivalent to those in the United States.

As usual, it was my job to send in the first team, to develop economic and electric load forecasts for each region of the country. Three of the men who worked for me—all experienced in international projects—were preparing to leave for Riyadh when word came down from our legal department that under the terms of the contract we were obligated to have a fully equipped office up and running in Riyadh within the next few weeks. This clause had apparently gone unnoticed for over a month. Our agreement with Treasury further stipulated that all equipment had to be manufactured either in the United States or in Saudi Arabia. Since Saudi Arabia did not have factories for producing such items, everything had to be sent from the States. To our chagrin, we discovered that long lines of tankers were queued up, waiting to get into ports on the Arabian Peninsula. It could take many months to get a shipment of supplies into the kingdom.

MAIN was not about to lose such a valuable contract over a couple of rooms of office furniture. At a conference of all the partners involved, we brainstormed for several hours. The solution we settled on was to charter a Boeing 747, fill it with supplies from Boston-area stores, and send it off to Saudi Arabia. I remember thinking that it would be fitting if the plane were owned by United Airlines and commanded by a certain pilot whose wife had played such a critical role in bringing the House of Saud around.

The deal between the United States and Saudi Arabia transformed the kingdom practically overnight. The goats were replaced by two hundred bright yellow American trash compactor trucks, provided under a $200 million contract with Waste Management, Inc.[2] In similar fashion, every sector of the Saudi economy was modernized, from agriculture and energy to education and communications. As Thomas Lippman observed in 2003:

> Americans have reshaped a vast, bleak landscape of nomads' tents and farmers' mud huts in their own image, right down to Starbucks on the corner and the wheelchair-accessible ramps in the newest public buildings. Saudi Arabia today is a country of expressways, computers, air-conditioned malls filled with the same glossy shops found in prosperous American suburbs, elegant hotels, fast-food restaurants, satellite tel-

evision, up-to-date hospitals, high-rise office towers, and amusement parks featuring whirling rides.[3]

The plans we conceived in 1974 set a standard for future negotiations with oil-rich countries. In a way, SAMA/JECOR was the next plateau after the one Kermit Roosevelt had established in Iran. It introduced an innovative level of sophistication to the arsenal of political-economic weapons used by a new breed of soldiers for global empire.

The Saudi Arabia Money-laundering Affair and the Joint Commission also set new precedents for international jurisprudence. This was very evident in the case of Idi Amin. When the notorious Ugandan dictator went into exile in 1979, he was given asylum in Saudi Arabia. Although he was considered a murderous despot responsible for the deaths of between one hundred thousand and three hundred thousand people, he retired to a life of luxury, complete with cars and domestic servants provided by the House of Saud. The United States quietly objected but refused to press the issue for fear of undermining its arrangement with the Saudis. Amin whiled away his last years fishing and taking strolls on the beach. In 2003, he died in Jiddah, succumbing to kidney failure at the age of eighty.[4]

More subtle and ultimately much more damaging was the role Saudi Arabia was allowed to play in financing international terrorism. The United States made no secret of its desire to have the House of Saud bankroll Osama bin Laden's Afghan war against the Soviet Union during the 1980s, and Riyadh and Washington together contributed an estimated $3.5 billion to the mujahideen.[5] However, U.S. and Saudi participation went far beyond this.

In late 2003, *U.S. News & World Report* conducted an exhaustive study titled, "The Saudi Connection." The magazine reviewed thousands of pages of court records, U.S. and foreign intelligence reports, and other documents, and interviewed dozens of government officials and experts on terrorism and the Middle East. Its findings include the following:

> The evidence was indisputable: Saudi Arabia, America's longtime ally and the world's largest oil producer, had somehow become, as a senior Treasury Department official put it, "the epicenter" of terrorist financing . . .
>
> Starting in the late 1980s—after the dual shocks of the Iranian revolution and the Soviet war in Afghanistan—Saudi Arabia's quasi-official charities became the primary source of funds for the fast-growing jihad movement. In some 20 countries the money was used to run paramilitary training camps, purchase weapons, and recruit new members . . .
>
> Saudi largess encouraged U.S. officials to look the other way, some veteran intelligence officers say. Billions of dollars in contracts, grants, and salaries have gone to a broad range of former U.S. officials who had dealt with the Saudis: ambassadors, CIA station chiefs, even cabinet secretaries . . .
>
> Electronic intercepts of conversations implicated members of the royal family in backing not only Al Qaeda but also other terrorist groups.[6]

After the 2001 attacks on the World Trade Center and the Pentagon, more evidence emerged about the covert relationships between Washington and Riyadh. In October 2003, *Vanity Fair* magazine disclosed information that had not previously been made public, in an in-depth report titled, "Saving the Saudis." The story that emerged about the relationship between the Bush family, the House of Saud, and the bin Laden family did not surprise me. I knew that those relationships went back at least to the time of the Saudi Arabian Money-laundering Affair, which began in

1974, and to George H. W. Bush's terms as U.S. Ambassador to the United Nations (from 1971 to 1973) and then as head of the CIA (from 1976 to 1977). What surprised me was the fact that the truth had finally made the press. *Vanity Fair* concluded:

> The Bush family and the House of Saud, the two most powerful dynasties in the world, have had close personal, business, and political ties for more than 20 years . . .
>
> In the private sector, the Saudis supported Harken Energy, a struggling oil company in which George W. Bush was an investor. Most recently, former president George H. W. Bush and his longtime ally, former Secretary of State James A. Baker III, have appeared before Saudis at fundraisers for the Carlyle Group, arguably the biggest private equity firm in the world. Today, former president Bush continues to serve as a senior adviser to the firm. . . .
>
> Just days after 9/11, wealthy Saudi Arabians, including members of the bin Laden family, were whisked out of the U.S. on private jets. No one will admit to clearing the flights, and the passengers weren't questioned. Did the Bush family's long relationship with the Saudis help make it happen?[7]

PART III: 1975–1981

CHAPTER 17

Panama Canal Negotiations
and Graham Greene

Saudi Arabia made many careers. Mine was already well on the way, but my successes in the desert kingdom certainly opened new doors for me. By 1977, I had built a small empire that included a staff of around twenty professionals headquartered in our Boston office, and a stable of consultants from MAIN's other departments and offices scattered across the globe. I had become the youngest partner in the firm's hundred-year history. In addition to my title of Chief Economist, I was named manager of Economics and Regional Planning. I was lecturing at Harvard and other venues, and newspapers were soliciting articles from me about current events.[1] I owned a sailing yacht that was docked in Boston Harbor next to the historic battleship *Constitution*, "Old Ironsides," renowned for subduing the Barbary pirates not long after the Revolutionary War. I was being paid an excellent salary and I had equity that promised to elevate me to the rarified heights of millionaire well before I turned forty. True, my marriage had fallen apart, but I was spending time with beautiful and fascinating women on several continents.

Bruno came up with an idea for an innovative approach to forecasting: an econometric model based on the writings of a turn-of-the-century Russian mathematician. The model involved assigning subjective probabilities to predictions that certain specific sectors of an economy would grow. I could see that this had the potential to be an ideal tool to justify the inflated rates of increase we liked to show in order to obtain large loans, and Bruno asked me to see what I could do with the concept.

I brought a young MIT mathematician, Dr. Nadipuram Prasad, into my department and gave him a budget. Within six months he developed the Markov method for econometric modeling. Together we hammered out a series of technical papers that presented Markov as a revolutionary method for forecasting the impact of infrastructure investment on economic development.

It was exactly what we wanted: a tool that scientifically "proved" we were doing countries a favor by helping them incur debts they would never be able to pay off. In addition, only a highly skilled econometrician with lots of time and money could possibly comprehend the intricacies of Markov or question its conclusions. The papers were published by several prestigious organizations, and we formally presented them at conferences and universities in a number of countries. The papers—and we—became famous throughout the industry.[2]

Omar Torrijos and I honored our secret agreement. I made sure our studies were honest and that our recommendations took into account the poor. Although I heard grumbling that my forecasts in Panama were not up to their usual inflated standards, and even that they smacked of socialism, the fact was that MAIN kept winning contracts from the Torrijos government. These contracts included a first—to provide innovative master plans that involved agriculture along with the more traditional infrastructure sectors. I also watched from the sidelines as Torrijos and Jimmy Carter set out to renegotiate the Canal Treaty.

The Canal negotiations generated great interest and great passions around the world. People everywhere waited to see whether the United States would do what most of the rest of the world believed was the right thing—allow the Panamanians to take control—or would instead try to reestablish our global version of Manifest Destiny, which had been shaken by our Vietnam debacle. For many, it appeared that a reasonable and compassionate man had been elected to the U.S. presidency at just the right time. However, the conservative bastions of Washington and the pulpits of the religious right rang with indignation. How could we give up this bulwark of national defense, this symbol of U.S. ingenuity, this ribbon of water that tied South America's fortunes to the whims of U.S. commercial interests?

During my trips to Panama, I became accustomed to staying at the Hotel Continental. However, on my fifth visit I moved across the street to the Hotel Panama because the Continental was undergoing renovations and the construction was very noisy. At first, I resented the inconvenience—the Continental had been my home away from home. But now the expansive lobby where I sat, with its rattan chairs and paddle-bladed wooden ceiling fans, was growing on me. It could have been the set of *Casablanca,* and I fantasized that Humphrey Bogart might stroll in at any moment. I set down the copy of the *New York Review of Books,* in which I had just finished reading a Graham Greene article about Panama, and stared up at those fans, recalling an evening almost two years earlier.

"Ford is a weak president who won't be reelected," Omar Torrijos predicted in 1975. He was speaking to a group of influential Panamanians. I was one of the few foreigners who had been invited to the elegant old club with its whirring ceiling fans. "That's the reason I decided to accelerate this Canal issue. It's a good time to launch an all-out political battle to win it back."

The speech inspired me. I returned to my hotel room and scratched out a letter that I eventually mailed to the *Boston*

Globe. Back in Boston, an editor responded by calling me at my office to request that I write an Op-Ed piece. "Colonialism in Panama Has No Place in 1975" took up nearly half the page opposite the editorials in the September 19, 1975, edition.

The article cited three specific reasons for transferring the Canal to Panama. First, "the present situation is unjust—a good reason for any decision." Second, "the existing treaty creates far graver security risks than would result from turning more control over to the Panamanians." I referenced a study conducted by the Interoceanic Canal Commission, which concluded that "traffic could be halted for two years by a bomb planted—conceivably by one man—in the side of Gatun Dam," a point General Torrijos himself had publicly emphasized. And third, "the present situation is creating serious problems for already-troubled United States–Latin American relations." I ended with the following:

> The best way of assuring the continued and efficient operation of the Canal is to help Panamanians gain control over and responsibility for it. In so doing, we could take pride in initiating an action that would reaffirm commitments to the cause of self-determination to which we pledged ourselves 200 years ago . . .
>
> Colonialism was in vogue at the turn of the century (early 1900s) as it had been in 1775. Perhaps ratification of such a treaty can be understood in the context of those times. Today it is without justification. Colonialism has no place in 1975. We, celebrating our bicentennial, should realize this, and act accordingly.[3]

Writing that piece was a bold move on my part, especially since I had recently been made a partner at MAIN. Partners were expected to avoid the press and certainly to refrain from publishing political diatribes on the editorial pages of New England's most prestigious newspaper. I received through interoffice mail a pile of nasty, mostly anonymous notes stapled to copies of the article. I was certain that I recognized the handwriting on one as that of Charlie Illingworth. My first project manager had been at MAIN for over ten years (compared to less than five for me) and was not yet a partner. A fierce skull and crossbones figured prominently on the note, and its message was simple: "Is this Commie really a partner in our firm?"

Bruno summoned me to his office and said, "You'll get loads of grief over this. MAIN's a pretty conservative place. But I want you to know I think you're smart. Torrijos will love it; I do hope you're sending him a copy. Good. Well, these jokers here in this office, the ones who think Torrijos is a Socialist, really won't give a damn as long as the work flows in."

Bruno had been right—as usual. Now it was 1977, Carter was in the White House, and serious Canal negotiations were under way. Many of MAIN's competitors had taken the wrong side and had been turned out of Panama, but our work had multiplied. And I was sitting in the lobby of the Hotel Panama, having just finished reading an article by Graham Greene in the *New York Review of Books*.

The article, "The Country with Five Frontiers," was a gutsy piece that included a discussion of corruption among senior officers in Panama's National Guard. The author pointed out that the general himself admitted to giving many of his staff special privileges, such as superior housing, because "If I don't pay them, the CIA will." The clear implication was that the U.S. intelligence community was determined to undermine the wishes of President Carter and, if necessary, would bribe Panama's military chiefs into sabotaging the treaty negotiations.[4] I could not help but wonder if the jackals had begun to circle Torrijos.

I had seen a photograph in the "People" section of *TIME* or *Newsweek* of Torrijos and Greene sitting together; the caption indicated that the writer was a special guest who had become a good friend. I wondered how the general felt about this novelist, whom he apparently trusted, writing such a critique.

Graham Greene's article raised another question, one that related to that day in 1972 when I had sat across a coffee table from Torrijos. At the time, I had assumed that Torrijos knew the foreign aid game was there to make him rich while shackling his country with debt. I had been sure he knew that the process was based on the assumption that men in power are corruptible, and that his decision not to seek personal benefit—but rather to use foreign aid to truly help his people—would be seen as a threat that might eventually topple the entire system. The world was watching this man; his actions had ramifications that reached far beyond Panama and would therefore not be taken lightly.

I had wondered how the corporatocracy would react if loans made to Panama helped the poor without contributing to impossible debts. Now I wondered whether Torrijos regretted the deal he and I had struck that day—and I wasn't quite sure how I felt about those deals myself. I had stepped back from my EHM role. I had played his game instead of mine, accepting his insistence on honesty in exchange for more contracts. In purely economic terms, it had been a wise business decision for MAIN. Nonetheless, it had been inconsistent with what Claudine had instilled in me; it was not advancing the global empire. Had it now unleashed the jackals?

I recalled thinking, when I left Torrijos's bungalow that day, that Latin American history is littered with dead heroes. A system based on corrupting public figures does not take kindly to public figures who refuse to be corrupted.

Then I thought my eyes were playing tricks. A familiar figure was walking slowly across the lobby. At first, I was so confused that I believed it was Humphrey Bogart, but Bogart was long deceased. Then I recognized the man ambling past me as one of the great figures in modern English literature, author of *The Power and the Glory*, *The Comedians*, *Our Man in Havana*, and of the article I had just set down on the table next to me. Graham Greene hesitated a moment, peered around, and headed for the coffee shop.

I was tempted to call out or to run after him, but I stopped myself. An inner voice said he needed his privacy; another warned that he would shun me. I picked up the *New York Review of Books* and was surprised a moment later to discover that I was standing in the doorway to the coffee shop.

I had breakfasted earlier that morning, and the maitre d' gave me an odd look. I glanced around. Graham Greene sat alone at a table near the wall. I pointed to the table beside him.

"Over there," I told the maitre d'. "Can I sit there for another breakfast?"

I was always a good tipper; the maitre d' smiled knowingly and led me to the table.

The novelist was absorbed in his newspaper. I ordered coffee and a croissant with honey. I wanted to discover Greene's thoughts about Panama, Torrijos, and the Canal affair, but had no idea how to initiate such a conversation. Then he looked up to take a sip from his glass.

"Excuse me," I said.

He glared at me—or so it seemed. "Yes?"

"I hate to intrude. But you are Graham Greene, aren't you?"

"Why, yes indeed." He smiled warmly. "Most people in Panama don't recognize me."

I gushed that he was my favorite novelist, and then gave him a brief life history, including my work at MAIN and my meetings with Torrijos. He asked if I was the consultant who had written an article about the United States getting out of Panama. "In the *Boston Globe*, if I recall correctly."

I was flabbergasted.

"A courageous thing to do, given your position," he said. "Won't you join me?"

I moved to his table and sat there with him for what must have been an hour and a half. I realized as we chatted how very close to Torrijos he had grown. He spoke of the general at times like a father speaking about his son.

"The general," he said, "invited me to write a book about his country. I'm doing just that. This one will be nonfiction—something a bit off the line for me."

I asked him why he usually wrote novels instead of nonfiction.

"Fiction is safer," he said. "Most of my subject matter is controversial. Vietnam. Haiti. The Mexican Revolution. A lot of publishers would be afraid to publish nonfiction about these matters." He pointed at the *New York Review of Books*, where it lay on the table I had vacated. "Words like those can cause a great deal of damage." Then he smiled. "Besides, I like to write fiction. It gives me much greater freedom." He looked at me intensely. "The important thing is to write about things that matter. Like your *Globe* article about the Canal."

His admiration for Torrijos was obvious. It seemed that Panama's head of state could impress a novelist every bit as much as he impressed the poor and dispossessed. Equally obvious was Greene's concern for his friend's life.

"It's a huge endeavor," he exclaimed, "taking on the Giant of the North." He shook his head sadly. "I fear for his safety."

Then it was time for him to leave.

"Must catch a flight to France," he said, rising slowly and shaking my hand. He peered into my eyes. "Why don't you write a book?" He gave me an encouraging nod. "It's in you. But remember, make it about things that matter." He turned and walked away. Then he stopped and came back a few steps into the restaurant.

"Don't worry," he said. "The general will prevail. He'll get the Canal back."

Torrijos did get it back. In that same year, 1977, he successfully negotiated new treaties with President Carter that transferred the Canal Zone and the Canal itself over to Panamanian control. Then the White House had to convince the U.S. Congress to ratify it. A long and arduous battle ensued. In the final tally, the Canal Treaty was ratified by a single vote. Conservatives swore revenge.

When Graham Greene's nonfiction book *Getting to Know the General* came out many years later, it was dedicated, "To the friends of my friend, Omar Torrijos, in Nicaragua, El Salvador, and Panama."[5]

CHAPTER 18

Iran's King of Kings

Between 1975 and 1978, I frequently visited Iran. Sometimes I commuted between Latin America or Indonesia and Tehran. The Shah of Shahs (literally, "King of Kings," his official title) presented a completely different situation from that in the other countries where we worked.

Iran was oil rich and, like Saudi Arabia, it did not need to incur debt in order to finance its ambitious list of projects. However, Iran differed significantly from Saudi Arabia in that its large population, while predominantly Middle Eastern and Muslim, was not Arabic. In addition, the country had a history of political turmoil—both internally and in its relationships with its neighbors. Therefore, we took a different approach: Washington and the business community joined forces to turn the shah into a symbol of progress.

We launched an immense effort to show the world what a strong, democratic friend of U.S. corporate and political interests could accomplish. Never mind his obviously undemocratic title or the less obvious fact of the CIA-orchestrated coup against his democratically elected premier; Washington and its European partners were determined to present the shah's government as an alternative to those in Iraq, Libya, China, Korea, and other nations where a powerful undercurrent of anti-Americanism was surfacing.

To all appearances, the shah was a progressive friend of the underprivileged. In 1962, he ordered large private landholdings broken up and turned over to peasant owners. The following year, he inaugurated his White Revolution, which involved an extensive agenda for socioeconomic reforms. The power of OPEC grew during the 1970s, and the shah became an increasingly influential world leader. At the same time, Iran developed one of the most powerful military forces in the Muslim Middle East.[1]

MAIN was involved in projects that covered most of the country, from tourist areas along the Caspian Sea in the north to secret military installations overlooking the Straits of Hormuz in the south. Once again, the focus of our work was to forecast regional development potentials and then to design electrical generating, transmission, and distribution systems that would provide the all-important energy required to fuel the industrial and commercial growth that would realize these forecasts.

I visited most of the major regions of Iran at one time or another. I followed the old caravan trail through the desert mountains, from Kirman to Bandar 'Abbas, and I roamed the ruins of Persepolis, the legendary palace of ancient kings and one of the wonders of the classical world. I toured the country's most famous and spectacular sites: Shiraz, Isfahan, and the magnificent tent city near Persepolis where the shah had been crowned. In the process, I developed a genuine love for this land and its complex people.

On the surface, Iran seemed to be a model example of Christian-Muslim cooperation. However, I soon learned that tranquil appearances may mask deep resentment.

Late one evening in 1977, I returned to my hotel room to find a note shoved under my door. I was shocked to discover that it was signed by a man named Yamin. I had never met him, but he had been described to me during a government briefing as a famous and most subversive radical. In beautifully crafted English script, the note invited me to meet him at a designated restaurant. However, there was a warning: I was to come only if I was interested in exploring a side of Iran that most people "in my position" never saw. I wondered whether Yamin knew what my true position was. I realized that I was taking a big risk; however, I could not resist the temptation to meet this enigmatic figure.

My taxi dropped me off in front of a tiny gate in a high wall—so high that I could not see the building behind it. A beautiful Iranian woman wearing a long black gown ushered me in and led me down a corridor illuminated by ornate oil lamps hanging from a low ceiling. At the end of this corridor, we entered a room that dazzled like the interior of a diamond, blinding me with its radiance. When my eyes finally adjusted, I saw that the walls were inlaid with semiprecious stones and mother-of-pearl. The restaurant was lighted by tall white candles protruding from intricately sculpted bronze chandeliers.

A tall man with long black hair, wearing a tailored navy blue suit, approached and shook my hand. He introduced himself as Yamin, in an accent that suggested he was an Iranian who had been educated in the British school system, and I was immediately struck by how little he looked like a subversive radical. He directed me past several tables where couples sat quietly eating, to a very private alcove; he assured me we could talk in complete confidentiality. I had the distinct impression that this restaurant catered to secret rendezvous. Ours, quite possibly, was the only non-amorous one that night.

Yamin was very cordial. During our discussion, it became obvious that he thought of me merely as an economic consultant, not as someone with ulterior motives. He explained that he had singled me out because he knew I had been a Peace Corps volunteer and because he had been told that I took every possible opportunity to get to know his country and to mix with its people.

"You are very young compared to most in your profession," he said. "You have a genuine interest in our history and our current problems. You represent our hope."

This, as well as the setting, his appearance, and the presence of so many others in the restaurant, gave me a certain degree of comfort. I had become accustomed to people befriending me, like Rasy in Java and Fidel in Panama, and I accepted it as a compliment and an opportunity. I knew that I stood out from other Americans because I was in fact infatuated with the places I visited. I have found that people warm to you very quickly if you open your eyes, ears, and heart to their culture.

Yamin asked if I knew about the Flowering Desert project.[2] "The shah believes that our deserts were once fertile plains and lush forests. At least, that's what he claims. During Alexander the Great's reign, according to this theory, vast armies swept across these lands, traveling with millions of goats and sheep. The animals ate all the grass and other vegetation. The disappearance of these plants caused a drought, and eventually the entire region became a desert. Now all we have to do, or so the shah says, is plant millions upon millions of trees. After that—presto—the rains will return and the desert will bloom again. Of course, in the process we will have to spend hundreds of millions of dollars." He smiled condescendingly. "Companies like yours will reap huge profits."

"I take it you don't believe in this theory."

"The desert is a symbol. Turning it green is about much more than agriculture."

Several waiters descended upon us with trays of beautifully presented Iranian food. Asking my permission first, Yamin proceeded to select an assortment from the various trays. Then he turned back to me.

"A question for you, Mr. Perkins, if I might be so bold. What destroyed the cultures of your own native peoples, the Indians?"

I responded that I felt there had been many factors, including greed and superior weapons.

"Yes. True. All of that. But more than anything else, did it not come down to a destruction of the environment?" He went on to explain how once forests and animals such as the buffalo are destroyed, and once people are moved onto reservations, the very foundations of cultures collapse.

"You see, it is the same here," he said. "The desert is our environment. The Flowering Desert project threatens nothing less than the destruction of our entire fabric. How can we allow this to happen?"

I told him that it was my understanding that the whole idea behind the project came from his people. He responded with a cynical laugh, saying that the idea was planted in the shah's mind by my own United States government, and that the shah was just a puppet of that government.

"A true Persian would never permit such a thing," Yamin said. Then he launched into a long dissertation about the relationship between his people—the Bedouins—and the desert. He emphasized the fact that many urbanized Iranians take their vacations in the desert. They set up tents large enough for the entire family and spend a week or more living in them.

"We—my people—are part of the desert. The people the shah claims to rule with that iron hand of his are not just *of* the desert. We *are* the desert."

After that, he told me stories about his personal experiences in the desert. When the evening was over, he escorted me back to the tiny door in the large wall. My taxi was waiting in the street outside. Yamin shook my hand and expressed his appreciation for the time I had spent with him. He again mentioned my young age and my openness, and the fact that my occupying such a position gave him hope for the future.

"I am so glad to have had this time with a man like you." He continued to hold my hand in his. "I would request of you only one more favor. I do not ask this lightly. I do it only because, after our time together tonight, I know it will be meaningful to you. You'll gain a great deal from it."

"What is it I can do for you?"

"I would like to introduce you to a dear friend of mine, a man who can tell you a great deal about our King of Kings. He may shock you, but I assure you that meeting him will be well worth your time."

CHAPTER 19

Confessions of a Tortured Man

Several days later, Yamin drove me out of Tehran, through a dusty and impoverished shantytown, along an old camel trail, and out to the edge of the desert. With the sun setting behind the city, he stopped his car at a cluster of tiny mud shacks surrounded by palm trees.

"A very old oasis," he explained, "dating back centuries before Marco Polo." He preceded me to one of the shacks. "The man inside has a PhD from one of your most prestigious universities. For reasons that will soon be clear, he must remain nameless. You can call him Doc."

He knocked on the wooden door, and there was a muffled response. Yamin pushed the door open and led me inside. The tiny room was windowless and lit only by an oil lamp on a low table in one corner. As my eyes adjusted, I saw that the dirt floor was covered with Persian carpets. Then the shadowy outline of a man began to emerge. He was seated in front of the lamp in a way that kept his features hidden. I could tell only that he was bundled in blankets and was wearing something around his head. He sat in a wheelchair, and other than the table, this was the only piece of furniture in the room. Yamin motioned for me to sit on a carpet. He went up and gently embraced the man, speaking a few words in his ear, then returned and sat at my side.

"I've told you about Mr. Perkins," he said. "We're both honored to have this opportunity to visit with you, sir."

"Mr. Perkins. You are welcome." The voice, with barely any detectable accent, was low and hoarse. I found myself leaning forward into the small space between us as he said, "You see before you a broken man. I have not always been so. Once I was strong like you. I was a close and trusted adviser to the shah." There was a long pause. "The Shah of Shahs, King of Kings." His tone of voice sounded, I thought, more sad than angry.

"I personally knew many of the world's leaders. Eisenhower, Nixon, de Gaulle. They trusted me to help lead this country into the capitalist camp. The shah trusted me, and," he made a sound that could have been a cough, but which I took for a laugh, "I trusted the shah. I believed his rhetoric. I was convinced that Iran would lead the Muslim world into a new epoch, that Persia would fulfill its promise. It seemed our destiny—the shah's, mine, all of ours who carried out the mission we thought we had been born to fulfill."

The lump of blankets moved; the wheelchair made a wheezing noise and turned slightly. I could see the outline of the man's face in profile, his shaggy beard, and—then it grabbed me—the flatness. He had no nose! I shuddered and stifled a gasp.

"Not a pretty sight, would you say, ah, Mr. Perkins? Too bad you can't see it in full light. It is truly grotesque." Again there was the sound of choking laughter. "But as I'm sure you can appreciate, I must remain anonymous. Certainly, you could learn my identity if you tried, although you might find that I am dead. Officially, I no longer exist. Yet I trust you won't try. You and your family are better off not knowing who I am. The arm of the shah and SAVAK reaches far."

The chair wheezed and returned to its original position. I felt a sense of relief, as though not seeing the profile somehow obliterated the violence that had been done. At the time, I did not know of this custom among some Islamic cultures. Individuals deemed to have brought dishonor or disgrace upon society or its leaders are punished by having their noses cut off. In this way, they are marked for life—as this man's face clearly demonstrated.

"I'm sure, Mr. Perkins, you're wondering why we invited you here." Without waiting for my response, the man in the wheelchair continued, "You see, this man who calls himself the King of Kings is in reality satanic. His father was deposed by your CIA with—I hate to say it—my help, because he was said to be a Nazi collaborator. And then there was the Mossadegh calamity. Today, our shah is on the route to surpassing Hitler in the realms of evil. He does this with the full knowledge and support of your government."

"Why is that?" I asked.

"Quite simple. He is your only real ally in the Middle East, and the industrial world rotates on the axle of oil that is the Middle East. Oh, you have Israel, of course, but that's actually a liability to you, not an asset. And no oil there. Your politicians must placate the Jewish vote, must get their money to finance campaigns. So you're stuck with Israel, I'm afraid. However, Iran is the key. Your oil companies—which carry even more power than the Jews—need us. You need our shah—or you think you do, just as you thought you needed South Vietnam's corrupt leaders."

"Are you suggesting otherwise? Is Iran the equivalent to Vietnam?"

"Potentially much worse. You see, this shah won't last much longer. The Muslim world hates him. Not just the Arabs, but Muslims everywhere—Indonesia, the United States, but mostly right here, his own Persian people." There was a thumping sound and I realized that he had struck the side of his chair. "He is evil! We Persians hate him." Then silence. I could hear only his heavy breathing, as though the exertion had exhausted him.

"Doc is very close to the mullahs," Yamin said to me, his voice low and calm. "There is a huge undercurrent among the religious factions here and it pervades most of our country, except for a handful of people in the commercial classes who benefit from the shah's capitalism."

"I don't doubt you," I said. "But I must say that during four visits here, I've seen nothing of it. Everyone I talk with seems to love the shah, to appreciate the economic upsurge."

"You don't speak Farsi," Yamin observed. "You hear only what is told to you by those men who benefit the most. The ones who have been educated in the States or in England end up working for the shah. Doc here is an exception—now."

He paused, seeming to ponder his next words. "It's the same with your press. They only talk with the few who are his kin, his circle. Of course, for the most part, your press is also controlled by oil. So they hear what they want to hear and write what their advertisers want to read."

"Why are we telling you all this, Mr. Perkins?" Doc's voice was even more hoarse than before, as if the effort of speaking and the emotions were draining what little energy the man had mustered for this meeting. "Because we'd like to convince you to get out and to persuade your company to stay away from our country. We want to warn you that although you may think you'll make a great deal of money here, it's an illusion. This government will not last." Again, I heard the sound of his hand thudding against the chair. "And when it goes, the one that replaces it will have no sympathy for you and your kind."

"You're saying we won't be paid?"

Doc broke down in a fit of coughing. Yamin went to him and rubbed his back. When the coughing ended, he spoke to Doc in Farsi and then came back to his seat.

"We must end this conversation," Yamin said to me. "In answer to your question: yes, you will not be paid. You'll do all that work, and when it comes time to collect your fees, the shah will be gone."

During the drive back, I asked Yamin why he and Doc wanted to spare MAIN the financial disaster he had predicted.

"We'd be happy to see your company go bankrupt. However, we'd rather see you leave Iran. Just one company like yours, walking away, could start a trend. That's what we're hoping. You see, we don't want a bloodbath here, but the shah must go, and we'll try anything that will make that easier. So we pray to Allah that you'll convince your Mr. Zambotti to get out while there is still time."

"Why me?"

"I knew during our dinner together, when we spoke of the Flowering Desert project, that you were open to the truth. I knew that our information about you was correct—you are a man between two worlds, a man in the middle."

It made me wonder just how much he did know about me.

⊕ CHAPTER 20

The Fall of a King

One evening in 1978, while I was sitting alone at the luxurious bar off the lobby of the Hotel InterContinental in Tehran, I felt a tap on my shoulder. I turned to see a heavyset Iranian in a business suit.

"John Perkins! You don't remember me?"

The former soccer player had gained a lot of weight, but the voice was unmistakable. It was my old Middlebury friend Farhad, whom I had not seen in more than a decade. We embraced and sat down together. It quickly became obvious that he knew all about me and about my work. It was equally obvious that he did not intend to share much about his own work.

"Let's get right to the point," he said as we ordered our second beers. "I'm flying to Rome tomorrow. My parents live there. I have a ticket for you on my flight. Things are falling apart here. You've got to get out." He handed me an airline ticket. I did not doubt him for a moment.

In Rome, we dined with Farhad's parents. His father, the retired Iranian general who once stepped in front of a would-be assassin's bullet to save the shah's life, expressed disillusionment with his former boss. He said that during the past few years the shah had showed his true colors, his arrogance and greed. The general blamed U.S. policy—particularly its backing of Israel, of corrupt leaders, and of despotic governments—for the hatred sweeping the Middle East, and he predicted that the shah would be gone within months.

"You know," he said, "you sowed the seeds of this rebellion in the early fifties, when you overthrew Mossadegh. You thought it very clever back then—as did I. But now it returns to haunt you—us."[1]

I was astounded by his pronouncements. I had heard something similar from Yamin and Doc, but coming from this man it took on new significance. By this time, everyone knew of the existence of a fundamentalist Islamic underground, but we had convinced ourselves that the shah was immensely popular among the majority of his people and was therefore politically invincible. The general, however, was adamant.

"Mark my words," he said solemnly, "the shah's fall will be only the beginning. It's a preview of where the Muslim world is headed. Our rage has smoldered beneath the sands too long. Soon it will erupt."

Over dinner, I heard a great deal about Ayatollah Ruhollah Khomeini. Farhad and his father made it clear that they did not support his fanatical Shiism, but they were obviously impressed by the inroads he had made against the shah. They told me that this cleric, whose given name translates to "inspired of God," was born into a family of dedicated Shiite scholars in a village near Tehran, in 1902.

Khomeini had made it a point not to become involved in the Mossadegh-shah struggles of the early 1950s, but he actively opposed the shah in the 1960s, criticizing the ruler so adamantly that he was banished to Turkey, then to the Shiite holy city of An Najaf in Iraq, where he became the acknowledged leader of the opposition. He sent out letters, articles, and tape-recorded messages urging Iranians to rise up, overthrow the shah, and create a clerical state.

Two days after that dinner with Farhad and his parents, news came out of Iran of bombings and riots. Ayatollah Khomeini and the mullahs had begun the offensive that would soon give them control. After that, things happened fast. The rage Farhad's father had described exploded in a violent Islamic uprising. The shah fled his country for Egypt in January 1979, and then, diagnosed with cancer, headed for a New York hospital.

Followers of the Ayatollah Khomeini demanded his return. In November 1979, a militant Islamic mob seized the United States Embassy in Tehran and held fifty-two American hostages for the next 444 days.[2] President Carter attempted to negotiate the release of the hostages. When this failed, he authorized a military rescue mission, launched in April 1980. It was a disaster, and it turned out to be the hammer that would drive the final nail into Carter's presidential coffin.

Tremendous pressure, exerted by U.S. commercial and political groups, forced the cancer-ridden shah to leave the United States. From the day he fled Tehran he had a difficult time finding sanctuary; all his former friends shunned him. However, General Torrijos exhibited his customary compassion and offered the shah asylum in Panama, despite a personal dislike of the shah's politics. The shah arrived and received sanctuary at the very same resort where the new Panama Canal Treaty had so recently been negotiated.

The mullahs demanded the shah's return in exchange for the hostages held in the U.S. Embassy. Those in Washington who had opposed the Canal Treaty accused Torrijos of corruption and collusion with the shah, and of endangering the lives of U.S. citizens. They too demanded that the shah be turned over to Ayatollah Khomeini. Ironically, until only a few weeks earlier, many of these same people had been the shah's staunchest supporters. The once-proud King of Kings eventually returned to Egypt, where he died of cancer.

Doc's prediction came true. MAIN lost millions of dollars in Iran, as did many of our competitors. Carter lost his bid for reelection. The Reagan-Bush administration marched into Washington with promises to free the hostages, to bring down the mullahs, to return democracy to Iran, and to set straight the Panama Canal situation.

For me, the lessons were irrefutable. Iran illustrated beyond any doubt that the United States was a nation laboring to deny the truth of our role in the world. It seemed incomprehensible that we could have been so misinformed about the shah and the tide of hatred that had surged against him. Even those of us in companies like MAIN, which had offices and personnel in the country, had not known. I felt certain that the NSA and the CIA must have seen what had been so obvious to Torrijos even as far back as my meeting with him in 1972, but that our own intelligence community had intentionally encouraged us all to close our eyes.

CHAPTER 21

Colombia: Keystone of Latin America

While Saudi Arabia, Iran, and Panama offered fascinating and disturbing studies, they also stood out as exceptions to the rule. Due to vast oil deposits in the first two and the Canal in the third, they did not fit the norm. Colombia's situation was more typical, and MAIN was the designer and lead engineering firm on a huge hydroelectric project there.

A Colombian college professor writing a book on the history of Pan-American relations once told me that Teddy Roosevelt had appreciated the significance of his country. Pointing at a map, the U.S. president and former Rough Rider reportedly described Colombia as "the keystone to the arch of South America." I have never verified that story; however, it is certainly true that on a map Colombia, poised at the top of the continent, appears to hold the rest of the continent together. It connects all the southern countries to the Isthmus of Panama and therefore to both Central and North America.

Whether Roosevelt actually described Colombia in those terms or not, he was only one of many presidents who understood its pivotal position. For nearly two centuries, the United States has viewed Colombia as a keystone—or perhaps more accurately, as a portal into the southern hemisphere for both business and politics.

The country also is endowed with great natural beauty: spectacular palm-lined beaches on both the Atlantic and Pacific coasts, majestic mountains, pampas that rival the Great Plains of the North American Midwest, and vast rain forests rich in biodiversity. The people, too, have a special quality, combining the physical, cultural, and artistic traits of diverse ethnic backgrounds ranging from the local Taironas to imports from Africa, Asia, Europe, and the Middle East.

Historically, Colombia has played a crucial role in Latin American history and culture. During the colonial period, Colombia was the seat of the viceroy for all Spanish territories north of Peru and south of Costa Rica. The great fleets of gold galleons set sail from its coastal city of Cartagena to transport priceless treasures from as far south as Chile and Argentina to ports in Spain. Many of the critical actions in the wars for independence occurred in Colombia; for example, forces under Simón Bolívar were victorious over Spanish royalists at the pivotal Battle of Boyacá, in 1819.

In modern times, Colombia has had a reputation for producing some of Latin America's most brilliant writers, artists, philosophers, and other intellectuals, as well as fiscally responsible and relatively democratic governments. It became the model for President Kennedy's nation-building programs throughout Latin America. Unlike Guatemala, its government was not tarnished with the reputation of being a CIA creation, and unlike Nicaragua, the government was an elected one, which presented an alternative to both right-wing dictators and Communists. Finally, unlike so many other countries, including powerful Brazil and Argentina, Colombia did not mistrust the United States. The image of Colombia as a reliable ally has continued, despite the blemish of its drug cartels.[1]

The glories of Colombia's history, however, are counterbalanced by hatred and violence. The seat of the Spanish viceroy was also home to the Inquisition. Magnificent forts, haciendas, and cities were constructed over the bones of Indian and African slaves. The treasures carried on the gold galleons, sacred objects and masterpieces of art that had been melted down for easy transport, were ripped from the hearts of ancient peoples. The proud cultures themselves were laid to waste by conquistador swords and diseases. More recently, a controversial presidential election in 1945 resulted in a deep division between political parties and led to *La Violencia* (1948–1957), during which more than two hundred thousand people died.

Despite the conflicts and ironies, both Washington and Wall Street historically have viewed Colombia as an essential factor in promoting Pan-American political and commercial interests. This is due to several factors, in addition to Colombia's critical geographic location, including the perception that leaders throughout the hemisphere look to Bogotá for inspiration and guidance, and the fact that the country is both a source of many products purchased in the United States—coffee, bananas, textiles, emeralds, flowers, oil, and cocaine—and a market for our goods and services.

One of the most important services we sold to Colombia during the late twentieth century was engineering and construction expertise. Colombia was typical of many places where I worked. It was relatively easy to demonstrate that the country could assume vast amounts of debt and then repay these debts from the benefits realized both from the projects themselves and from the country's natural resources. Thus, huge investments in electrical power grids, highways, and telecommunications would help Colombia open up its vast gas and oil resources and its largely undeveloped Amazonian territories; these projects, in turn, would generate the income necessary to pay off the loans, plus interest.

That was the theory. However, the reality, consistent with our true intent around the world, was to subjugate Bogotá, to further the global empire. My job, as it had been in so many places, was to present the case for exceedingly large loans. Colombia did not have the benefit of a Torrijos; therefore, I felt I had no choice but to develop inflated economic and electric load forecasts.

With the exception of the occasional bouts of guilt over my job, Colombia became a personal refuge for me. Ann and I had spent a couple of months there in the early 1970s, and had even made a down payment on a small coffee farm located in the mountains along the Caribbean coast. I think our time together during that period came as close as anything could to healing the wounds we had inflicted on each other over the preceding years. Ultimately, however, the wounds went too deep, and it was not until after our marriage fell apart that I became truly acquainted with the country.

During the 1970s, MAIN had been awarded a number of contracts to develop various infrastructure projects, including a network of hydroelectric facilities and the distribution systems to transport the electricity from deep in the jungle to cities high in the mountains. I was given an office in the coastal city of Barranquilla, and it was there, in 1977, that I met a beautiful Colombian woman who would become a powerful agent of change in my life.

Paula had long blonde hair and striking green eyes—not what most foreigners expect in a Colombian. Her mother and father had emigrated from northern Italy, and in keeping with her heritage, she became a fashion designer. She went a step further, however, and built a small factory where her creations were transformed into clothes, which she then sold at upscale boutiques throughout the country, as well as in Panama and Venezuela. She was a deeply compassionate person who helped me get through some of the personal trauma of my broken marriage and begin dealing with some of my attitudes toward women, which had affected me so negatively. She also taught me a great deal about the consequences of the actions I took in my job.

As I have said before, life is composed of a series of coincidences over which we have no control. For me, those included being raised as the son of a teacher at an all-male prep school in rural New Hampshire, meeting Ann and her Uncle Frank, the Vietnam War, and meeting Einar Greve. However, once we are presented with such coincidences, we face choices. How we respond, the actions we take in the face of coincidences, makes all the difference. For example, excelling at that school, marrying Ann, entering the Peace Corps, and choosing to become an economic hit man—all these decisions had brought me to my current place in life.

Paula was another coincidence, and her influence would lead me to take actions that changed the course of my life. Until I met her, I had pretty much gone along with the system. I often found myself questioning what I was doing, sometimes feeling guilty about it, yet I always discovered a way to rationalize staying in the system. Perhaps Paula just happened along at the right time. It is possible that I would have taken the plunge anyway, that my experiences in Saudi Arabia, Iran, and Panama would have nudged me into action. But I am certain that even as one woman, Claudine, had been instrumental in persuading me to join the ranks of EHMs, another, Paula, was the catalyst I needed at that time. She convinced me to go deep inside myself and see that I would never be happy as long as I continued in that role.

CHAPTER 22

American Republic Versus Global Empire

"I'll be frank," Paula said one day, while we were sitting in a coffee shop. "The Indians and all the farmers who live along the river you're damming hate you. Even people in the cities, who aren't directly affected, sympathize with the guerrillas who've been attacking your construction camp. Your government calls these people Communists, terrorists, and narcotics traffickers, but the truth is they're just people with families who live on lands your company is destroying."

I had just told her about Manuel Torres. He was an engineer employed by MAIN and one of the men recently attacked by guerrillas at our hydroelectric dam construction site. Manuel was a Colombian citizen who had a job because of a policy prohibiting us from sending U.S. citizens to that site. Some of us, including our Colombian counterparts, referred to it as the Colombians are Expendable doctrine, and it symbolized an attitude I had grown to hate. My feelings toward such policies were making it increasingly difficult for me to live with myself.

"According to Manuel, they fired AK-47s into the air and at his feet," I told Paula. "He sounded calm when he told me about it, but

I know he was almost hysterical. They didn't shoot anyone. Just gave them that letter and sent them downriver in their boats."

"My God," Paula exclaimed. "The poor man was terrified."

"Of course he was." I told her that I had asked Manuel whether he thought they were FARC or M-19, referring to two of the most infamous Colombian guerrilla groups.

"And?"

"He said, neither. But he told me that he believes what they said in that letter."

Paula picked up the newspaper I had brought and read the letter aloud.

"'We, who work every day just to survive, swear on the blood of our ancestors that we will never allow dams across our rivers. We are simple Indians and mestizos, but we would rather die than stand by as our land is flooded. We warn our Colombian brothers: stop working for the construction companies.'" She set the paper down. "What did you say to him?"

I hesitated, but only for a moment. "I had no choice. I had to toe the company line. I asked him if he thought that sounds like a letter a farmer would write."

She sat watching me, patiently.

"He just shrugged." Our eyes met. "Oh, Paula, I detest myself for playing this role."

"What did you do next?" she pressed.

"I slammed my fist on the desk. I intimidated him. I asked him whether farmers with AK-47s made any sense to him. Then I asked if he knew who invented the AK-47."

"Did he?"

"Yes, but I could hardly hear his answer. 'A Russian,' he said. Of course, I assured him that he was right, that the inventor had been a Communist named Kalashnikov, a highly decorated officer in the Red Army. I brought him around to understand that the people who wrote that note were Communists."

"Do you believe that?" she asked.

Her question stopped me. How could I answer, honestly? I recalled Iran and the time Yamin described me as a man caught between two worlds, a man in the middle. In some ways, I wished I had been in that camp when the guerrillas attacked, or that I was one of the guerrillas. An odd feeling crept over me, a sort of jealousy for Yamin and Doc and the Colombian rebels. These were men with convictions. They had chosen real worlds, not a no-man's territory somewhere between.

"I have a job to do," I said at last.

She smiled gently.

"I hate it," I continued. I thought about the men whose images had come to me so often over the years, Tom Paine and other Revolutionary War heroes, pirates and frontiersmen. They stood at the edges, not in the middle. They had taken stands and lived with the consequences. "Every day I come to hate my job a little more."

She took my hand. "Your job?"

Our eyes met and held. I understood the implication. "Myself."

She squeezed my hand and nodded slowly. I felt an immediate sense of relief, just admitting it.

"What will you do, John?"

I had no answer. The relief turned into defensiveness. I stammered out the standard justifications: that I was trying to do good, that I was exploring ways to change the system from within, and—the old standby—that if I quit, someone even worse would fill my shoes. But I could see from the way she watched me that she was not buying it. Even worse, I knew that I was not buying it either. She had forced me to understand the essential truth: it was not my job, but me, that was to blame.

"What about you?" I asked at last. "What do you believe?"

She gave a little sigh and released my hand, asking, "You trying to change the subject?"

I nodded.

"Okay," she agreed. "Under one condition. That we'll return to it another day." She picked up a spoon and appeared to examine it.

"I know that some of the guerrillas have trained in Russia and China." She lowered the spoon into her *café con leche,* stirred, and then slowly licked the spoon. "What else can they do? They need to learn about modern weapons and how to fight the soldiers who've gone through your schools. Sometimes they sell cocaine in order to raise money for supplies. How else can they buy guns? They're up against terrible odds. Your World Bank doesn't help them defend themselves. In fact, it forces them into this position." She took a sip of coffee. "I believe their cause is just. The electricity will help only a few, the wealthiest Colombians, and thousands will die because the fish and water are poisoned, after you build that dam of yours."

Hearing her speak so compassionately about the people who opposed us—me—caused my flesh to crawl. I found myself clawing at my forearms.

"How do you know so much about the guerrillas?" Even as I asked it, I had a sinking feeling, a premonition that I did not want to know the answer.

"I went to school with some of them," she said. She hesitated, pushed her cup away. "My brother joined the movement."

There it was. I felt absolutely deflated. I thought I knew all about her, but this . . . I had the fleeting image of a man coming home to find his wife in bed with another man.

"How come you never told me?"

"Seemed irrelevant. Why would I? It isn't something I brag about." She paused. "I haven't seen him for two years. He has to be very careful."

"How do you know he's alive?"

"I don't, except recently the government put him on a wanted list. That's a good sign."

I was fighting the urge to be judgmental or defensive. I hoped she could not discern my jealousy. "How did he become one of them?" I asked.

Fortunately, she kept her eyes on the coffee cup. "Demonstrating outside the offices of an oil company—Occidental, I think. He was protesting drilling on indigenous lands, in the forests of a tribe facing extinction—him and a couple dozen of his friends. They were attacked by the army, beaten, and thrown into prison—for doing nothing illegal, mind you, just standing outside that building waving placards and singing." She glanced out a nearby window. "They kept him in jail for nearly six months. He never did tell us what happened there, but when he came out he was a different person."

It was the first of many similar conversations with Paula, and I now know that these discussions set the stage for what was to follow. My soul was torn apart, yet I was still ruled by my wallet and by those other weaknesses the NSA had identified when they profiled me a decade earlier, in 1968. By forcing me to see this and to confront the deeper feelings behind my fascination with pirates and other rebels, Paula helped me along the trail toward salvation.

Beyond my own personal dilemmas, my times in Colombia also helped me comprehend the distinction between the old American republic and the new global empire. The republic offered hope to the world. Its foundation was moral and philosophical rather than materialistic. It was based on concepts of equality and justice for all. But it also could be pragmatic, not merely a utopian dream but also a living, breathing, magnanimous entity. It could open its arms to shelter the downtrodden. It was an inspiration and at the same time a force to reckon with; if needed, it could swing into action, as it had during World War II, to defend the principles for which it stood. The very institutions—the big corporations, banks, and government bureaucracies—that threaten the republic could be used instead to institute fundamental changes in the world. Such institutions possess the communications networks and transportation systems necessary to end disease, starvation, and even wars—if only they could be convinced to take that course.

The global empire, on the other hand, is the republic's nemesis. It is self-centered, self-serving, greedy, and materialistic, a system based on mercantilism. Like empires before, its arms open only to accumulate resources, to grab everything in sight and stuff its insatiable maw. It will use whatever means it deems necessary to help its rulers gain more power and riches.

Of course, in learning to understand this distinction I also developed a clearer sense of my own role. Claudine had warned me; she had honestly outlined what would be expected of me if I accepted the job MAIN offered. Yet, it took the experience of working in countries like Indonesia, Panama, Iran, and Colombia in order for me to understand the deeper implications. And it took the patience, love, and personal stories of a woman like Paula.

I was loyal to the American republic, but what we were perpetrating through this new, highly subtle form of imperialism was the financial equivalent of what we had attempted to accomplish militarily in Vietnam. If Southeast Asia had taught us that armies have limitations, the economists had responded by devising a better plan, and the foreign aid agencies and the private contractors who served them (or, more appropriately, were served by them) had become proficient at executing that plan.

In countries on every continent, I saw how men and women working for U.S. corporations—though not officially part of the EHM network—participated in something far more pernicious than anything envisioned in conspiracy theories. Like many of MAIN's engineers, these workers were blind to the consequences of their actions, convinced that the sweatshops and factories that made shoes and automotive parts for their companies were helping the poor climb out of poverty, instead of simply burying them deeper in a type of slavery reminiscent of medieval manors and southern plantations. Like those earlier manifestations of exploitation, modern serfs or slaves were socialized into believing they were better off than the unfortunate souls who lived on the margins, in the dark hollows of Europe, in the jungles of Africa, or in the wilds of the American frontier.

The struggle over whether I should continue at MAIN or should quit had become an open battlefield. There was no doubt that my conscience wanted out, but that other side, what I liked to think of as my business-school persona, was not so sure. My own empire kept expanding; I added employees, countries, and shares of stock to my various portfolios and to my ego. In addition to the seduction of the money and lifestyle, and the adrenaline high of power, I often recalled Claudine warning me that once I was in I could never get out.

Of course, Paula sneered at this. "What would she know?"

I pointed out that Claudine had been right about a great many things.

"That was a long time ago. Lives change. Anyway, what difference does it make? You're not happy with yourself. What can Claudine or anyone else do to make things worse than that?"

It was a refrain Paula often came back to, and I eventually agreed. I admitted to her and to myself that all the money, adventure, and glamour no longer justified the turmoil, guilt, and stress. As a MAIN partner, I was becoming wealthy, and I knew that if I stayed longer I would be permanently trapped.

One day, while we were strolling along the beach near the old Spanish fort at Cartagena, a place that had endured countless pirate attacks, Paula hit upon an approach that had not occurred to me. "What if you never say anything about the things you know?" she asked.

"You mean . . . just keep quiet?"

"Exactly. Don't give them an excuse to come after you. In fact, give them every reason to leave you alone, to not muddy the water."

It made a great deal of sense—I wondered why it never occurred to me before. I would not write books or do anything else to expose the truth as I had come to see it. I would not be a crusader; instead, I would just be a person, concentrate on enjoying life, travel for pleasure, perhaps even start a family with someone like Paula. I had had enough; I simply wanted out.

"Everything Claudine taught you is a deception," Paula added.

"Your life's a lie." She smiled condescendingly. "Have you looked at your own résumé recently?"

I admitted that I had not.

"Do," she advised. "I read the Spanish version the other day. If it's anything like the English one, I think you'll find it very interesting."

⊕ CHAPTER 23

The Deceptive Résumé

While I was in Colombia, word arrived that Jake Dauber had retired as MAIN's president. As expected, chairman and CEO Mac Hall appointed Bruno as Dauber's replacement. The phone lines between Boston and Barranquilla went crazy. Everyone predicted that I, too, would soon be promoted; after all, I was one of Bruno's most trusted protégés.

These changes and rumors were an added incentive for me to review my own position. While still in Colombia, I followed Paula's advice and read the Spanish version of my résumé. It shocked me. Back in Boston, I pulled out both the English original and a November 1978 copy of *MAINLINES*, the corporate magazine; that edition featured me in an article titled, "Specialists Offer MAIN's Clients New Services." (See pages 157 and 158.)

I once had taken great pride in that résumé and that article, and yet now, seeing them as Paula did, I felt a growing sense of anger and depression. The material in these documents represented intentional deceptions, if not lies. And these documents carried a deeper significance, a reality that reflected our times and reached to the core of our current march to global empire:

they epitomized a strategy calculated to convey appearances, to shield an underlying reality. In a strange way, they symbolized the story of my life, a glossy veneer covering synthetic surfaces.

Of course, it did not give me any great comfort to know that I had to take much of the responsibility for what was included in my résumé. According to standard operating procedures, I was required to constantly update both a basic résumé and a file with pertinent backup information about clients served and the type of work done. If a marketing person or project manager wanted to include me in a proposal or to use my credentials in some other way, he could massage this basic data in a manner that emphasized his particular needs.

For instance, he might choose to highlight my experience in the Middle East, or in making presentations before the World Bank and other multinational forums. Whenever this was done, that person was supposed to get my approval before actually publishing the revised résumé. However, since like many other MAIN employees I traveled a great deal, exceptions were frequently made. Thus, the résumé Paula suggested I look at, and its English counterpart, were completely new to me, although the information certainly was included in my file.

At first glance, my résumé seemed innocent enough. Under *Experience*, it stated that I had been in charge of major projects in the United States, Asia, Latin America, and the Middle East, and it provided a laundry list of the types of projects: development planning, economic forecasting, energy demand forecasting, and so on. This section ended by describing my Peace Corps work in Ecuador; however, it omitted any reference to the Peace Corps itself, leaving the impression that I had been the professional manager of a construction materials company, instead of a volunteer assisting a small cooperative composed of illiterate Andean peasant brick makers.

Following that was a long list of clients. This list included the International Bank for Reconstruction and Development (the official name of the World Bank); the Asian Development Bank; the government of Kuwait; the Iranian Ministry of Energy; the

Arabian-American Oil Company of Saudi Arabia; Instituto de Recursos Hidraulicos y Electrificación; Perusahaan Umum Listrik Negara; and many others. But the one that caught my attention was the final entry: U.S. Treasury Department, Kingdom of Saudi Arabia. I was amazed that such a listing had ever made it to print, even though it was obviously part of my file.

Setting aside the résumé for a moment, I turned to the *MAINLINES* article. I clearly recalled my interview with its author, a very talented and well-intentioned young woman. She had given it to me for my approval before publishing it. I remembered feeling gratified that she had painted such a flattering portrait of me, and I immediately approved it. Once again, the responsibility fell on my shoulders. The article began:

> Looking over the faces behind the desks, it's easy to tell that Economics and Regional Planning is one of the most recently formed and rapidly growing disciplines at MAIN...
>
> While several people were influential in getting the economics group started, it basically came about through the efforts of one man, John Perkins, who is now head of the group.
>
> Hired as an assistant to the head load forecaster in January, 1971, John was one of the few economists working for MAIN at the time. For his first assignment, he was sent as part of an 11-man team to do an electricity demand study in Indonesia.

The article briefly summarized my previous work history, described how I had "spent three years in Ecuador," and then continued with the following:

> It was during this time that John Perkins met Einar Greve (a former employee) [he had since left MAIN to

EXPERIENCE

John M. Perkins is Manager of the Economics Department of the Power and Environmental Systems Division.

Since joining MAIN, Mr. Perkins has been in charge of major projects in the United States, Asia, Latin America and the Middle East. This work has included development planning, economic forecasting, energy demand forecasting, marketing studies, plant siting, fuel allocation analysis, economic feasibility studies, environmental and economic impact studies, investment planning and management consulting. In addition, many projects have involved training clients in the use of techniques developed by Mr. Perkins and his staff.

Recently Mr. Perkins has been in charge of a project to design computer program packages for 1) projecting energy demand and quantifying the relationships between economic development and energy production, 2) evaluating environmental and socio-economic impacts of projects, and 3) applying Markov and econometric models to national and regional economic planning.

Prior to joining MAIN, Mr. Perkins spent three years in Ecuador conducting marketing studies and organizing and managing a construction materials company. He also conducted studies of the feasibility of organizing credit and savings cooperatives throughout Ecuador.

EDUCATION

Bachelor of Arts in Business Administration
Boston University
Post Graduate Studies:
Model Building, Engineering Economics,
Econometrics, Probability Methods

LANGUAGES

English, Spanish

PROFESSIONAL AFFILIATIONS

American Economic Association
Society for International Development

PUBLICATIONS

"A Markov Process Applied to Forecasting the Demand for Electricity"
"A Macro Approach to Energy Forecasting"
"A Model for Describing the Direct and Indirect Interrelationships between the Economy and the Environment"
"Electric Energy from Interconnected Systems"
"Markov Method Applied to Planning"

JOHN M. PERKINS

CREDENTIALS

Forecasting Studies
Marketing Studies
Feasibility Studies
Site Selection Studies
Economic Impact Studies
Investment Planning
Fuel Supply Studies
Economic Development Planning
Training Programs
Project Management
Allocation Planning
Management Consulting

Clients served:

o Arabian-American Oil Company, Saudi Arabia
o Asian Development Bank
o Boise Cascade Corporation
o City Service Corporation
o Dayton Power & Light Company
o General Electric Company
o Government of Kuwait
o Instituto de Recursos Hidraulicos y Electrificacion, Panama
o Inter-American Development Bank
o International Bank for Reconstruction and Development
o Ministry of Energy, Iran
o New York Times
o Power Authority of the State of New York
o Perusahaan Umum Listrik Negara, Indonesia
o South Carolina Electric and Gas Company
o Technical Association of the Pulp and Paper Industry
o Union Camp Corporation
o U.S. Treasury Dept., Kingdom of Saudi Arabia

The Deceptive Résumé   157

Specialists offer MAIN's clients new services

by Pauline Ouellette

Looking over the faces behind the desks, it's easy to tell that Economics and Regional Planning is one of the most recently formed and rapidly growing disciplines at MAIN. To date, there are about 20 specialists in this group, gathered over a seven-year period. These specialists include not only economists, but city planners, demographers, market specialists and MAIN's first sociologist.

While several people were influential in getting the economics group started, it basically came about through the efforts of one man, **John Perkins,** who is now head of the group.

Hired as an assistant to the head load forecaster in January, 1971, John was one of the few economists working for MAIN at the time. For his first assignment, he was sent as part of an 11-man team to do an electricity demand study in Indonesia.

"They wanted to see if I could survive there for three months," he said laughing reminiscently. But with his background, John had no trouble "surviving." He had just spent three years in Ecuador with a Construction Materials Co-op helping the Quechua Indians, direct descendants of the Incas. The

Indians, John said, were being exploited in their work as brick makers so he was asked by an Ecuadorian agency to form a co-op. He then rented a truck to help them sell their bricks directly to the consumers. As a result, profits rapidly increased by 60%. The profits were divided among the members of the co-op which, after 2½ years, included 200 families.

It was during this time that John Perkins met **Einar Greve** (a former employee) who was working in the town of Paute, Ecuador, on a hydroelectric project for MAIN. The two became friendly and, through continual correspondence, John was offered a position with MAIN.

About a year later, John became the head load forecaster and, as the demands from clients and institutions such as the World Bank grew, he realized that more economists were needed at MAIN. "While MAIN is an engineering firm," he said, "the clients were telling us we had to be more than that." He hired more economists in 1973 to meet the clients' needs and, as a result, formed the discipline which brought him the title of Chief Economist.

John's latest project involves

agricultural development in Panama from where he recently returned after a month's stay. It was in Panama that MAIN conducted its first sociological study through **Martha Hayes,** MAIN's first sociologist. Marti spent 1½ months in Panama to determine the impact of the project on people's lives and cultures. Specialists in agriculture and other related fields were also hired in conjunction with this study.

The expansion of Economics and Regional Planning has been fast paced, yet John feels he has been lucky in that each individual hired has been a hard working professional. As he spoke to me from across his desk, the interest and support he holds for his staff was evident and admirable.

MAINLINES   November 1978

become president of the Tucson Gas & Electric Company] who was working in the town of Paute, Ecuador, on a hydroelectric project for MAIN. The two became friendly and, through continual correspondence, John was offered a position with MAIN.

About a year later, John became the head load forecaster and, as the demands from clients and institutions such as the World Bank grew, he realized that more economists were needed at MAIN.

None of the statements in either document were outright lies—the backup for both documents was on the record, in my file; however, they conveyed a perception that I now found to be twisted and sanitized. And in a culture that worships official documents, they perpetrated something that was even more sinister. Outright lies can be refuted. Documents like those two were impossible to refute because they were based on glimmers of truth, not open deceptions, and because they were produced by a corporation that had earned the trust of other corporations, international banks, and governments.

This was especially true of the résumé because it was an official document, as opposed to the article, which was a bylined interview in a magazine. The MAIN logo, appearing on the bottom of the résumé and on the covers of all the proposals and reports that résumé was likely to grace, carried a lot of weight in the world of international business; it was a seal of authenticity that elicited the same level of confidence as those stamped on diplomas and framed certificates hanging in doctors' and lawyers' offices.

These documents portrayed me as a very competent economist, head of a department at a prestigious consulting firm, who was traveling around the globe conducting a broad range of studies that would make the world a more civilized and prosperous place. The deception was not in what was stated, but in what was omitted. If I put on an outsider's hat—took a purely objective look—I had to admit that those omissions raised many questions.

For example, there was no mention of my recruitment by the NSA or of Einar Greve's connection with the Army and his role as an NSA liaison. There obviously was no discussion of the fact that I had been under tremendous pressure to produce highly inflated economic forecasts, or that much of my job revolved around arranging huge loans that countries like Indonesia and Panama could never repay. There was no praise for the integrity of my predecessor, Howard Parker, nor any acknowledgment that I became the head load forecaster because I was willing to provide the biased studies expected of me, rather than—like Howard—saying what I believed was true and getting fired as a result. Most puzzling was that final entry, under the list of my clients: U.S. Treasury Department, Kingdom of Saudi Arabia.

I kept returning to that line, and I wondered how people would interpret it. They might well ask what is the connection between the U.S. Department of the Treasury and Saudi Arabia. Perhaps some would take it as a typo, two separate lines erroneously compressed into one. Most readers, though, would never guess the truth, that it had been included for a specific reason. It was there so that those in the inner circle of the world where I operated would understand that I had been part of the team that crafted the deal of the century, the deal that changed the course of world history but never reached the newspapers. I helped create a covenant that guaranteed continued oil for America, safeguarded the rule of the House of Saud, and assisted in the financing of Osama bin Laden and the protection of international criminals like Uganda's Idi Amin. That single line in my résumé spoke to those in the know. It said that MAIN's chief economist was a man who could deliver.

The final paragraph of the *MAINLINES* article was a personal observation by the author, and it struck a raw nerve:

The expansion of Economics and Regional Planning has been fast paced, yet John feels he has been lucky in that each individual hired has been a hard-working professional. As he spoke to me from across his desk, the interest and support he holds for his staff was evident and admirable.

The fact was that I had never thought of myself as a bona fide economist. I had graduated with a bachelor of science in business administration from Boston University, emphasis on marketing. I had always been lousy in mathematics and statistics. At Middlebury College, I had majored in American literature; writing had come easily to me. My status as chief economist and as manager of Economics and Regional Planning could not be attributed to my capabilities in either economics or planning; rather, it was a function of my willingness to provide the types of studies and conclusions my bosses and clients wanted, combined with a natural acumen for persuading others through the written word. In addition, I was clever enough to hire very competent people, many with master's degrees and a couple with PhDs, acquiring a staff who knew a whole lot more about the technicalities of my business than I did. Small wonder that the author of that article concluded that "the interest and support he holds for his staff was evident and admirable."

I kept these two documents and several other similar ones in the top drawer of my desk, and I returned to them frequently. Afterward, I sometimes found myself outside my office, wandering among the desks of my staff, looking at those men and women who worked for me and feeling guilty about what I had done to them, and about the role we all played in widening the gap between rich and poor. I thought about the people who starved each day while my staff and I slept in first-class hotels, ate at the finest restaurants, and built up our financial portfolios.

I thought about the fact that people I trained had now joined the ranks of EHMs. I had brought them in. I had recruited them and trained them. But it had not been the same as when I joined. The world had shifted and the corporatocracy had progressed. We had gotten better or more pernicious. The people who worked for me were a different breed from me. There had been no NSA polygraphs or Claudines in their lives. No one had spelled it out for them, what they were expected to do to carry on the mission of global empire. They had never heard the term economic hit man or even EHM, nor had they been told they were in for life. They simply had learned from my example and from my system of rewards and punishments. They knew that they were expected to produce the types of studies and results I wanted. Their salaries, Christmas bonuses, indeed their very jobs, depended on pleasing me.

I, of course, had done everything I could imagine to lighten their burden. I had written papers, given lectures, and taken every possible opportunity to convince them of the importance of optimistic forecasts, of huge loans, of infusions of capital that would spur GNP growth and make the world a better place. It had required less than a decade to arrive at this point where the seduction, the coercion, had taken a much more subtle form, a sort of gentle style of brainwashing. Now these men and women who sat at desks outside my office overlooking Boston's Back Bay were going out into the world to advance the cause of global empire. In a very real sense, I had created them, even as Claudine had created me. But unlike me, they had been kept in the dark.

Many nights I lay awake, thinking, fretting about these things. Paula's reference to my résumé had opened a Pandora's box, and I often felt jealous of my employees for their naiveté. I had intentionally deceived them, and in so doing, had protected them from their own consciences. They did not have to struggle with the moral issues that haunted me.

I also thought a great deal about the idea of integrity in business, about appearances versus reality. Certainly, I told myself, people have deceived each other since the beginning of history. Legend and folklore are full of tales about distorted truths and fraudulent deals: cheating rug merchants, usurious moneylenders, and tailors willing to convince the emperor that his clothes are invisible only to him.

However, much as I wanted to conclude that things were the same as they always had been, that the facade of my MAIN résumé and the reality behind it were merely reflections of human nature, I knew in my heart this was not the case. Things had changed. I now understood that we have reached a new level of deception, one that will lead to our own destruction—not only morally, but also physically, as a culture—unless we make significant changes soon.

The example of organized crime seemed to offer a metaphor. Mafia bosses often start out as street thugs. But over time, the ones who make it to the top transform their appearance. They take to wearing impeccably tailored suits, owning legitimate businesses, and wrapping themselves in the cloak of upstanding society. They support local charities and are respected by their communities. They are quick to lend money to those in desperate straits. Like the John Perkins in the MAIN résumé, these men appear to be model citizens. However, beneath this patina is a trail of blood. When the debtors cannot pay, hit men move in to demand their pound of flesh. If this is not granted, the jackals close in with baseball bats. Finally, as a last resort, out come the guns.

I realized that my gloss as chief economist, head of Economics and Regional Planning, was not the simple deception of a rug dealer, not something of which a buyer can beware. It was part of a sinister system aimed not at outfoxing an unsuspecting customer, but rather at promoting the most subtle and effective form of imperialism the world has ever known. Every one of the people on my staff also held a title—financial analyst, sociologist, economist, lead economist, econometrician, shadow pricing expert, and so forth—and yet none of those titles indicated that every one of them was, in his or her own way, an EHM, that every one of them was serving the interests of global empire.

Nor did the fact of those titles among my staff suggest that we were just the tip of the iceberg. Every major international company—from ones that marketed shoes and sporting goods to those that manufactured heavy equipment—had its own EHM equivalents. The march had begun and it was rapidly encircling the planet. The hoods had discarded their leather jackets, dressed up in business suits, and taken on an air of respectability. Men and women were descending from corporate headquarters in New York, Chicago, San Francisco, London, and Tokyo, streaming across every continent to convince corrupt politicians to allow their countries to be shackled to the corporatocracy, and to induce desperate people to sell their bodies to sweatshops and assembly lines.

It was disturbing to understand that the unspoken details behind the written words of my résumé and of that article defined a world of smoke and mirrors intended to keep us all shackled to a system that is morally repugnant and ultimately self-destructive. By getting me to read between the lines, Paula had nudged me to take one more step along a path that would ultimately transform my life.

⊕ CHAPTER 24

Ecuador's President Battles Big Oil

My work in Colombia and Panama gave me many opportunities to stay in touch with and to visit the first country to be my home away from home. Ecuador had suffered under a long line of dictators and right-wing oligarchies manipulated by U.S. political and commercial interests. In a way, the country was the quintessential banana republic, and the corporatocracy had made major inroads there.

The serious exploitation of oil in the Ecuadorian Amazon basin began in the late 1960s, and it resulted in a buying spree in which the small club of families who ran Ecuador played into the hands of the international banks. They saddled their country with huge amounts of debt, backed by the promise of oil revenues. Roads and industrial parks, hydroelectric dams, transmission and distribution systems, and other power projects sprang up all over the country. International engineering and construction companies struck it rich—once again.

One man whose star was rising over this Andean country was the exception to the rule of political corruption and complicity with the corporatocracy. Jaime Roldós was a university professor and attorney in his late thirties, whom I had met on several occasions. He was charismatic and charming. Once, I impetuously offered to fly to Quito and provide free consulting services any time he asked. I said it partially in jest, but also because I would gladly have done it on my own vacation time—I liked him and, as I was quick to tell him, was always looking for a good excuse to visit his country. He laughed and offered me a similar deal, saying that whenever I needed to negotiate my oil bill, I could call on him.

He had established a reputation as a populist and a nationalist, a person who believed strongly in the rights of the poor and in the responsibility of politicians to use a country's natural resources prudently. When he began campaigning for the presidency in 1978, he captured the attention of his countrymen and of citizens in every nation where foreign interests exploited oil—or where people desired independence from the influences of powerful outside forces. Roldós was the rare modern politician who was not afraid to oppose the status quo. He went after the oil companies and the not-so-subtle system that supported them.

For instance, I heard that he accused the Summer Institute of Linguistics (SIL), an evangelical missionary group from the United States, of sinister collusion with the oil companies. I was familiar with SIL missionaries from my Peace Corps days. The organization had entered Ecuador, as it had so many other countries, with the professed goal of studying, recording, and translating indigenous languages.

SIL had been working extensively with the Huaorani tribe in the Amazon basin area, during the early years of oil exploration, when a disturbing pattern appeared to emerge. While it might have been a coincidence (and no link was ever proved), stories were told in many Amazonian communities that when seismologists reported to corporate headquarters that a certain region had characteristics indicating a high probability of oil beneath the surface, some SIL members went in and encouraged the indigenous people to move from that land, onto missionary reservations; there they would receive free food, shelter, clothes, medical treatment, and missionary-style education. The condition was that, according to these stories, they had to deed their lands to the oil companies.

Rumors abounded that SIL missionaries used an assortment of underhanded techniques to persuade the tribes to abandon their homes and move to the missions. A frequently repeated story was that they had donated food heavily laced with laxatives—then offered medicines to cure the diarrhea epidemic. Throughout Huaorani territory, SIL airdropped false-bottomed food baskets containing tiny radio transmitters; the rumor was that receivers at highly sophisticated communications stations, manned by U.S. military personnel at the army base in Shell, tuned in to these transmitters. Whenever a member of the tribe was bitten by a poisonous snake or became seriously ill, an SIL representative arrived with antivenom or the proper medicines—often in oil company helicopters.

During the early days of oil exploration, five missionaries were found dead with Huaorani spears protruding from their bodies. Later, the Huaoranis claimed they did this to send a message to keep missionaries out. The message went unheeded. In fact, it ultimately had the opposite effect. Rachel Saint, the sister of one of the murdered men, toured the United States, appearing on national television in order to raise money and support for SIL and the oil companies, who she claimed were helping the "savages" become civilized and educated.

According to some sources, SIL received funding from the Rockefeller charities. Family scion John D. Rockefeller had founded Standard Oil—which later divested into the majors, including Chevron, Exxon, and Mobil.[1]

Roldós struck me as a man who walked the path blazed by Torrijos. Both stood up to the world's strongest superpower. Torrijos wanted to take back the Canal, while Roldós's strongly nationalistic position on oil threatened the world's most influential companies. Like Torrijos, Roldós was not a Communist, but rather stood for the right of his country to determine its own destiny. And as they had with Torrijos, pundits predicted that big business and Washington would never tolerate Roldós as president, that if elected he would meet a fate similar to that of Guatemala's Arbenz or Chile's Allende.

It seemed to me that the two men together might spearhead a new movement in Latin American politics and that this movement might form the foundation of changes that could affect every nation on the planet. These men were not Castros or Gadhafis. They were not associated with Russia or China or, as in Allende's case, with the international Socialist movement. They were popular, intelligent, charismatic leaders who were pragmatic instead of dogmatic. They were nationalistic but not anti-American. If corporatocracy was built on three pillars—major corporations, international banks, and colluding governments—Roldós and Torrijos held out the possibility of removing the pillar of government collusion.

A major part of the Roldós platform was what came to be known as the Hydrocarbons Policy. This policy was based on the premise that Ecuador's greatest potential resource was petroleum and that all future exploitation of that resource should be done in a manner that would bring the greatest benefit to the largest percentage of the population. Roldós was a firm believer in the state's obligation to assist the poor and disenfranchised. He expressed hope that the Hydrocarbons Policy could in fact be used as a vehicle for bringing about social reform. He had to walk a fine line, however, because he knew that in Ecuador, as in so many other countries, he could not be elected without the support of at least some of the most influential families, and that even if he should manage to win without them, he would never see his programs implemented without their support.

I was personally relieved that Carter was in the White House during this crucial time. Despite pressures from Texaco and other oil interests, Washington stayed pretty much out of the picture. I knew this would not have been the case under most other administrations—Republican or Democrat.

More than any other issue, I believe it was the Hydrocarbons Policy that convinced Ecuadorians to send Jaime Roldós to the Presidential Palace in Quito—their first democratically elected president after a long line of dictators. He outlined the basis of this policy in his August 10, 1979, inaugural address:

> We must take effective measures to defend the energy resources of the nation. The State (must) maintain the diversification of its exports and not lose its economic independence . . . Our decisions will be inspired solely by national interests and in the unrestricted defense of our sovereign rights.[2]

Once in office, Roldós had to focus on Texaco, since by that time it had become the main player in the oil game. It was an extremely rocky relationship. The oil giant did not trust the new president and did not want to be part of any policy that would set new precedents. It was very aware that such policies might serve as models in other countries.

A speech delivered by a key adviser to Roldós, José Carvajal, summed up the new administration's attitude:

> If a partner [Texaco] does not want to take risks, to make investments for exploration, or to exploit the areas of an oil concession, the other partner has the right to make those investments and then to take over as the owner . . .
>
> We believe our relations with foreign companies have to be just; we have to be tough in the struggle; we have to be prepared for all kinds of pressures, but we should not display fear or an inferiority complex in negotiating with those foreigners.[3]

On New Year's Day, 1980, I made a resolution. It was the beginning of a new decade. In twenty-eight days, I would turn thirty-five. I resolved that during the next year I would make a major change in my life and that in the future I would try to model myself after modern heroes like Jaime Roldós and Omar Torrijos.

In addition, something shocking had happened months earlier. From a profitability standpoint, Bruno had been the most successful president in MAIN's history. Nonetheless, suddenly and without warning, Mac Hall had fired him.

⊕ **CHAPTER 25**

I Quit

Mac Hall's firing of Bruno hit MAIN like an earthquake. It caused turmoil and dissension throughout the company. Bruno had his share of enemies, but even some of them were dismayed. To many employees it was obvious that the motive had been jealousy. During discussions across the lunch table or around the coffee wagon, people often confided that they thought Hall felt threatened by this man who was more than fifteen years his junior and who had taken the firm to new levels of profitability.

"Hall couldn't allow Bruno to go on looking so good," one man said. "Hall had to know that it was just a matter of time before Bruno would take over and the old man would be out to pasture."

As if to prove such theories, Hall appointed Paul Priddy as the new president. Paul had been a vice president at MAIN for years and was an amiable, nuts-and-bolts engineer. In my opinion, he was also lackluster, a yes-man who would bow to the chairman's whims and would never threaten him with stellar profits. My opinion was shared by many others.

For me, Bruno's departure was devastating. He had been a personal mentor and a key factor in our international work. Priddy, on the other hand, had focused on domestic jobs and knew little if anything about the true nature of our overseas roles. I had to question where the company would go from here. I called Bruno at his home and found him philosophical.

"Well, John, he knew he had no cause," he said of Hall, "so I demanded a very good severance package, and I got it. Mac controls a huge block of voting stock, and once he made his move there was nothing I could do." Bruno indicated that he was considering several offers of high-level positions at multinational banks that had been our clients.

I asked him what he thought I should do.

"Keep your eyes open," he advised. "Mac Hall has lost touch with reality, but no one will tell him so—especially not now, after what he did to me."

In late March 1980, still smarting from the firing, I took a sailing vacation in the Virgin Islands. I was joined by "Mary," a young woman who also worked for MAIN. Although I did not think about it when I chose the location, I now know that the region's history was a factor in helping me make a decision that would start to fulfill my New Year's resolution. The first inkling occurred early one afternoon as we rounded St. John Island and tacked into Sir Francis Drake Channel, which separates the American from the British Virgin Islands.

The channel was named, of course, after the English scourge of the Spanish gold fleets. That fact reminded me of the many times during the past decade when I had thought about pirates and other historical figures, men like Drake and Sir Henry Morgan, who robbed and plundered and exploited and yet were lauded—even knighted—for their activities. I had often asked myself why, given that I had been raised to respect such people, I should have qualms about exploiting countries like Indonesia, Panama, Colombia, and Ecuador. So many of my heroes—Ethan Allen, Thomas Jefferson, George Washington, Daniel Boone, Davy Crockett, Lewis and Clark, to name just a few—had exploited Indians, slaves, and lands that did not belong to them, and I had drawn upon their examples to assuage my guilt. Now, tacking up Sir Francis Drake Channel, I saw the folly of my past rationalizations.

I remembered some things I had conveniently ignored over the years. Ethan Allen spent several months in fetid and cramped British prison ships, much of the time locked into thirty pounds of iron shackles, and then more time in an English dungeon. He was a prisoner of war, captured at the 1775 Battle of Montreal while fighting for the same sorts of freedom Jaime Roldós and Omar Torrijos now sought for their people. Thomas Jefferson, George Washington, and all the other Founding Fathers had risked their lives for similar ideals. Winning the revolution was no foregone conclusion; they understood that if they lost, they would be hanged as traitors. Daniel Boone, Davy Crockett, and Lewis and Clark also had endured great hardships and made many sacrifices.

And Drake and Morgan? I was a bit hazy about that period in history, but I remembered that Protestant England had seen itself sorely threatened by Catholic Spain. I had to admit to the possibility that Drake and Morgan had turned to piracy in order to strike at the heart of the Spanish empire, at those gold ships, to defend the sanctity of England, rather than out of a desire for self-aggrandizement.

As we sailed up that channel, tacking back and forth into the wind, inching closer to the mountains rising from the sea—Great Thatch Island to the north and St. John to the south—I could not erase these thoughts from my mind. Mary handed me a beer and turned up the volume on a Jimmy Buffett song. Yet, despite the beauty that surrounded me and the sense of freedom that sailing usually brings, I felt angry. I tried to brush it off. I chugged down the beer.

The emotion would not leave. I was angered by those voices from history and the way I had used them to rationalize my own greed. I was furious at my parents, and at Tilton—that self-righteous prep school on the hill—for imposing all that history on me. I popped open another beer. I could have killed Mac Hall for what he had done to Bruno.

A wooden boat with a rainbow flag sailed past us, its sails billowing out on both sides, downwinding through the channel. A half dozen young men and women shouted and waved at us, hippies in brightly colored sarongs, one couple stark naked on the foredeck. It was obvious from the boat itself and the look about them that they lived aboard, a communal society, modern pirates, free, uninhibited.

I tried to wave back but my hand would not obey. I felt overcome with jealousy.

Mary stood on the deck, watching them as they faded into the distance at our stern. "How would you like that life?" she asked.

And then I understood. It was not about my parents, Tilton, or Mac Hall. It was my *life* I hated. Mine. The person responsible, the one I loathed, was me.

Mary shouted something. She was pointing over the starboard bow. She stepped closer to me. "Leinster Bay," she said. "Tonight's anchorage."

There it was, nestled into St. John Island, a cove where pirate ships had lain in wait for the gold fleet when it passed through this very body of water. I sailed in closer, then handed the tiller over to Mary and headed up to the foredeck. As she navigated the boat around Watermelon Cay and into the beautiful bay, I lowered and bagged the jib and hauled the anchor out of its locker. She deftly dropped the mainsail. I nudged the anchor over the side; the chain rattled down into the crystal clear water and the boat drifted to a stop.

After we settled in, Mary took a swim and a nap. I left her a note and rowed the dinghy ashore, beaching it just below the ruins of an old sugar plantation. I sat there next to the water for a long time, trying not to think, concentrating on emptying myself of all emotion. But it did not work.

Late in the afternoon, I struggled up the steep hill and found myself standing on the crumbling walls of this ancient plantation, looking down at our anchored sloop. I watched the sun sink toward the Caribbean. It all seemed very idyllic, yet I knew that the plantation surrounding me had been the scene of untold misery; hundreds of African slaves had died here—forced at gunpoint to build the stately mansion, to plant and harvest the cane, and to operate the equipment that turned raw sugar into the basic ingredient of rum. The tranquility of the place masked its history of brutality, even as it masked the rage that surged within me.

The sun disappeared behind a mountain-ridged island. A vast magenta arch spread across the sky. The sea began to darken, and I came face-to-face with the shocking fact that I too had been a slaver, that my job at MAIN had not been just about using debt to draw poor countries into the global empire. My inflated forecasts were not merely vehicles for assuring that when my country needed oil we could call in our pound of flesh, and my position as a partner was not simply about enhancing the firm's profitability. My job was also about people and their families, people akin to the ones who had died to construct the wall I sat on, people I had exploited.

For ten years, I had been the heir of those slavers who had marched into African jungles and hauled men and women off to waiting ships. Mine had been a more modern approach, subtler— I never had to see the dying bodies, smell the rotting flesh, or hear the screams of agony. But what I had done was every bit as sinister, and because I could remove myself from it, because I could cut myself off from the personal aspects, the bodies, the flesh, and the screams, perhaps in the final analysis I was the greater sinner.

I glanced again at the sloop where it rode at anchor, straining against the outflowing tide. Mary was lounging on the deck, probably drinking a margarita and waiting to hand one to me. In that moment, seeing her there in that last light of the day, so relaxed, so trusting, I was struck by what I was doing to her and to all the others who worked for me, the ways I was turning them into EHMs. I was doing to them what Claudine had done to me, but without Claudine's honesty. I was seducing them through raises and promotions to be slavers, and yet they, like me, were also being shackled to the system. They too were enslaved.

I turned away from the sea and the bay and the magenta sky. I closed my eyes to the walls that had been built by slaves torn from their African homes. I tried to shut it all out. When I opened my eyes, I was staring at a large gnarled stick, as thick as a baseball bat and twice as long. I leaped up, grabbed the stick, and began slamming it against the stone walls. I beat on those walls until I collapsed from exhaustion. I lay in the grass after that, watching the clouds drift over me.

Eventually I made my way back down to the dinghy. I stood there on the beach, looking out at our sailboat anchored in the azure waters, and I knew what I had to do. I knew that if I ever went back to my former life, to MAIN and all it represented, I would be lost forever. The raises, the pensions, the insurance and perks, the equity . . . The longer I stayed, the more difficult it was to get out. I had become a slave. I could continue to beat myself up as I had beat on those stone walls, or I could escape.

Two days later I returned to Boston. On April 1, 1980, I walked into Paul Priddy's office and resigned.

PART IV:
1981–PRESENT

CHAPTER 26

Ecuador's Presidential Death

Leaving MAIN was no easy matter; Paul Priddy refused to believe me. "April Fool's," he winked.

I assured him that I was serious. Recalling Paula's advice that I should do nothing to antagonize anyone or to give cause for suspicion that I might expose my EHM work, I emphasized that I appreciated everything MAIN had done for me but that I needed to move on. I had always wanted to write about the people that MAIN had introduced me to around the world, but nothing political. I said I wanted to freelance for *National Geographic* and other magazines, and to continue to travel. I declared my loyalty to MAIN and swore that I would sing its praises at every opportunity. Finally, Paul gave in.

After that, everyone else tried to talk me out of resigning. I was reminded frequently about how good I had it, and I was even accused of insanity. I came to understand that no one wanted to accept the fact that I was leaving voluntarily, at least in part, because it forced them to look at themselves. If I were not crazy for leaving, then they might have to consider their own sanity in staying. It was easier to see me as a person who had departed from his senses.

Particularly disturbing were the reactions of my staff. In their eyes, I was deserting them, and there was no strong heir apparent. However, I had made up my mind. After all those years of vacillation, I now was determined to make a clean sweep.

Unfortunately, it did not quite work out that way. True, I no longer had a job, but since I had been far from a fully vested partner, the cash-out of my stock was not sufficient for retirement. Had I stayed at MAIN another few years, I might have become the forty-year-old millionaire I had once envisioned; however, at thirty-five I had a long way to go to accomplish that objective. It was a cold and dreary April in Boston.

Then one day Paul Priddy called and pleaded with me to come to his office. "One of our clients is threatening to drop us," he said. "They hired us because they wanted you to represent them on the expert witness stand."

I thought a lot about it. By the time I sat across the desk from Paul, I had made my decision. I named my price—a retainer that was more than three times what my MAIN salary had been. To my surprise, he agreed, and that started me on a new career.

For the next several years, I was employed as a highly paid expert witness—primarily for U.S. electric utility companies seeking to have new power plants approved for construction by public utilities commissions. One of my clients was the Public Service Company of New Hampshire. My job was to justify, under oath, the economic feasibility of the highly controversial Seabrook nuclear power plant.

Although I was no longer directly involved with Latin America, I continued to follow events there. As an expert witness, I had lots of time between appearances on the stand. I kept in touch with Paula and renewed old friendships from my Peace Corps days in Ecuador—a country that had suddenly jumped to center stage in the world of international oil politics.

Jaime Roldós was moving forward. He took his campaign promises seriously and he was launching an all-out attack on the oil companies. He seemed to see clearly the things that many others on both sides of the Panama Canal either missed or chose to ignore. He understood the underlying currents that threatened to turn the world into a global empire and to relegate the citizens of his country to a very minor role, bordering on servitude. As I read the newspaper articles about him, I was impressed not only by his commitment, but also by his ability to perceive the deeper issues. And the deeper issues pointed to the fact that we were entering a new epoch of world politics.

In November 1980, Carter lost the U.S. presidential election to Ronald Reagan. The Panama Canal Treaty he had negotiated with Torrijos, and the situation in Iran, especially the hostages held at the U.S. Embassy and the failed rescue attempt, were major factors. However, something subtler was also happening. A president whose greatest goal was world peace and who was dedicated to reducing U.S. dependence on oil was replaced by a man who believed that the United States' rightful place was at the top of a world pyramid held up by military muscle, and that controlling oil fields wherever they existed was part of our Manifest Destiny. A president who installed solar panels on White House roofs was replaced by one who, immediately upon occupying the Oval Office, had them removed.

Carter may have been an ineffective politician, but he had a vision for America that was consistent with the one defined in our Declaration of Independence. In retrospect, he now seems naively archaic, a throwback to the ideals that molded this nation and drew so many of our grandparents to her shores. When we compare him to his immediate predecessors and successors, he is an anomaly. His worldview was inconsistent with that of the EHMs.

Reagan, on the other hand, was most definitely a global empire builder, a servant of the corporatocracy. At the time of his election, I found it fitting that he was a Hollywood actor, a man who had followed orders passed down from moguls, who knew how to take direction. That would be his signature. He would cater to the men who shuttled back and forth from corporate CEO offices to bank boards and into the halls of government. He would serve the men who appeared to serve him but who in fact ran the government— men like Vice President George H. W. Bush, Secretary of State George Shultz, Secretary of Defense Caspar Weinberger, Richard Cheney, Richard Helms, and Robert McNamara. He would advocate what those men wanted: an America that controlled the world and all its resources, a world that answered to the commands of that America, a U.S. military that would enforce the rules as they were written by America, and an international trade and banking system that supported America as CEO of the global empire.

As I looked into the future, it seemed we were entering a period that would be very good to the EHMs. It was another twist of fate that I had chosen this moment in history to drop out. The more I reflected on it, however, the better I felt about it. I knew that my timing was right.

As for what this meant in the long term, I had no crystal ball; however, I knew from history that empires do not endure and that the pendulum always swings in both directions. From my perspective, men like Roldós offered hope. I was certain that Ecuador's new president understood many of the subtleties of the current situation. I knew that he had been a Torrijos admirer and had applauded Carter for his courageous stand on the Panama Canal issue. I felt certain that Roldós would not falter. I could only hope that his fortitude would light a candle for the leaders of other countries, who needed the type of inspiration he and Torrijos could provide.

Early in 1981, the Roldós administration formally presented his new hydrocarbons law to the Ecuadorian Congress. If implemented, it would reform the country's relationship to oil companies. By many standards, it was considered revolutionary and even radical. It certainly aimed to change the way business was conducted. Its influence would stretch far beyond Ecuador, into much of Latin America and throughout the world.[1]

The oil companies reacted predictably—they pulled out all the stops. Their public relations people went to work to vilify Jaime Roldós, and their lobbyists swept into Quito and Washington, briefcases full of threats and payoffs. They tried to paint the first democratically elected president of Ecuador in modern times as another Castro. But Roldós would not cave in to intimidation. He responded by denouncing the conspiracy between politics and oil—and religion. Although he offered no tangible proof, he openly accused the Summer Institute of Linguistics of colluding with the oil companies and then, in an extremely bold move, he ordered SIL out of the country.[2]

Only weeks after sending his legislative package to Congress and a couple of days after expelling the SIL missionaries, Roldós warned all foreign interests, including but not limited to oil companies, that unless they implemented plans that would help Ecuador's people, they would be forced to leave his country. He delivered a major speech at the Atahualpa Olympic Stadium in Quito and then headed off to a small community in southern Ecuador.

He died there in a fiery airplane crash, on May 24, 1981.[3]

The world was shocked. Latin Americans were outraged. Newspapers throughout the hemisphere blazed, "CIA Assassination!" In addition to the fact that Washington and the oil companies hated him, many circumstances appeared to support these allegations, and such suspicions were heightened as more facts became known. Nothing was ever proven, but eyewitnesses claimed that Roldós, forewarned about an attempt on his life, had taken precautions, including traveling in two airplanes. At the last moment, it was said, one of his security officers had convinced him to board the decoy airplane. It had blown up.

Despite world reaction, the news hardly made the U.S. press.

Osvaldo Hurtado took over as Ecuador's president. Under his administration, the Summer Institute of Linguistics continued working in Ecuador, and SIL members were granted special visas. By the end of the year, he had launched an ambitious program to increase oil drilling by Texaco and other foreign companies in the Gulf of Guayaquil and the Amazon basin.[4]

Omar Torrijos, in eulogizing Roldós, referred to him as "brother." He also confessed to having nightmares about his own assassination; he saw himself dropping from the sky in a gigantic fireball. It was prophetic.

CHAPTER 27

Panama: Another Presidential Death

I was stunned by Roldós's death, but perhaps I should not have been. I was anything but naive. I knew about Arbenz, Mossadegh, Allende—and about many other people whose names never made the newspapers or history books but whose lives were destroyed and sometimes cut short because they stood up to the corporatocracy. Nevertheless, I was shocked. It was just so very blatant.

I had concluded, after our phenomenal success in Saudi Arabia, that such wantonly overt actions were things of the past. I thought the jackals had been relegated to zoos. Now I saw that I was wrong. I had no doubt that Roldós's death had not been an accident. It had all the markings of a CIA-orchestrated assassination. I understood that it had been executed so blatantly in order to send a message. The new Reagan administration, complete with its fast-draw Hollywood cowboy image, was the ideal vehicle for delivering such a message. The jackals were back, and they wanted Omar Torrijos and everyone else who might consider joining an anti-corporatocracy crusade to know it.

But Torrijos was not buckling. Like Roldós, he refused to be intimidated. He, too, expelled the Summer Institute of Linguistics, and he adamantly refused to give in to the Reagan administration's demands to renegotiate the Canal Treaty.

Two months after Roldós's death, Omar Torrijos's nightmare came true; he died in a plane crash. It was July 31, 1981.

Latin America and the world reeled. Torrijos was known across the globe; he was respected as the man who had forced the United States to relinquish the Panama Canal to its rightful owners, and who continued to stand up to Ronald Reagan. He was a champion of human rights, the head of state who had opened his arms to refugees across the political spectrum, including the shah of Iran, a charismatic voice for social justice who, many believed, would be nominated for the Nobel Peace Prize. Now he was dead. "CIA Assassination!" once again headlined articles and editorials.

Graham Greene began his book *Getting to Know the General*, the one that grew out of the trip when I met him at the Hotel Panama, with the following paragraph:

> In August 1981, my bag was packed for my fifth visit to Panama when the news came to me over the telephone of the death of General Omar Torrijos Herrera, my friend and host. The small plane in which he was flying to a house which he owned at Coclesito in the mountains of Panama had crashed, and there were no survivors. A few days later the voice of his security guard, Sergeant Chuchu, alias José de Jesús Martínez, ex-professor of Marxist philosophy at Panama University, professor of mathematics and a poet, told me, "There was a bomb in that plane. I *know* there was a bomb in the plane, but I can't tell you why over the telephone."[1]

People everywhere mourned the death of this man who had earned a reputation as defender of the poor and defenseless, and they clamored for Washington to open investigations into CIA activities. However, this was not about to happen. There were men who hated Torrijos, and the list included people with immense power. From what I heard, he was considered a liability by President Reagan, Vice President Bush, Secretary of Defense Weinberger, and the Joint Chiefs of Staff, as well as by the CEOs of many powerful corporations.

The military chiefs were especially incensed by provisions in the Torrijos-Carter Treaty that forced them to close the School of the Americas and the U.S. Southern Command's tropical warfare center. The chiefs thus had a serious problem. Either they had to figure out some way to get around the new treaty, or they needed to find another country that would be willing to harbor these facilities—an unlikely prospect in the closing decades of the twentieth century. Of course, there was also another option: dispose of Torrijos and renegotiate the treaty with his successor.

Among Torrijos's corporate enemies were the huge multinationals. Most had close ties to U.S. politicians and were involved in exploiting Latin American labor forces and natural resources—oil, lumber, tin, copper, bauxite, and agricultural lands. They included manufacturing firms, communications companies, shipping and transportation conglomerates, and engineering and other technologically oriented corporations.

The Bechtel Group, Inc., whose senior officers included George Shultz and Caspar Weinberger, was a prime example of the cozy relationship between private companies and the U.S. government. I knew Bechtel well; we at MAIN often worked closely with the company, and its chief architect became a close personal friend. Bechtel was the United States' most influential engineering and construction company. Many people in high positions at Bechtel despised Torrijos because he brazenly courted a Japanese plan to replace Panama's existing canal with a new, more efficient one.[2] Such a move not only would transfer ownership from the United States to Panama but also would exclude Bechtel from participating in the most exciting and potentially lucrative engineering project of the century.

Torrijos stood up to these men, and he did so with grace, charm, and a wonderful sense of humor. Now he was dead, and he had been replaced by a protégé, Manuel Noriega, a man who lacked Torrijos's wit, charisma, and intelligence, and a man who many suspected had no chance against the Reagans, Bushes, and Bechtels of the world.

I was personally devastated by the tragedy. I spent many hours reflecting on my conversations with Torrijos. Late one night, I sat for a long time staring at his photo in a magazine and recalling my first night in Panama, riding in a cab through the rain, stopping before his gigantic billboard picture. "Omar's ideal is freedom; the missile is not invented that can kill an ideal!" The memory of that inscription sent a shudder through me, even as it had on that stormy night.

I could not have known back then that Torrijos would collaborate with Carter to return the Panama Canal to the people who rightfully deserved to own it, or that this victory, along with his attempts to reconcile differences between Latin American Socialists and the dictators, would so infuriate the Reagan-Bush administration that it would seek to assassinate him, as testimony to Senate inquiries would later reveal.[3] I could not have known that on another dark night he would be killed during a routine flight in his Twin Otter, or that most of the world outside the United States would have no doubt that Torrijos's death at the age of fifty-two was just one more in a series of CIA assassinations.

Had Torrijos lived, he undoubtedly would have sought to quell the growing violence that has plagued so many Central and South American nations. Based on his record, we can assume that he would have tried to work out an arrangement to mitigate international oil company destruction of the Amazon regions of Ecuador, Colombia, and Peru. One result of such action would be the alleviation of the terrible conflicts that Washington refers to as terrorist and drug wars, but which Torrijos would have seen as actions taken by desperate people to protect their families and homes. Most important, I feel certain that he would have served as a role model for a new generation of leaders in the Americas, Africa, and Asia—something the CIA, the NSA, and the EHMs could not allow.

CHAPTER 28

My Energy Company, Enron,
and George W. Bush

At the time of Torrijos's death, I had not seen Paula for several months. I was dating other women, including Winifred Grant, a young environmental planner I had met at MAIN, and whose father happened to be chief architect at Bechtel. Paula was dating a Colombian journalist. We remained friends but agreed to sever our romantic ties.

I struggled with my job as an expert witness, particularly in justifying the Seabrook nuclear power plant. It often seemed as though I had sold out again, slipping back into an old role simply for the sake of money. Winifred was an immense help to me during this period. She was an avowed environmentalist, yet she understood the practical necessities of providing ever-increasing amounts of electricity. She had grown up in the Berkeley area of San Francisco's East Bay and had graduated from UC Berkeley. She was a freethinker whose views on life contrasted with those of my puritanical parents and of Ann.

Our relationship developed. Winifred took a leave of absence from MAIN, and together we sailed my boat down the Atlantic coast toward Florida. We took our time, frequently leaving the boat in different ports so I could fly off to provide expert witness testimony. Eventually, we sailed into West Palm Beach, Florida, and rented an apartment. We married, and our daughter, Jessica, was born on May 17, 1982. I was thirty-six, considerably older than all the other men who hung out in Lamaze class.

Part of my job on the Seabrook case was to convince the New Hampshire Public Service Commission that nuclear power was the best and most economical choice for generating electricity in the state. Unfortunately, the longer I studied the issue, the more I began to doubt the validity of my own arguments. The literature was constantly changing at that time, reflecting a growth in research, and the evidence increasingly indicated that many alternative forms of energy were technically superior and more economical than nuclear power.

The balance also was beginning to shift away from the old theory that nuclear power was safe. Serious questions were being raised about the integrity of backup systems, the training of operators, the human tendency to make mistakes, equipment fatigue, and the inadequacy of nuclear waste disposal. I personally became uncomfortable with the position I was expected to take—was paid to take—under oath in what amounted to a court of law. At the same time, I was becoming convinced that some of the emerging technologies offered electricity-generating methods that could actually help the environment. This was particularly true in the area of generating electricity from substances previously considered waste products.

One day I informed my bosses at the New Hampshire utility company that I could no longer testify on their behalf. I gave up this very lucrative career and decided to create a company that would move some of the new technologies off the drawing boards and put the theories into practice. Winifred supported me one hundred percent, despite the uncertainties of the venture and the fact that, for the first time in her life, she was now starting a family.

Several months after Jessica's birth in 1982, I founded Independent Power Systems (IPS), a company whose mission included developing environmentally beneficial power plants and establishing models to inspire others to do likewise. It was a high-risk business, and most of our competitors eventually failed. However, "coincidences" came to our rescue. In fact, I was certain that many times someone stepped in to help, that I was being rewarded for my past service and for my commitment to silence.

Bruno Zambotti had accepted a high-level position at the Inter-American Development Bank. He agreed to serve on the IPS board and to help finance the fledgling company. We received backing from Bankers Trust; ESI Energy; Prudential Insurance Company; Chadbourne and Parke (a major Wall Street law firm, in which former U.S. senator, presidential candidate, and secretary of state Ed Muskie, was a partner); and Riley Stoker Corporation (an engineering firm, owned by Ashland Oil Company, which designed and built highly sophisticated and innovative power plant boilers). We even had backing from the U.S. Congress, which singled out IPS for exemption from a specific tax, and in the process gave us a distinct advantage over our competitors.

In 1986, IPS and Bechtel simultaneously—but independently of each other—began construction of power plants that used highly innovative, state-of-the-art technologies for burning waste coal without producing acid rain. By the end of the decade these two plants had revolutionized the utility industry, directly contributing to new national antipollution laws by proving once and for all that many so-called waste products actually can be converted into electricity, and that coal can be burned without creating acid rain, thereby dispelling long-standing utility company claims to the contrary. Our plant also established that such unproven, state-of-the-art technologies could be financed by a small independent company, through Wall Street and other conventional means.[1] As an added benefit, the IPS power plant sent vented heat to a three and one-half–acre hydroponic green-house, rather than into cooling ponds or cooling towers.

My role as IPS president gave me an inside track on the energy industry. I dealt with some of the most influential people in the business: lawyers, lobbyists, investment bankers, and high-level executives at the major firms. I also had the advantage of a father-in-law who had spent over thirty years at Bechtel, had risen to the position of chief architect, and now was in charge of building a city in Saudi Arabia—a direct result of the work I had done in the early 1970s, during the Saudi Arabian Money-laundering Affair. Winifred grew up near Bechtel's San Francisco world headquarters and was also a member of the corporate family; her first job after graduating from UC Berkeley was at Bechtel.

The energy industry was undergoing major restructuring. The big engineering firms were jockeying to take over—or at least to compete with—the utility companies that previously had enjoyed the privileges of local monopolies. Deregulation was the watchword of the day, and rules changed overnight. Opportunities abounded for ambitious people to take advantage of a situation that baffled the courts and Congress. Industry pundits dubbed it the "Wild West of Energy" era.

One casualty of this process was MAIN. As Bruno predicted, Mac Hall had lost touch with reality and no one dared tell him so. Paul Priddy never asserted control, and MAIN's management not only failed to take advantage of the changes sweeping the industry but also made a series of fatal mistakes. Only a few years after Bruno delivered record profits, MAIN dropped its EHM role and was in dire financial straits. The partners sold MAIN to one of the large engineering and construction firms that had played its cards right.

While I had received almost thirty dollars a share for my stock in 1980, the remaining partners settled for less than half that amount, approximately four years later. Thus did one hundred years of proud service end in humiliation. I was sad to see the company fold, but I felt vindicated that I had gotten out when I did. The MAIN name continued under the new ownership for a while, but then it was dropped. The logo that had once carried such weight in countries around the globe fell into oblivion.

MAIN was one example of a company that did not cope well in the changing atmosphere of the energy industry. At the opposite end of the spectrum was a company we insiders found fascinating: Enron. One of the fastest-growing organizations in the business, it seemed to come out of nowhere and immediately began putting together mammoth deals. Most business meetings open with a few moments of idle chatter while the participants settle into their seats, pour themselves cups of coffee, and arrange their papers; in those days the idle chatter often centered on Enron. No one outside the company could fathom how Enron was able to accomplish such miracles. Those on the inside simply smiled at the rest of us, and kept quiet. Occasionally, when pressed, they talked about new approaches to management, about "creative financing," and about their commitment to hiring executives who knew their way through the corridors of power in capitals across the globe.

To me, this all sounded like a new version of old EHM techniques. The global empire was marching forward at a rapid pace.

For those of us interested in oil and the international scene, there was another frequently discussed topic: the vice president's son, George W. Bush. His first energy company, Arbusto (Spanish for *bush*), was a failure that ultimately was rescued through a 1984 merger with Spectrum 7. Then Spectrum 7 found itself poised at the brink of bankruptcy, and was purchased, in 1986, by Harken Energy Corporation; G. W. Bush was retained as a board member and consultant with an annual salary of $120,000.[2]

We all assumed that having a father who was the U.S. vice president factored into this hiring decision, since the younger Bush's record of accomplishment as an oil executive certainly did not warrant it. It also seemed no coincidence that Harken took this opportunity to branch out into the international field for the first time in its corporate history, and to begin actively searching for oil investments in the Middle East. *Vanity Fair* magazine reported, "Once Bush took his seat on the board, wonderful things started to happen to Harken—new investments, unexpected sources of financing, serendipitous drilling rights."[3]

In 1989, Amoco was negotiating with the government of Bahrain for offshore drilling rights. Then Vice President Bush was elected president. Shortly thereafter, Michael Ameen—a State Department consultant assigned to brief the newly confirmed U.S. ambassador to Bahrain, Charles Hostler—arranged for meetings between the Bahraini government and Harken Energy. Suddenly, Amoco was replaced by Harken. Within a few weeks, the price of Harken Energy stock increased by over twenty percent, from $4.50 to $5.50 per share.[4]

Even seasoned energy people were shocked by what had happened in Bahrain. "I hope G. W. isn't up to something his father will pay for," said a lawyer friend of mine who specialized in the energy industry and also was a major supporter of the Republican Party. We were enjoying cocktails at a bar around the corner from Wall Street, high atop the World Trade Center. He expressed dismay. "I wonder if it's really worth it," he continued, shaking his head sadly. "Is the son's career worth risking the presidency?"

I was less surprised than my peers, but I suppose I had a unique perspective. I had worked for the governments of Kuwait, Saudi Arabia, Egypt, and Iran, I was familiar with Middle Eastern politics, and I knew that Bush, just like the Enron executives, was part of the network I and my EHM colleagues had created; they were the feudal lords and plantation masters.[5]

CHAPTER 29

I Take a Bribe

During this time in my life, I came to realize that we truly had entered a new era in world economics. Events set in motion while Robert McNamara—the man who had served as one of my models—reigned as secretary of defense and president of the World Bank had escalated beyond my gravest fears. McNamara's Keynesian-inspired approach to economics, and his advocacy of aggressive leadership, had become pervasive. The EHM concept had expanded to include all manner of executives in a wide variety of businesses. They may not have been recruited or profiled by the NSA, but they were performing similar functions.

The only difference now was that the corporate executive EHMs did not necessarily involve themselves with the use of funds from the international banking community. While the old branch, my branch, continued to thrive, the new version took on aspects that were even more sinister. During the 1980s, young men and women rose up through the ranks of middle management believing that any means justified the end: an enhanced bottom line. Global empire was simply a pathway to increased profits.

The new trends were typified by the energy industry, where I worked. The Public Utility Regulatory Policy Act (PURPA) was passed by Congress in 1978, went through a series of legal challenges, and finally became law in 1982. Congress originally envisioned the law as a way to encourage small, independent companies like mine to develop alternative fuels and other innovative approaches to producing electricity. Under this law, the major utility companies were required to purchase energy generated by the smaller companies, at fair and reasonable prices. This policy was a result of Carter's desire to reduce U.S. dependence on oil—all oil, not just imported oil. The intent of the law was clearly to encourage both alternative energy sources and the development of independent companies that reflected America's entrepreneurial spirit. However, the reality turned out to be something very different.

During the 1980s and into the 1990s, the emphasis switched from entrepreneurship to deregulation. I watched as most of the other small independents were swallowed up by the large engineering and construction firms, and by the public utility companies themselves. The latter found legal loopholes that allowed them to create holding companies, which could own both the regulated utility companies and the unregulated independent energy-producing corporations. Many of them launched aggressive programs to drive the independents into bankruptcy and then purchase them. Others simply started from scratch and developed their own equivalent of the independents.

The idea of reducing our oil dependence fell by the wayside. Reagan was deeply indebted to the oil companies; Bush had made his own fortune as an oilman. And most of the key players and cabinet members in these two administrations were either part of the oil industry or were part of the engineering and construction companies so closely tied to it. Moreover, in the final analysis, oil and construction were not partisan; many Democrats had profited from and were beholden to them also.

IPS continued to maintain a vision of environmentally beneficial energy. We were committed to the original PURPA goals, and we seemed to lead a charmed life. We were one of the few independents that not only survived but also thrived. I have no doubt that the reason for this was because of my past services to the corporatocracy.

What was going on in the energy field was symbolic of a trend that was affecting the whole world. Concerns about social welfare, the environment, and other quality-of-life issues took a backseat to greed. In the process, an overwhelming emphasis was placed on promoting private businesses. At first, this was justified on theoretical bases, including the idea that capitalism was superior to and would deter communism. Eventually, however, such justification was unneeded. It was simply accepted a priori that there was something inherently better about projects owned by wealthy investors rather than by governments. International organizations such as the World Bank bought into this notion, advocating deregulation and privatization of water and sewer systems, communications networks, utility grids, and other facilities that up until then had been managed by governments.

As a result, it was easy to expand the EHM concept into the larger community, to send executives from a broad spectrum of businesses on missions previously reserved for the few of us recruited into an exclusive club. These executives fanned out across the planet. They sought the cheapest labor pools, the most accessible resources, and the largest markets. They were ruthless in their approach. Like the EHMs who had gone before them— like me, in Indonesia, in Panama, and in Colombia—they found ways to rationalize their misdeeds. And like us, they ensnared communities and countries. They promised affluence, a way for countries to use the private sector to dig themselves out of debt. They built schools and highways, donated telephones, televisions, and medical services. In the end, however, if they found cheaper workers or more accessible resources elsewhere, they left. When they abandoned a community whose hopes they had raised, the consequences were often devastating, but they apparently did this without a moment's hesitation or a nod to their own consciences.

I had to wonder, though, what all this was doing to their psyches, whether they had their moments of doubt, as I had had mine. Did they ever stand next to a befouled canal and watch a young woman try to bathe while an old man defecated upriver? Were there no Howard Parkers left to ask the tough questions?

Although I enjoyed my IPS successes and my life as a family man, I could not fight my moments of severe depression. I was now the father of a young girl, and I feared for the future she would inherit. I was weighed down with guilt for the part I had played.

I also could look back and see a very disturbing historical trend. The modern international financial system was created near the end of World War II, at a meeting of leaders from many countries, held in Bretton Woods, New Hampshire—my home state. The World Bank and the International Monetary Fund were formed in order to reconstruct a devastated Europe, and they achieved remarkable success. The system expanded rapidly, and it was soon sanctioned by every major U.S. ally and hailed as a panacea for oppression. It would, we were assured, save us all from the evil clutches of communism.

But I could not help wondering where all this would lead us. By the late 1980s, with the collapse of the Soviet Union and the world Communist movement, it became apparent that deterring communism was not the goal; it was equally obvious that the global empire, which was rooted in capitalism, would have free reign. As Jim Garrison, president of the State of the World forum, observes:

> Taken cumulatively, the integration of the world as a
> whole, particularly in terms of economic globalization
> and the mythic qualities of "free market" capitalism,
> represents a veritable "empire" in its own right . . . No

nation on earth has been able to resist the compelling magnetism of globalization. Few have been able to escape the "structural adjustments" and "conditionalities" of the World Bank, the International Monetary Fund, or the arbitrations of the World Trade Organization, those international financial institutions that, however inadequate, still determine what economic globalization means, what the rules are, and who is rewarded for submission and punished for infractions. Such is the power of globalization that within our lifetime we are likely to see the integration, even if unevenly, of all national economies in the world into a single global, free market system.[1]

As I mulled over these issues, I decided it was time to write a tell-all book, *Conscience of an Economic Hit Man*, but I made no attempt to keep the work quiet. Even today, I am not the sort of writer who writes in isolation. I find it necessary to discuss the work I am doing. I receive inspiration from other people, and I call upon them to help me remember and put into perspective events of the past. I like to read sections of the materials I am working on to friends, so I may hear their reactions. I understand that this may be risky, yet I know no other way for me to write. Thus, it was no secret that I was writing a book about my time with MAIN.

One afternoon in 1987, another former MAIN partner contacted me and offered me an extremely lucrative consulting contract with Stone & Webster Engineering Corporation (SWEC). At that time, SWEC was one of the world's premier engineering and construction companies, and it was trying to forge a place for itself in the changing environment of the energy industry. My contact explained that I would report to their new subsidiary, an independent energy-development branch modeled after companies like my own IPS. I was relieved to learn that I would not be asked to get involved in any international or EHM-type projects.

In fact, he told me, I would not be expected to do very much at all. I was one of the few people who had founded and managed a successful independent energy company, and I had an excellent reputation in the industry. SWEC's primary interest was to use my résumé and to include me on its list of advisers, which was legal and was consistent with standard industry practices. The offer was especially attractive to me because, due to a number of circumstances, I was considering selling IPS. The idea of joining the SWEC stable and receiving a spectacular retainer was welcome.

The day he hired me, the CEO of SWEC took me out to a private lunch. We chatted informally for some time, and as we did so I realized that a side of me was eager to get back into the consulting business, to leave behind the responsibilities of running a complicated energy company, of being responsible for over a hundred people when we were constructing a facility, and of dealing with all the liabilities associated with building and operating power plants. I had already envisioned how I would spend the substantial retainer I knew he was about to offer me. I had decided to use it, among other things, to create a nonprofit organization.

Over dessert, my host brought up the subject of the one book I had already published, *The Stress-Free Habit*. He told me he had heard wonderful things about it. Then he looked me squarely in the eye. "Do you intend to write any more books?" he asked.

My stomach tightened. Suddenly, I understood what this was all about. I did not hesitate. "No," I said. "I don't intend to try to publish any more books at this time."

"I'm glad to hear that," he said. "We value our privacy at this company. Just like at MAIN."

"I understand that."

He sat back and, smiling, seemed to relax. "Of course, books like your last one, about dealing with stress and such things, are perfectly acceptable. Sometimes they can even further a man's career. As a consultant to SWEC, you are perfectly free to publish that sort of thing." He looked at me as though expecting a response.

"That's good to know."

"Yes, perfectly acceptable. However, it goes without saying that you'll never mention the name of this company in your books, and that you will not write about anything that touches on the nature of our business here or the work you did at MAIN. You will not mention political subjects or any dealings with international banks and development projects." He peered at me. "Simply a matter of confidentiality."

"It goes without saying," I assured him. For an instant, my heart seemed to stop beating. An old feeling returned, similar to ones I had experienced around Howard Parker in Indonesia, while driving through Panama City beside Fidel, and while sitting in a Colombian coffee shop with Paula. I was selling out—again. This was not a bribe in the legal sense—it was perfectly aboveboard and legitimate for this company to pay to include my name on their roster, to call upon me for advice or to show up at a meeting from time to time, but I understood the real reason I was being hired.

He offered me an annual retainer that was equivalent to an executive's salary.

Later that afternoon I sat in an airport, stunned, waiting for my flight back to Florida. I felt like a prostitute. Worse than that, I felt I had betrayed my daughter, my family, and my country. And yet, I told myself, I had little choice. I feared that if I had not accepted this offer, unfortunate consequences would have followed.

CHAPTER 30

The United States Invades Panama

Torrijos was dead, but Panama continued to hold a special place in my heart. Living in South Florida, I had access to many sources of information about current events in Central America. Torrijos's legacy lived on, even if it was filtered through people who were not graced with his compassionate personality and strength of character. Attempts to settle differences throughout the hemisphere continued after his death, as did Panama's determination to force the United States to live up to the terms of the Canal Treaty.

Torrijos's successor, Manuel Noriega, at first appeared committed to following in his mentor's footsteps. I never met Noriega personally, but by all accounts, he initially endeavored to further the cause of Latin America's poor and oppressed. One of his most important projects was the continued exploration of prospects for building a new canal, to be financed and constructed by the Japanese. Predictably, he encountered a great deal of resistance from Washington and from private U.S. companies. As Noriega himself writes:

> Secretary of State George Shultz was a former execu-
> tive of the multinational construction company Bech-

tel; Defense Secretary Caspar Weinberger had been a Bechtel vice president. Bechtel would have liked nothing better than to earn the billions of dollars in revenue that canal construction would generate ... The Reagan and Bush administrations feared the possibility that Japan might dominate an eventual canal construction project; not only was there a misplaced concern about security, there was also the question of commercial rivalry. U.S. construction firms stood to lose billions of dollars.[1]

But Noriega was no Torrijos. He did not have his former boss's charisma or integrity. Over time, he developed an unsavory reputation for corruption and drug dealing, and was even suspected of arranging the assassination of a political rival, Hugo Spadafora.

Noriega built his reputation as a colonel heading up the Panamanian Defense Forces' G-2 unit, the military intelligence command that was the national liaison with the CIA. In this capacity, he developed a close relationship with CIA Director William J. Casey. The CIA used this connection to further its agenda throughout the Caribbean and Central and South America. For example, when the Reagan administration wanted to give Castro advance warning of the 1983 U.S. invasion of Grenada, Casey turned to Noriega, asking him to serve as messenger. The colonel also helped the CIA infiltrate Colombian and other drug cartels.

By 1984, Noriega had been promoted to general and commander in chief of the Panamanian Defense Forces. It is reported that when Casey arrived in Panama City that year and was met at the airport by the local CIA chief, he asked, "Where's my boy? Where's Noriega?" When the general visited Washington, the two men met privately at Casey's house. Many years later, Noriega would admit that his close bond with Casey made him feel invincible. He believed that the CIA, like G-2, was the strongest branch of its country's government. He was convinced that Casey would protect him, despite Noriega's stance on the Panama Canal Treaty and U.S. Canal Zone military bases.[2]

Thus, while Torrijos had been an international icon for justice and equality, Noriega became a symbol of corruption and decadence. His notoriety in this regard was assured when, on June 12, 1986, the *New York Times* ran a front-page article with the headline, "Panama Strongman Said to Trade in Drugs and Illicit Money." The exposé, written by a Pulitzer Prize–winning reporter, alleged that the general was a secret and illegal partner in several Latin American businesses; that he had spied on and for both the United States and Cuba, acting as a sort of double agent; that G-2, under his orders, had in fact beheaded Hugo Spadafora; and that Noriega had personally directed "the most significant drug running in Panama." This article was accompanied by an unflattering portrait of the general, and a follow-up the next day included more details.[3]

Compounding his other problems, Noriega was also saddled with a U.S. president who suffered from an image problem, what journalists referred to as George H. W. Bush's "wimp factor."[4] This took on special significance when Noriega adamantly refused to consider a fifteen-year extension for the School of the Americas. The general's memoirs provide an interesting insight:

> As determined and proud as we were to follow
> through with Torrijos's legacy, the United States didn't
> want any of this to happen. They wanted an extension
> or a renegotiation for the installation [School of the
> Americas], saying that with their growing war prepa-
> rations in Central America, they still needed it. But
> that School of the Americas was an embarrassment to
> us. We didn't want a training ground for death squads
> and repressive right-wing militaries on our soil.[5]

Perhaps, therefore, the world should have anticipated it, but in fact the world was stunned when, on December 20, 1989, the

United States attacked Panama with what was reported to be the largest airborne assault on a city since World War II.[6] It was an unprovoked attack on a civilian population. Panama and her people posed absolutely no threat to the United States or to any other country. Politicians, governments, and press around the world denounced the unilateral U.S. action as a clear violation of international law.

Had this military operation been directed against a country that had committed mass murder or other human rights crimes—Pinochet's Chile, Stroessner's Paraguay, Somosa's Nicaragua, D'Aubuisson's El Salvador, or Saddam's Iraq, for example—the world might have understood. But Panama had done nothing of the sort; it had merely dared to defy the wishes of a handful of powerful politicians and corporate executives. It had insisted that the Canal Treaty be honored, it had held discussions with social reformers, and it had explored the possibility of building a new canal with Japanese financing and construction companies. As a result, it suffered devastating consequences. As Noriega puts it:

> I want to make it very clear: the destabilization campaign launched by the United States in 1986, ending with the 1989 Panama invasion, was a result of the U.S. rejection of any scenario in which future control of the Panama Canal might be in the hands of an independent, sovereign Panama—supported by Japan . . . Shultz and Weinberger, meanwhile, masquerading as officials operating in the public interest and basking in popular ignorance about the powerful economic interests they represented, were building a propaganda campaign to shoot me down.[7]

Washington's stated justification for the attack was based on one man. The United States' sole rationale for sending its young men and women to risk their lives and consciences killing innocent people, including untold numbers of children, and setting fire to huge sections of Panama City, was Noriega. He was characterized as evil, as the enemy of the people, as a drug-trafficking monster, and as such he provided the administration with an excuse for the massive invasion of a country with two million inhabitants—which coincidentally happened to sit on one of the most valuable pieces of real estate in the world.

I found the invasion disturbing to the point of driving me into a depression that lasted many days. I knew that Noriega had bodyguards, yet I could not help believing that the jackals could have taken him out, as they had Roldós and Torrijos. Most of his bodyguards, I suspected, had been trained by U.S. military personnel and probably could have been paid either to look the other way or to carry out an assassination themselves.

The more I thought and read about the invasion, therefore, the more convinced I became that it signaled a U.S. policy turn back toward the old methods of empire building, that the Bush administration was determined to go one better than Reagan and to demonstrate to the world that it would not hesitate to use massive force in order to achieve its ends. It also seemed that the goal in Panama, in addition to replacing the Torrijos legacy with a puppet administration favorable to the United States, was to frighten countries like Iraq into submission.

David Harris, a contributing editor at the *New York Times Magazine* and the author of many books, has an interesting observation. In his 2001 book *Shooting the Moon*, he states:

> Of all the thousands of rulers, potentates, strongmen, juntas, and warlords the Americans have dealt with in all corners of the world, General Manuel Antonio Noriega is the only one the Americans came after like this. Just once in its 225 years of formal national existence has the United States ever invaded another country and carried its ruler back to the United States to face

trial and imprisonment for violations of American law committed on that ruler's own native foreign turf.[8]

Following the bombardment, the United States suddenly found itself in a delicate situation. For a while, it seemed as though the whole thing would backfire. The Bush administration might have quashed the wimp rumors, but now it faced the problem of legitimacy, of appearing to be a bully caught in an act of terrorism. It was disclosed that the U.S. Army had prohibited the press, the Red Cross, and other outside observers from entering the heavily bombed areas for three days, while soldiers incinerated and buried the casualties. The press asked questions about how much evidence of criminal and other inappropriate behavior was destroyed, and about how many died because they were denied timely medical attention, but such questions were never answered.

We shall never know many of the facts about the invasion, nor shall we know the true extent of the massacre. Defense Secretary Richard Cheney claimed a death toll between five hundred and six hundred, but independent human rights groups estimated it at three thousand to five thousand, with another twenty-five thousand left homeless.[9] Noriega was arrested, flown to Miami, and sentenced to forty years' imprisonment; at that time, he was the only person in the United States officially classified as a prisoner of war.[10]

The world was outraged by this breach of international law and by the needless destruction of a defenseless people at the hands of the most powerful military force on the planet, but few in the United States were aware of either the outrage or the crimes Washington had committed. Press coverage was very limited. A number of factors contributed to this, including government policy, White House phone calls to publishers and television executives, congresspeople who dared not object, lest the wimp factor become their problem, and journalists who thought the public needed heroes rather than objectivity.

One exception was Peter Eisner, a *Newsday* editor and Associated Press reporter who covered the Panama invasion and continued to analyze it for many years. In *The Memoirs of Manuel Noriega: America's Prisoner*, published in 1997, Eisner writes:

> The death, destruction and injustice wrought in the name of fighting Noriega—and the lies surrounding that event—were threats to the basic American principles of democracy . . . Soldiers were ordered to kill in Panama and they did so after being told they had to rescue a country from the clamp of a cruel, depraved dictator; once they acted, the people of their country (the U.S.) marched lockstep behind them.[11]

After lengthy research, including interviews with Noriega in his Miami prison cell, Eisner states:

> On the key points, I do not think the evidence shows Noriega was guilty of the charges against him. I do not think his actions as a foreign military leader or a sovereign head of state justify the invasion of Panama or that he represented a threat to U.S. national security.[12]

Eisner concludes:

> My analysis of the political situation and my reporting in Panama before, during, and after the invasion brought me to the conclusion that the U.S. invasion of Panama was an abominable abuse of power. The invasion principally served the goals of arrogant American

politicians and their Panamanian allies, at the expense of unconscionable bloodshed.[13]

The Arias family and the pre-Torrijos oligarchy, which had served as U.S. puppets from the time when Panama was torn from Colombia until Torrijos took over, were reinstated. The new Canal Treaty became a moot point. In essence, Washington once again controlled the waterway, despite anything the official documents said.

As I reflected on those incidents and all that I had experienced while working for MAIN, I found myself asking the same questions over and over: How many decisions—including ones of great historical significance that impact millions of people—are made by men and women who are driven by personal motives rather than by a desire to do the right thing? How many of our top government officials are driven by personal greed instead of national loyalty? How many wars are fought because a president does not want his constituents to perceive him as a wimp?

Despite my promises to SWEC's president, my frustration and feelings of impotence about the Panama invasion prodded me into resuming work on my book, except now I decided to focus on Torrijos. I saw his story as a way to expose many of the injustices that infect our world, and as a way to rid myself of my guilt. This time, however, I was determined to keep silent about what I was doing, rather than seeking advice from friends and peers.

As I worked on the book, I was stunned by the magnitude of what we EHMs had accomplished, in so many places. I tried to concentrate on a few countries that stood out, but the list of places where I had worked and which were worse off afterward was astounding. I also was horrified by the extent of my own corruption. I had done a great deal of soul searching, yet I realized that while I was in the midst of it I had been so focused on my daily activities that I had not seen the larger perspective. Thus, when I was in Indonesia I fretted over the things Howard Parker and I discussed, or the issues raised by Rasy's young Indonesian friends. While I was working in Panama, I was deeply affected by the implications of what I had seen during Fidel's introduction of the slums, the Canal Zone, and the discotheque. In Iran, my conversations with Yamin and Doc troubled me immensely. Now, the act of writing this book gave me an overview. I understood how easy it had been not to see the larger picture and therefore to miss the true significance of my actions.

How simple this sounds, and how self-evident; yet, how insidious the nature of these experiences. For me it conjures the image of a soldier. In the beginning, he is naive. He may question the morality of killing other people, but mostly he has to deal with his own fear, has to focus on survival. After he kills his first enemy, he is overwhelmed with emotions. He may wonder about the family of the dead man and feel a sense of remorse. But as time goes on and he participates in more battles, kills more people, he becomes hardened. He is transformed into a professional soldier.

I had become a professional soldier. Admitting that fact opened the door for a better understanding of the process by which crimes are committed and empires are built. I could now comprehend why so many people have committed atrocious acts—how, for example, good, family-loving Iranians could work for the shah's brutal secret police, how good Germans could follow the orders of Hitler, how good American men and women could bomb Panama City.

As an EHM, I never drew a penny directly from the NSA or any other government agency; MAIN paid my salary. I was a private citizen, employed by a private corporation. Understanding this helped me see more clearly the emerging role of the corporate executive-as-EHM. A whole new class of soldier was emerging on the world scene, and these people were becoming desensitized to their own actions. I wrote:

Today, men and women are going into Thailand, the
Philippines, Botswana, Bolivia, and every other coun-

try where they hope to find people desperate for work. They go to these places with the express purpose of exploiting wretched people—people whose children are severely malnourished, even starving, people who live in shantytowns and have lost all hope of a better life, people who have ceased to even dream of another day. These men and women leave their plush offices in Manhattan or San Francisco or Chicago, streak across continents and oceans in luxurious jetliners, check into first-class hotels, and dine at the finest restaurants the country has to offer. Then they go searching for desperate people.

Today, we still have slave traders. They no longer find it necessary to march into the forests of Africa looking for prime specimens who will bring top dollar on the auction blocks in Charleston, Cartagena, and Havana. They simply recruit desperate people and build a factory to produce the jackets, blue jeans, tennis shoes, automobile parts, computer components, and thousands of other items they can sell in the markets of their choosing. Or they may elect not even to own the factory themselves; instead, they hire a local businessman to do all their dirty work for them.

These men and women think of themselves as upright. They return to their homes with photographs of quaint sites and ancient ruins, to show to their children. They attend seminars where they pat each other on the back and exchange tidbits of advice about dealing with the eccentricities of customs in far-off lands. Their bosses hire lawyers who assure them that what they are doing is perfectly legal. They have a cadre of psychotherapists and other human resource experts at their disposal to convince them that they are helping those desperate people.

The old-fashioned slave trader told himself that he was dealing with a species that was not entirely human, and that he was offering them the opportunity to become Christianized. He also understood that slaves were fundamental to the survival of his own society, that they were the foundation of his economy. The modern slave trader assures herself (or himself) that the desperate people are better off earning one dollar a day than no dollars at all, and that they are receiving the opportunity to become integrated into the larger world community. She also understands that these desperate people are fundamental to the survival of her company, that they are the foundation for her own lifestyle. She never stops to think about the larger implications of what she, her lifestyle, and the economic system behind them are doing to the world—or of how they may ultimately impact her children's future.

CHAPTER 31

An EHM Failure in Iraq

My role as president of IPS in the 1980s, and as a consultant to SWEC in the late 1980s and throughout much of the 1990s, gave me access to information about Iraq that was not available to most people. Indeed, during the 1980s the majority of Americans knew little about the country. It simply was not on their radar screen. However, I was fascinated by what was going on there.

I kept in touch with old friends who worked for the World Bank, USAID, the IMF, or one of the other international financial organizations, and with people at Bechtel, Halliburton, and the other major engineering and construction companies, including my own father-in-law. Many of the engineers employed by IPS subcontractors and other independent power companies were also involved in projects in the Middle East. I was very aware that the EHMs were hard at work in Iraq.

The Reagan and Bush administrations were determined to turn Iraq into another Saudi Arabia. There were many compelling reasons for Saddam Hussein to follow the example of the House of Saud. He had only to observe the benefits they had reaped from the Money-laundering Affair. Since that deal was struck, modern cities had risen from the Saudi desert, Riyadh's garbage-collecting goats had been transformed into sleek trucks, and now the Saudis enjoyed the fruits of some of the most advanced technologies in the world: state-of-the-art desalinization plants, sewage treatment systems, communications networks, and electric utility grids.

Saddam Hussein undoubtedly was aware that the Saudis also enjoyed special treatment when it came to matters of international law. Their good friends in Washington turned a blind eye to many Saudi activities, including the financing of fanatical groups—many of which were considered by most of the world to be radicals bordering on terrorism—and the harboring of international fugitives. In fact, the United States actively sought and received Saudi Arabian financial support for Osama bin Laden's Afghan war against the Soviet Union. The Reagan and Bush administrations not only encouraged the Saudis in this regard, but also they pressured many other countries to do the same—or at least to look the other way.

The EHM presence in Baghdad was very strong during the 1980s. They believed that Saddam eventually would see the light, and I had to agree with this assumption. After all, if Iraq reached an accord with Washington similar to that of the Saudis, Saddam could basically write his own ticket in ruling his country, and might even expand his circle of influence throughout that part of the world.

It hardly mattered that he was a pathological tyrant, that he had the blood of mass murders on his hands, or that his mannerisms and brutal actions conjured images of Adolph Hitler. The United States had tolerated and even supported such men many times before. We would be happy to offer him U.S. government securities in exchange for petrodollars, for the promise of continued oil supplies, and for a deal whereby the interest on those securities was used to hire U.S. companies to improve infrastructure systems throughout Iraq, to create new cities, and to turn the deserts into oases. We would be willing to sell him tanks and fighter planes and to build him chemical and nuclear power plants, as we had done in so many other countries, even if these technologies could conceivably be used to produce advanced weaponry.

Iraq was extremely important to us, much more important than was obvious on the surface. Contrary to common public opinion, Iraq is not simply about oil. It is also about water and geopolitics. Both the Tigris and Euphrates rivers flow through Iraq; thus, of all the countries in that part of the world, Iraq controls the most important sources of increasingly critical water resources. During the 1980s, the importance of water—politically as well as economically—was becoming obvious to those of us in the energy and engineering fields. In the rush toward privatization, many of the major companies that had set their sights on taking over the small independent power companies now looked toward privatizing water systems in Africa, Latin America, and the Middle East.

In addition to oil and water, Iraq is situated in a very strategic location. It borders Iran, Kuwait, Saudi Arabia, Jordan, Syria, and Turkey, and it has a coastline on the Persian Gulf. It is within easy missile-striking distance of both Israel and the former Soviet Union. Military strategists equate modern Iraq to the Hudson River valley during the French and Indian War and the American Revolution. In the eighteenth century, the French, British, and Americans knew that whoever controlled the Hudson River valley controlled the continent. Today, it is common knowledge that whoever controls Iraq holds the key to controlling the Middle East.

Above all else, Iraq presented a vast market for American technology and engineering expertise. The fact that it sits atop one of the world's most extensive oil fields (by some estimates, even greater than Saudi Arabia's) assured that it was in a position to finance huge infrastructure and industrialization programs. All the major players—engineering and construction companies; computer systems suppliers; aircraft, missile, and tank manufacturers; and pharmaceutical and chemical companies—were focused on Iraq.

However, by the late 1980s it was apparent that Saddam was not buying into the EHM scenario. This was a major frustration and a great embarrassment to the first Bush administration. Like Panama, Iraq contributed to George H. W. Bush's wimp image. As Bush searched for a way out, Saddam played into his hands. In August 1990, he invaded the oil-rich sheikhdom of Kuwait. Bush responded with a denunciation of Saddam for violating international law, even though it had been less than a year since Bush himself had staged the illegal and unilateral invasion of Panama.

It was no surprise when the president finally ordered an all-out military attack. Five hundred thousand U.S. troops were sent in as part of an international force. During the early months of 1991, an aerial assault was launched against Iraqi military and civilian targets. It was followed by a one hundred–hour land assault that routed the outgunned and desperately inferior Iraqi army. Kuwait was safe. A true despot had been chastised, though not brought to justice. Bush's popularity ratings soared to 90 percent among the American people.

I was in Boston attending meetings at the time of the Iraq invasion—one of the few occasions when I was actually asked to do something for SWEC. I vividly recall the enthusiasm that greeted Bush's decision. Naturally, people throughout the Stone & Webster organization were excited, though not only because we had taken a stand against a murderous dictator. For them, a U.S. victory in Iraq offered possibilities for huge profits, promotions, and raises.

The excitement was not limited to those of us in businesses that would directly benefit from war. People across the nation seemed almost desperate to see our country reassert itself militarily. I believe there were many reasons for this attitude, including the philosophical change that occurred when Reagan defeated

Carter, the Iranian hostages were released, and Reagan announced his intention to renegotiate the Panama Canal Treaty. Bush's invasion of Panama stirred the already smoldering flames.

Beneath the patriotic rhetoric and the calls for action, however, I believe a much more subtle transformation was occurring in the way U.S. commercial interests—and therefore most of the people who worked for American corporations—viewed the world. The march toward global empire had become a reality in which much of the country participated. The dual ideas of globalization and privatization were making significant inroads into our psyches.

In the final analysis, this was not solely about the United States. The global empire had become just that; it reached across all borders. What we had previously considered U.S. corporations were now truly international, even from a legal standpoint. Many of them were incorporated in a multitude of countries; they could pick and choose from an assortment of rules and regulations under which to conduct their activities, and a multitude of globalizing trade agreements and organizations made this even easier. Words like *democracy, socialism,* and *capitalism* were becoming almost obsolete. Corporatocracy had become a fact, and it increasingly exerted itself as the single major influence on world economies and politics.

In a strange turn of events, I succumbed to the corporatocracy when I sold IPS in November 1990. It was a lucrative deal for my partners and me, but we sold out mainly because Ashland Oil Company put tremendous pressure on us. I knew from experience that fighting them would be extremely costly in many ways, while selling would make us wealthy. However, it did strike me as ironic that an oil company would become the new owners of my alternative energy company; part of me felt like a traitor.

SWEC demanded very little of my time. Occasionally, I was asked to fly to Boston for meetings or to help prepare a proposal.

I was sometimes sent to places like Rio de Janeiro, to hobnob with the movers and shakers there. Once, I flew to Guatemala on a private jet. I frequently called project managers to remind them that I was on the payroll and available. Receiving all that money for doing so very little rubbed at my conscience. I knew the business well and wanted to contribute something useful. But it simply was not on the agenda.

The image of being a man in the middle haunted me. I wanted to take some action that would justify my existence and that might turn all the negatives of my past into something positive. I continued to work surreptitiously—and very irregularly—on *Conscience of an Economic Hit Man,* and yet I did not deceive myself into believing that it would ever be published.

In 1991, I began guiding small groups of people into the Amazon to spend time with and learn from the Shuars, who were eager to share their knowledge about environmental stewardship and indigenous healing techniques. During the next few years, the demand for these trips increased rapidly and resulted in the formation of a nonprofit organization, Dream Change Coalition. Dedicated to changing the way people from industrialized countries see the earth and our relationship to it, Dream Change developed a following around the world and empowered people to create organizations with similar missions in many countries. *TIME* magazine selected it as one of thirteen organizations whose Web sites best reflect the ideals and goals of Earth Day.[1]

Throughout the 1990s, I became increasingly involved in the nonprofit world, helping to create several organizations and serving on the board of directors of others. Many of these grew out of the work of highly dedicated people at Dream Change and involved working with indigenous people in Latin America—the Shuars and Achuars of the Amazon, the Quechuas of the Andes, the Mayas in Guatemala—or teaching people in the United States and Europe about these cultures. SWEC approved of this philanthropic work; it was consistent with SWEC's own commitment to the United Way. I also wrote more books, always careful to focus on indigenous teachings and to avoid references to my EHM activities. Besides alleviating my boredom, these measures helped me keep in touch with Latin America and the political issues that were dear to me.

But try as I might to convince myself that my nonprofit and writing activities provided a balance, that I was making amends for my past activities, I found this increasingly difficult. In my heart, I knew I was shirking my responsibilities to my daughter. Jessica was inheriting a world where millions of children are born saddled with debts they will never be able to repay. And I had to accept responsibility for it.

My books grew in popularity, especially one titled, *The World Is As You Dream It*. Its success led to increasing demands for me to give workshops and lectures. Sometimes, standing in front of an audience in Boston or New York or Milan, I was struck by the irony. If the world is as you dream it, why had I dreamed such a world? How had I managed to play such an active role in manifesting such a nightmare?

In 1997, I was commissioned to teach a weeklong Omega Institute workshop in the Caribbean, at a resort on St. John Island. I arrived late at night. When I awoke the next morning, I walked onto a tiny balcony and found myself looking out at the very bay where, seventeen years earlier, I had made the decision to quit MAIN. I collapsed into a chair, overcome with emotion.

Throughout the week, I spent much of my free time on that balcony, looking down at Leinster Bay, trying to understand my feelings. I came to realize that although I had quit, I had not taken the next step, and that my decision to remain in the middle was exacting a devastating toll. By the end of the week, I had concluded that the world around me was not one that I wanted to dream, and that I needed to do exactly what I was instructing my students to do: to change my dreams in ways that reflected what I really wanted in my life.

When I returned home, I gave up my corporate consulting practice. The president of SWEC who had hired me was now retired. A new man had come aboard, one who was younger than me and was apparently unconcerned about me telling my story. He had initiated a cost-cutting program and was happy not to have to pay me that exorbitant retainer any longer.

I decided to complete the book I had been working on for so long, and just making the decision brought a wonderful sense of relief. I shared my ideas about writing with close friends, mostly people in the nonprofit world who were involved with indigenous cultures and rain forest preservation. To my surprise, they were dismayed. They feared that speaking out would undermine my teaching work and jeopardize the nonprofit organizations I supported. Many of us were helping Amazon tribes protect their lands from oil companies; coming clean, I was told, could undermine my credibility, and might set back the whole movement. Some even threatened to withdraw their support.

So, once again, I stopped writing. Instead, I focused on taking people deep into the Amazon, showing them a place and a tribe that are mostly untouched by the modern world. In fact, that is where I was on September 11, 2001.

CHAPTER 32

September 11 and Its Aftermath for Me, Personally

On September 10, 2001, I was traveling down a river in the Ecuadorian Amazon with Shakaim Chumpi, the coauthor of my book *Spirit of the Shuar*. We were leading a group of sixteen North Americans to his community deep in the rain forest. The visitors had come to learn about his people and to help them preserve their precious rain forests.

Shakaim had fought as a soldier in the recent Ecuador-Peru conflict. Most people in the major oil-consuming nations have never heard about this war, yet it was fought primarily to provide them with oil. Although the border between these two countries was disputed for many years, only recently did a resolution become urgent. The reason for the urgency was that the oil companies needed to know with which country to negotiate in order to win concessions for specific tracts of the oil-rich lands. Borders had to be defined.

The Shuars formed Ecuador's first line of defense. They proved themselves to be ferocious fighters, often overcoming superior numbers and better-equipped forces. The Shuars did not know anything about the politics behind the war or that its resolution would open the door to oil companies. They fought because they come from a long tradition of warriors and because they were not about to allow foreign soldiers onto their lands.

As we paddled down the river, watching a flock of chattering parrots fly overhead, I asked Shakaim whether the truce was still holding.

"Yes," he said, "but I'm afraid I must tell you that we are now preparing to go to war with you." He went on to explain that, of course, he did not mean me personally or the people in our group. "You are our friends," he assured me. He was, he said, referring to our oil companies and to the military forces that would come into his jungle to defend them.

"We've seen what they did to the Huaorani tribe. They destroyed their forests, polluted the rivers, and killed many people, including children. Today, the Huaorani hardly exist as a people anymore. We won't let that happen to us. We won't allow oil companies into our territory, any more than we would the Peruvians. We have all sworn to fight to the last man."[1]

That night our group sat around a fire in the center of a beautiful Shuar longhouse built from split bamboo slats placed in the ground and covered with a thatched roof. I told them about my conversation with Shakaim. We all wondered how many other people in the world felt similarly about our oil companies and our country. How many, like the Shuars, were terrified that we would come into their lives and destroy their culture and their lands? How many hated us?

The next morning, I went down to the little office where we kept our two-way radio. I needed to arrange for pilots to fly in and pick us up in a few days. As I was talking with them, I heard a shout.

"My God!" the man on the other end of the radio exclaimed. "New York is under attack." He turned up the commercial radio that had been playing music in the background. During the next half hour, we received a minute-by-minute account of the events unfolding in the United States. Like everyone else, it was a moment I shall never forget.

When I returned to my home in Florida, I knew I had to visit Ground Zero, the former site of the World Trade Center towers, so I arranged to fly to New York. I checked into my uptown hotel in early afternoon. It was a sunny November day, unseasonably balmy. I strolled along Central Park, filled with enthusiasm, then headed for a part of the city where once I had spent a lot of time, the area near Wall Street now known as Ground Zero.

As I approached, my enthusiasm was replaced with a sense of horror. The sights and smells were overwhelming—the incredible destruction; the twisted and melted skeletons of those once-great buildings; the debris; the rancid odor of smoke, charred ruins, and burnt flesh. I had seen it all on TV, but being here was different.

I had not been prepared for this—especially not for the people. Two months had passed and still they stood around, those who lived or worked nearby, those who had survived. An Egyptian man was loitering outside his small shoe repair shop, shaking his head in disbelief.

"Can't get used to it," he muttered. "I lost many customers, many friends. My nephew died up there." He pointed at the blue sky. "I think I saw him jump. I don't know . . . So many were jumping, holding hands and flapping their arms as though they could fly."

It came as a surprise, the way people talked with one another. In New York City. And it went beyond language. Their eyes met. Although somber, they exchanged looks of compassion, half-smiles that spoke more than a million words.

But there was something else, a sense about the place itself. At first, I couldn't figure it out; then it struck me: the light. Lower Manhattan had been a dark canyon, back in the days when I made the pilgrimage to this part of town to raise capital for IPS, when I used to plot strategy with my investment bankers over dinner at

Windows on the World. You had to go that high, to the top of the World Trade Center, if you wanted to see light. Now, here it was at street level. The canyon had been split wide open, and we who stood on the street beside the ruins were warmed by the sunshine. I couldn't help wondering if the view of the sky, of the light, had helped people open their hearts. I felt guilty just thinking such thoughts.

I turned the corner at Trinity Church and headed down Wall Street. Back to the old New York, enveloped in shadow. No sky, no light. People hurried along the sidewalk, ignoring one another. A cop screamed at a stalled car.

I sat down on the first steps I came to, at number fourteen. From somewhere, the sounds of giant fans or an air blower rose above the other noises. It seemed to come from the massive stone wall of the New York Stock Exchange building. I watched the people. They hustled up and down the street, leaving their offices, hurrying home, or heading to a restaurant or bar to discuss business. A few walked in tandem and chatted with each other. Most, though, were alone and silent. I tried to make eye contact; it didn't happen.

The wail of a car alarm drew my attention down the street. A man rushed out of an office and pointed a key at the car; the alarm went silent. I sat there quietly for a few long moments. After a while, I reached into my pocket and pulled out a neatly folded piece of paper covered with statistics.

Then I saw him. He shuffled along the street, staring down at his feet. He had a scrawny gray beard and wore a grimy overcoat that looked especially out of place on this warm afternoon on Wall Street. I knew he was Afghan.

He glanced at me. Then, after only a second of hesitation, he started up the steps. He nodded politely and sat down beside me, leaving a yard or two between us. From the way he looked straight ahead, I realized it would be up to me to begin the conversation.

"Nice afternoon."

"Beautiful." His accent was thick. "Times like these, we want sunshine."

"You mean because of the World Trade Center?"

He nodded.

"You're from Afghanistan?"

He stared at me. "Is it so obvious?"

"I've traveled a lot. Recently, I visited the Himalayas, Kashmir."

"Kashmir." He pulled at his beard. "Fighting."

"Yes, India and Pakistan, Hindus and Muslims. Makes you wonder about religion, doesn't it?"

His eyes met mine. They were deep brown, nearly black. They struck me as wise and sad. He turned back toward the New York Stock Exchange building. With a long gnarled finger, he pointed at the building.

"Or maybe," I agreed, "it's about economics, not religion."

"You were a soldier?"

I couldn't help but chuckle. "No. An economic consultant." I handed him the paper with the statistics. "These were my weapons."

He reached over and took them. "Numbers."

"World statistics."

He studied the list, then gave a little laugh. "I can't read." He handed it back to me.

"The numbers tell us that twenty-four thousand people die every day from hunger."

He whistled softly, then took a moment to think about this, and sighed. "I was almost one of them. I had a little pomegranate farm near Kandahar. Russians arrived and mujahideen hid behind trees and in water ditches." He raised his hands and pointed them like a rifle. "Ambushing." He lowered his hands. "All my trees and ditches were destroyed."

"After that, what did you do?"

He nodded at the list I held. "Does it show beggars?"

It did not, but I thought I remembered. "About eighty million in the world, I believe."

"I was one." He shook his head, seemed lost in thought. We sat in silence for a few minutes before he spoke again. "I do not like beggaring. My child dies. So I raise poppies."

"Opium?"

He shrugged. "No trees, no water. The only way to feed our families."

I felt a lump in my throat, a depressing sense of sadness combined with guilt. "We call raising opium poppies evil, yet many of our wealthiest people owe their fortunes to the drug trade."

His eyes met mine and seemed to penetrate my soul. "You were a soldier," he stated, nodding his head to confirm this simple fact. Then he rose slowly to his feet and hobbled down the steps. I wanted him to stay, but I felt powerless to say anything. I managed to get to my feet and start after him. At the bottom of the steps I was stopped by a sign. It included a picture of the building where I had been seated. At the top, it notified passersby that the sign had been erected by Heritage Trails of New York. It said:

> The Mausoleum of Halicarnassus piled on top of the
> bell tower of St. Mark's in Venice, at the corner of Wall
> and Broad—that's the design concept behind 14 Wall
> Street. In its day the world's tallest bank building, the
> 539-foot-high skyscraper originally housed the head-
> quarters of Bankers Trust, one of the country's wealth-
> iest financial institutions.

I stood there in awe and looked up at this building. Shortly after the turn of the last century, 14 Wall Street had played the role the World Trade Center would later assume; it had been the very symbol of power and economic domination. It had also housed Bankers Trust, one of the firms I had employed to finance my energy company. It was an essential part of my heritage—the heritage, as the old Afghan man so aptly put it, of a soldier.

That I had ended up here this day, talking with him, seemed an odd coincidence. Coincidence. The word stopped me. I thought about how our reactions to coincidences mold our lives. How should I react to this one?

Continuing to walk, I scanned the heads in the crowd, but I could find no sign of him. At the next building, there was an immense statue shrouded in blue plastic. An engraving on the building's stone face revealed that this was Federal Hall, 26 Wall Street, where on April 30, 1789, George Washington had taken the oath of office as first president of the United States. This was the exact spot where the first man given the responsibility to safeguard life, liberty, and the pursuit of happiness for all people was sworn in. So close to Ground Zero; so close to Wall Street.

I went on around the block, to Pine Street. There I came face-to-face with the world headquarters of Chase, the bank David Rockefeller built, a bank seeded with oil money and harvested by men like me. This bank, an institution that served the EHMs and that was a master at promoting global empire, was in many ways the very symbol of the corporatocracy.

I recalled reading that the World Trade Center was a project started by David Rockefeller in 1960, and that in recent years the complex had been considered an albatross. It had the reputation of being a financial misfit, unsuited to modern fiber-optic and Internet technologies, and burdened with an inefficient and costly elevator system. Those two towers once had been nicknamed David and Nelson. Now the albatross was gone.

I kept walking, slowly, almost reluctantly. Despite the warmth of the afternoon, I felt a chill, and I realized that a strange anxiousness, a foreboding, had taken hold of me. I could not identify its source and I tried to brush it off, picking up my pace. I eventually found myself once again looking at that smoldering hole, the twisted metal, that great scar in the earth. I leaned against a building that had escaped the destruction and stared into the pit. I tried to imagine the people rushing out of the collapsing tower and the firefighters dashing in to help them. I tried to think about the people who had jumped, the desperation they felt. But none of these things came to me.

Instead, I saw Osama bin Laden accepting money, and weapons worth millions of dollars, from a man employed by a consulting company under contract to the United States government. Then I saw myself sitting at a computer with a blank screen.

I looked around, away from Ground Zero, at the New York streets that had avoided the fire and now were returning to normal. I wondered what the people who walked those streets today thought about all this—not simply about the destruction of the towers, but also about the ruined pomegranate farms and the twenty-four thousand who starve every single day. I wondered if they thought about such things at all, if they could tear themselves away from their jobs and gas-guzzling cars and their interest payments long enough to consider their own contribution to the world they were passing on to their children. I wondered what they knew about Afghanistan—not the Afghanistan on television, the one littered with U.S. military tents and tanks, but the old man's Afghanistan. I wondered what those twenty-four thousand who die every day think.

And then I saw myself again, sitting before a blank computer screen.

I forced my attention back to Ground Zero. At the moment, one thing was certain: my country was thinking about revenge, and it was focusing on countries like Afghanistan. But I was thinking about all the other places in the world where people hate our companies, our military, our policies, and our march toward global empire.

I wondered, What about Panama, Ecuador, Indonesia, Iran, Guatemala, most of Africa?

I pushed myself off the wall I had been leaning against and started walking away. A short, swarthy man was waving a newspaper in the air and shouting in Spanish. I stopped.

"Venezuela on the brink of revolution!" he yelled above the noise of the traffic, the honking horns, and the milling people.

I bought his paper and stood there for a moment scanning the lead article. It was about Hugo Chávez, Venezuela's democratically elected, anti-American president, and the undercurrent of hatred generated by U.S. policies in Latin America.

What about Venezuela?

CHAPTER 33

Venezuela: Saved by Saddam

I had watched Venezuela for many years. It was a classic example of a country that rose from rags to riches as a result of oil. It was also a model of the turmoil oil wealth foments, of the disequilibrium between rich and poor, and of a country shamelessly exploited by the corporatocracy. It had become the epitome of a place where old-style EHMs like me converged with the new-style, corporate version.

The events I read about in the newspaper that day at Ground Zero were a direct result of the 1998 elections, when the poor and disenfranchised of Venezuela elected Hugo Chávez by a landslide as their president.[1] He immediately instituted drastic measures, taking control of the courts and other institutions and dissolving the Venezuelan Congress. He denounced the United States for its "shameless imperialism," spoke out forcefully against globalization, and introduced a hydrocarbons law that was reminiscent, even in name, to the one Jaime Roldós had brought to Ecuador shortly before his airplane went down. The law doubled the royalties charged to foreign oil companies. Then Chávez defied the traditional independence of the state-owned oil company, Petróleos de

Venezuela, by replacing its top executives with people loyal to him.[2]

Venezuelan oil is crucial to economies around the world. In 2002 the nation was the world's fourth-largest oil exporter and the number-three supplier to the United States.[3] Petróleos de Venezuela, with forty thousand employees and $50 billion a year in sales, provides 80 percent of the country's export revenue. It is by far the most important factor in Venezuela's economy.[4] By taking over the industry, Chávez had thrust himself onto the world stage as a major player.

Many Venezuelans saw this as destiny, the completion of a process that began eighty years earlier. On December 14, 1922, a huge oil blowout had gushed from the earth near Maracaibo. One hundred thousand barrels of crude sprayed into the air each day for the next three days, and this single geologic event changed Venezuela forever. By 1930, the country was the world's largest oil exporter. Venezuelans looked to oil as a solution to all their problems.

Oil revenues during the next forty years enabled Venezuela to evolve from one of the most impoverished nations in the world to one of the wealthiest in Latin America. All of the country's vital statistics improved: health care, education, employment, longevity, and infant survival rates. Businesses prospered.

During the 1973 OPEC oil embargo, petroleum prices skyrocketed and Venezuela's national budget quadrupled. The EHMs went to work. The international banks flooded the country with loans that paid for vast infrastructure and industrial projects and for the highest skyscrapers on the continent. Then, in the 1980s, the corporate-style EHMs arrived. It was an ideal opportunity for them to cut their fledgling teeth. The Venezuelan middle class had become sizable, and provided a ripe market for a vast array of products, yet there was still a very large poor sector available to labor in the sweatshops and factories.

Then oil prices crashed, and Venezuela could not repay its debts. In 1989, the IMF imposed harsh austerity measures and pressured Caracas to support the corporatocracy in many other ways. Venezuelans reacted violently; riots killed over two hundred people. The illusion of oil as a bottomless source of support was shattered. Between 1978 and 2003, Venezuela's per capita income plummeted by over 40 percent.[5]

As poverty increased, resentment intensified. Polarization resulted, with the middle class pitted against the poor. As so often occurs in countries whose economies depend on oil production, demographics radically shifted. The sinking economy took its toll on the middle class, and many fell into the ranks of the poor.

The new demographics set the stage for Chávez—and for conflict with Washington. Once in power, the new president took actions that challenged the Bush administration. Just before the September 11 attacks, Washington was considering its options. The EHMs had failed; was it time to send in the jackals?

Then 9/11 changed all priorities. President Bush and his advisers focused on rallying the world community to support U.S. activities in Afghanistan and an invasion of Iraq. On top of that, the U.S. economy was in the middle of a recession. Venezuela was relegated to a back burner. However, it was obvious that at some point Bush and Chávez would come to blows. With Iraqi and other Middle Eastern oil supplies threatened, Washington could not afford to ignore Venezuela for long.

Wandering around Ground Zero and Wall Street, meeting the old Afghan man, and reading about Chávez's Venezuela brought me to a point I had avoided for many years, and it forced me to take a hard look at the consequences of the things I had done over the past three decades. I could not possibly deny the role I had played or the fact that my work as an EHM now affected my daughter's generation in very negative ways. I knew I could no longer postpone taking action to atone for what I had done. I had to come clean about my life, in a manner that would help people wake up to the fact of corporatocracy and understand why so much of the world hates us.

I started writing once again, but as I did so, it seemed to me that my story was too old. Somehow, I needed to bring it up to date. I considered traveling to Afghanistan, Iraq, and Venezuela and writing a contemporary commentary on those three countries. They seemed to embody an irony of current world affairs: each had undergone traumatic political turmoil and ended up with leaders who left a great deal to be desired (a cruel and despotic Taliban, a psychopathic Saddam, and an economically inept Chávez), yet in no case did the corporatocracy respond by attempting to solve the deeper problems of these countries. Rather, the response was simply to undermine leaders who stood in the way of our oil policies. In many respects, Venezuela was the most intriguing case because, while military intervention had already occurred in Afghanistan and appeared inevitable in Iraq, the administration's response to Chávez remained a mystery. As far as I was concerned, the issue was not about whether Chávez was a good leader; it was about Washington's reaction to a leader who stood in the way of the corporatocracy's march to global empire.

Before I had time to organize such a trip, however, circumstances once again intervened. My nonprofit work took me to South America several times in 2002. A Venezuelan family whose businesses were going bankrupt under the Chávez regime joined one of my trips to the Amazon. We became close friends, and I heard their side of the story. I also met with Latin Americans from the other end of the economic spectrum, who considered Chávez a savior. The events unfolding in Caracas were symptomatic of the world we EHMs had created.

By December 2002, the situation in both Venezuela and in Iraq reached crisis points. The two countries were evolving into perfect counterpoints for each other. In Iraq, all the subtle efforts—both the EHMs and the jackals—had failed to force Saddam to comply, and now we were preparing for the ultimate solution, invasion. In Venezuela, the Bush administration was bringing Kermit Roosevelt's Iranian model into play. As the *New York Times* reported,

> Hundreds of thousands of Venezuelans filled the streets here today to declare their commitment to a national strike, now in its 28th day, to force the ouster of President Hugo Chávez.
>
> The strike, joined by an estimated 30,000 oil workers, threatens to wreak havoc on this nation, the world's fifth-largest oil producer, for months to come . . .
>
> In recent days, the strike has reached a kind of stalemate. Mr. Chávez is using nonstriking workers to try to normalize operations at the state-owned oil company. His opponents, led by a coalition of business and labor leaders, contend, though, that their strike will push the company, and thus the Chávez government, to collapse.[6]

This was exactly how the CIA brought down Mossadegh and replaced him with the shah. The analogy could not have been stronger. It seemed history was uncannily repeating itself, fifty years later. Five decades, and still oil was the driving force.

Chávez's supporters continued to clash with his opponents. Several people, it was reported, were shot to death and dozens more were wounded. The next day, I talked with an old friend who for many years had been involved with the jackals. Like me, he had never worked directly for any government, but he had led clandestine operations in many countries. He told me that a private contractor had approached him to foment strikes in Caracas and to bribe military officers—many of whom had been trained at the School of the Americas—to turn against their elected president. He had turned down the offer, but he confided, "The man who took the job knows what he's doing."[7]

Oil company executives and Wall Street feared a rise in oil prices and a decline in American inventories. Given the Middle East situation, I knew the Bush administration was doing everything in its power to overthrow Chávez. Then came the news that they had succeeded; Chávez had been ousted. The *New York Times* took this turn of events as an opportunity to provide a historical perspective—and also to identify the man who appeared to play the Kermit Roosevelt role in contemporary Venezuela:

The United States . . . supported authoritarian regimes throughout Central and South America during and after the Cold War in defense of its economic and political interests.

In tiny Guatemala, the Central Intelligence Agency mounted a coup overthrowing the democratically elected government in 1954, and it backed subsequent right-wing governments against small leftist rebel groups for four decades. Roughly 200,000 civilians died.

In Chile, a CIA-supported coup helped put Gen. Augusto Pinochet in power from 1973 to 1990. In Peru, a fragile democratic government is still unraveling the agency's role in a decade of support for the now-deposed and disgraced president, Alberto K. Fujimori, and his disreputable spy chief, Vladimiro L. Montesinos.

The United States had to invade Panama in 1989 to topple its narco-dictator, Manuel A. Noriega, who, for almost 20 years, was a valued informant for American intelligence. And the struggle to mount an unarmed opposition against Nicaragua's leftists in the 1980s by any means necessary, including selling arms to Iran for cold cash, led to indictments against senior Reagan administration officials.

Among those investigated back then was Otto J. Reich, a veteran of Latin American struggles. No charges were ever filed against Mr. Reich. He later became United States Ambassador to Venezuela and now serves as assistant secretary of state for inter-American affairs by presidential appointment. The fall of Mr. Chávez is a feather in his cap.[8]

If Mr. Reich and the Bush administration were celebrating the coup against Chávez, the party was suddenly cut short. In an amazing turnabout, Chávez regained the upper hand and was back in power less than seventy-two hours later. Unlike Mossadegh in Iran, Chávez had managed to keep the military on his side, despite all attempts to turn its highest-ranking officers against him. In addition, he had the powerful state oil company on his side. Petróleos de Venezuela defied the thousands of striking workers and made a comeback.

Once the dust cleared, Chávez tightened his government's grip on oil company employees, purged the military of the few disloyal officers who had been persuaded to betray him, and forced many of his key opponents out of the country. He demanded twenty-year prison terms for two prominent opposition leaders, Washington-connected operatives who had directed the nationwide strike.[9]

In the final analysis, the entire sequence of events was a calamity for the Bush administration. As the *Los Angeles Times* reported,

> Bush administration officials acknowledged Tuesday that they had discussed the removal of Venezuelan President Hugo Chávez for months with military and civilian leaders from Venezuela ... The administration's handling of the abortive coup has come under increasing scrutiny.[10]

It was obvious that not only had the EHMs failed, but so had the jackals. Venezuela in 2003 turned out to be very different from Iran in 1953. I wondered if this was a harbinger or simply an anomaly—and what Washington would do next.

At least for the time being, I believe a serious crisis was averted in Venezuela—and Chávez was saved—by Saddam Hussein. The Bush administration could not take on Afghanistan, Iraq, and Venezuela all at once. At the moment, it had neither the military muscle nor the political support to do so. I knew, however, that such circumstances could change quickly, and that President Chávez was likely to face fierce opposition in the near future. Nonetheless, Venezuela was a reminder that not much had changed in fifty years—except the outcome.

CHAPTER 34

Ecuador Revisited

Venezuela was a classic case. However, as I watched events unfolding there, I was struck by the fact that the truly significant battle lines were being drawn in yet another country. They were significant not because they represented more in terms of dollars or human lives, but because they involved issues that went far beyond the materialistic goals that generally define empires. These battle lines extended beyond the armies of bankers, business executives, and politicians, deep into the soul of modern civilization. And they were being established in a country I had come to know and love, the one where I had first worked as a Peace Corps volunteer: Ecuador.

In the years since I first went there, in 1968, this tiny country had evolved into the quintessential victim of the corporatocracy. My contemporaries and I, and our modern corporate equivalents, had managed to bring it to virtual bankruptcy. We loaned it billions of dollars so it could hire our engineering and construction firms to build projects that would help its richest families. As a result, in those three decades, the official poverty level grew from 50 to 70 percent, under- or unemployment increased from 15 to 70 percent, public debt increased from $240 million to $16 billion, and the share of national resources allocated to the poorest citizens declined from 20 percent to 6 percent. Today, Ecuador must devote nearly 50 percent of its national budget simply to paying off its debts—instead of to helping the millions of its citizens who are officially classified as dangerously impoverished.[1]

The situation in Ecuador clearly demonstrates that this was not the result of a conspiracy; it was a process that had occurred during both Democratic and Republican administrations, a process that had involved all the major multinational banks, many corporations, and foreign aid missions from a multitude of countries. The United States played the lead role, but we had not acted alone.

During those three decades, thousands of men and women participated in bringing Ecuador to the tenuous position it found itself in at the beginning of the millennium. Some of them, like me, had been aware of what they were doing, but the vast majority had merely performed the tasks they had been taught in business, engineering, and law schools, or had followed the lead of bosses in my mold, who demonstrated the system by their own greedy example and through rewards and punishments calculated to perpetuate it. Such participants saw the parts they played as benign, at worst; in the most optimistic view, they were helping an impoverished nation.

Although unconscious, deceived, and—in many cases—self-deluded, these players were not members of any clandestine conspiracy; rather, they were the product of a system that promotes the most subtle and effective form of imperialism the world has ever witnessed. No one had to go out and seek men and women who could be bribed or threatened—they had already been recruited by companies, banks, and government agencies. The bribes consisted of salaries, bonuses, pensions, and insurance policies; the threats were based on social mores, peer pressure, and unspoken questions about the future of their children's education.

The system had succeeded spectacularly. By the time the new millennium rolled in, Ecuador was thoroughly entrapped. We had her, just as a Mafia don has the man whose daughter's wedding and small business he has financed and then refinanced. Like any good Mafiosi, we had taken our time. We could afford to be patient, knowing that beneath Ecuador's rain forests lies a sea of oil, knowing that the proper day would come.

That day had already arrived when, in early 2003, I wound my way from Quito to the jungle town of Shell in my Subaru Outback. Chávez had reestablished himself in Venezuela. He had defied George W. Bush and had won. Saddam was standing his ground and was preparing to be invaded. Oil supplies were depleted to their lowest level in nearly three decades, and the prospects of taking more from our prime sources looked bleak—and therefore, so did the health of the corporatocracy's balance sheets. We needed an ace in the hole. It was time to cut away our Ecuadorian pound of flesh.

As I drove past the monster dam on the Pastaza River, I realized that here in Ecuador the battle was not simply the classic struggle between the rich of the world and the impoverished, between those who exploit and the exploited. These battle lines would ultimately define who we are as a civilization. We were poised to force this tiny country to open its Amazon rain forests to our oil companies. The devastation that would result was immeasurable.

If we insisted on collecting the debt, the repercussions would go far beyond our abilities to quantify them. It was not just about the destruction of indigenous cultures, human lives, and hundreds of thousands of species of animals, reptiles, fish, insects, and plants, some of which might contain the undiscovered cures to any number of diseases. It was not just that rain forests absorb the deadly greenhouse gases produced by our industries, give off the oxygen that is essential to our lives, and seed the clouds that ultimately create a large percentage of the world's fresh water. It went beyond all the standard arguments made by ecologists for saving such places, and reached deep into our souls.

If we pursued this strategy, we would continue an imperialist pattern that had begun long before the Roman Empire. We decry slavery, but our global empire enslaves more people than the Romans and all the other colonial powers before us. I wondered how we could execute such a shortsighted policy in Ecuador and still live with our collective conscience.

Peering through the window of the Subaru at the deforested slopes of the Andes, an area that during my Peace Corps days had been lush with tropical growth, I was suddenly surprised by another realization. It dawned on me that this view of Ecuador as a significant battle line was purely personal, that in fact every country where I had worked, every country with resources coveted by the empire, was equally significant. I had my own attachment to this one, which stemmed from those days back in the late 1960s when I lost my innocence here. However, it was subjective, my personal bias.

Though the Ecuadorian rain forests are precious, as are the indigenous people and all the other life forms that inhabit them, they are no more precious than the deserts of Iran and the Bedouins of Yamin's heritage. No more precious than the mountains of Java, the seas off the coast of the Philippines, the steppes of Asia, the savannas of Africa, the forests of North America, the icecaps of the Arctic, or hundreds of other threatened places. Every one of these represents a battle line, and every one of them forces us to search the depths of our individual and collective souls.

I was reminded of a statistic that sums it all up: The income ratio of the one-fifth of the world's population in the wealthiest countries to the one-fifth in the poorest countries went from 30 to 1 in 1960 to 74 to 1 in 1995.[2] And the World Bank, the U.S. Agency for International Development, the IMF, and the rest of the banks, corporations, and governments involved in international "aid" continue to tell us that they are doing their jobs, that progress has been made.

So here I was in Ecuador again, in the country that was just one of many battle lines but that holds a special place in my heart. It was 2003, thirty-five years after I had first arrived as a member of a U.S. organization that bears the word *peace* in its name. This time, I had come in order to try to prevent a war that for three decades I had helped to provoke.

It would seem that events in Afghanistan, Iraq, and Venezuela might be enough to deter us from another conflict; yet, in Ecuador the situation was very different. This war would not require the U.S. Army, for it would be fought by a few thousand indigenous warriors equipped only with spears, machetes, and single-shot, muzzle-loaded rifles. They would face off against a modern Ecuadorian army, a handful of U.S. Special Forces advisers, and jackal-trained mercenaries hired by the oil companies. This would be a war, like the 1995 conflict between Ecuador and Peru, that most people in the United States would never hear about, and recent events had escalated the probability of such a war.

In December 2002, oil company representatives accused an indigenous community of taking a team of its workers hostage; they suggested that the warriors involved were members of a terrorist group, with implications of possible ties to al-Qaeda. It was an issue made especially complicated because the oil company had not received government permission to begin drilling. However, the company claimed its workers had the right to perform preliminary, nondrilling investigations—a claim vehemently disputed by the indigenous groups a few days later, when they shared their side of the story.

The oil workers, tribal representatives insisted, had trespassed on lands where they were not allowed; the warriors had carried no weapons, nor had they threatened the oil workers with violence of any sort. In fact, they had escorted the workers to their village, where they offered them food and *chicha*, a local beer.

While their visitors feasted, the warriors persuaded the workers' guides to paddle away. However, the tribe claimed, the workers were never held against their will; they were free to go wherever they pleased.[3]

Driving down that road, I remembered what the Shuars had told me in 1990 when, after selling IPS, I returned to offer to help them save their forests. "The world is as you dream it," they had said, and then pointed out that we in the North had dreamed of huge industries, lots of cars, and gigantic skyscrapers. Now we had discovered that our vision had in fact been a nightmare that would ultimately destroy us all.

"Change that dream," the Shuars had advised me. Yet here it was, more than a decade later, and despite the work of many people and nonprofit organizations, including the ones I had worked with, the nightmare had reached new and horrifying proportions.

When my Outback finally pulled into the jungle town of Shell, I was hustled off to a meeting. The men and women who attended represented many tribes: Kichwa, Shuar, Achuar, Shiwiar, and Zaparo. Some had walked for days through the jungle, others had flown in on small planes, funded by nonprofits. A few wore their traditional kilts, face paint, and feathered headbands, though most attempted to emulate the townspeople, wearing slacks, T-shirts, and shoes.

Representatives from the community accused of taking hostages spoke first. They told us that shortly after the workers returned to the oil company, over a hundred Ecuadorian soldiers arrived in their small community. They reminded us that this was at the beginning of a special season in the rain forests, the fruiting of the *chonta*. A tree sacred to indigenous cultures, its fruit comes but once a year and signals the start of the mating season for many of the region's birds, including rare and endangered species. As they flock to it, the birds are extremely vulnerable. The tribes enforce strict policies forbidding the hunting of these birds during chonta season.

"The timing of the soldiers couldn't have been worse," a woman explained. I felt her pain and that of her companions as they told their tragic stories about how the soldiers ignored the prohibitions. They shot down the birds for sport and for food. In addition, they raided family gardens, banana groves, and manioc fields, often irreparably destroying the sparse topsoil. They used explosives in the rivers for fishing, and they ate family pets. They confiscated the local hunters' guns and blowguns, dug improper latrines, polluted the rivers with fuel oil and solvents, sexually molested women, and neglected to properly dispose of garbage, which attracted insects and vermin.

"We had two choices," a man said. "We could fight, or we could swallow our pride and do our best to repair the damage. We decided it was not yet the time to fight." He described how they had attempted to compensate for the military's abuses by encouraging their own people to go without food. He called it a fast, but in fact it sounded closer to voluntary starvation. Old people and children became malnourished and grew sick.

They spoke about threats and bribes. "My son," a woman said, "speaks English as well as Spanish and several indigenous dialects. He worked as a guide and translator for an ecotourist company. They paid him a decent salary. The oil company offered him ten times as much. What could he do? Now he writes letters denouncing his old company and all the others who come to help us, and in his letters calls the oil companies our friends." She shook her body, like a dog shaking off water. "He is no longer one of us. My son . . ."

An elderly man wearing the traditional toucan-feather headdress of a shaman stood up. "You know about those three we elected to represent us against the oil companies, who died in that plane crash? Well, I'm not going to stand here and tell you what so many say, that the oil companies caused the crash. But I can tell you that those three deaths dug a big hole in our organization. The oil companies lost no time filling that hole with their people."

Another man produced a contract and read it. In exchange for three hundred thousand dollars, it ceded a vast territory over to a lumber company. It was signed by three tribal officials.

"These aren't their real signatures," he said. "I ought to know; one is my brother. It's another type of assassination. To discredit our leaders."

It seemed ironic and strangely appropriate that this was taking place in a region of Ecuador where the oil companies had not yet been given permission to drill. They had drilled in many areas around this one, and the indigenous people had seen the results, had witnessed the destruction of their neighbors. As I sat there listening, I asked myself how the citizens of my country would react if gatherings like this were featured on CNN or the evening news.

The meetings were fascinating and the revelations deeply disturbing. But something else also happened, outside the formal setting of those sessions. During breaks, at lunch, and in the evening, when I talked with people privately, I frequently was asked why the United States was threatening Iraq. The impending war was discussed on the front pages of Ecuadorian newspapers that made their way into this jungle town, and the coverage was very different from coverage in the States. It included references to the Bush family's ownership of oil companies, and to Vice President Cheney's role as former CEO of Halliburton.

These newspapers were read to men and women who had never attended school. Everyone seemed to take an interest in this issue. Here I was, in the Amazon rain forest, among illiterate people many in North America consider "backward," even "savages," and yet probing questions were being asked that struck at the heart of the global empire.

Driving out of Shell, back past the hydroelectric dam and high into the Andes, I kept thinking about the difference between what I had seen and heard during this visit to Ecuador and what I had become accustomed to in the United States. It seemed that Amazonian tribes had a great deal to teach us, that despite all our schooling and our many hours reading magazines and watching television news, we lacked an awareness they had somehow found. This line of thinking made me think of "The Prophecy of the Condor and Eagle," which I have heard many times throughout Latin America, and of similar prophecies I have encountered around the world.

Nearly every culture I know prophesies that in the late 1990s we entered a period of remarkable transition. At monasteries in the Himalayas, ceremonial sites in Indonesia, and indigenous reservations in North America, from the depths of the Amazon to the peaks of the Andes and into the ancient Mayan cities of Central America, I have heard that ours is a special moment in human history, and that each of us was born at this time because we have a mission to accomplish.

The titles and words of the prophecies differ slightly. They tell variously of a New Age, the Third Millennium, the Age of Aquarius, the Beginning of the Fifth Sun, or the end of old calendars and the commencement of new ones. Despite the varying terminologies, however, they have a great deal in common, and "The Prophecy of the Condor and Eagle" is typical. It states that back in the mists of history, human societies divided and took two different paths: that of the condor (representing the heart, intuitive and mystical) and that of the eagle (representing the brain, rational and material). In the 1490s, the prophecy said, the two paths would converge and the eagle would drive the condor to the verge of extinction. Then, five hundred years later, in the 1990s, a new epoch would begin, one in which the condor and eagle will have the opportunity to reunite and fly together in the same sky, along the same path. If the condor and eagle accept this opportunity, they will create a most remarkable offspring, unlike any ever seen before.

"The Prophecy of the Condor and Eagle" can be taken at many levels—the standard interpretation is that it foretells the sharing of indigenous knowledge with the technologies of science, the balancing of yin and yang, and the bridging of northern and southern cultures. However, most powerful is the message it offers about consciousness; it says that we have entered a time when we can benefit from the many diverse ways of seeing ourselves and the world, and that we can use these as a springboard to higher levels of awareness. As human beings, we can truly wake up and evolve into a more conscious species.

The condor people of the Amazon make it seem so obvious that if we are to address questions about the nature of what it is to be human in this new millennium, and about our commitment to evaluating our intentions for the next several decades, then we need to open our eyes and see the consequences of our actions—the actions of the eagle—in places like Iraq and Ecuador. We must shake ourselves awake. We who live in the most powerful nation history has ever known must stop worrying so much about the outcome of soap operas, football games, quarterly balance sheets, and the daily Dow Jones averages, and must instead reevaluate who we are and where we want our children to end up. The alternative to stopping to ask ourselves the important questions is simply too dangerous.

CHAPTER 35

Piercing the Veneer

Shortly after I returned home from Ecuador in 2003, the United States invaded Iraq for the second time in a little over a decade. The EHMs had failed. The jackals had failed. So young men and women were sent to kill and die among the desert sands. One important question the invasion raised, but one that I figured few Americans would be in a position to consider, was what this would mean for the royal House of Saud. If the United States took over Iraq, which according to many estimates has more oil than Saudi Arabia, there would seem to be little need to continue honoring the pact we struck with the Saudi royal family in the 1970s, the deal that originated with the Saudi Arabian Money-laundering Affair.

The end of Saddam, like the end of Noriega in Panama, would change the formula. In the case of Panama, once we had reinstated our puppets, we controlled the Canal, regardless of the terms of the treaty Torrijos and Carter had negotiated. Once we controlled Iraq, then, could we break OPEC? Would the Saudi royal family become irrelevant in the arena of global oil politics? A few pundits were already questioning why Bush attacked Iraq rather than funneling all of our resources into pursuing al-Qaeda in Afghanistan. Could it be that from the point of view of this administration—this oil family—establishing oil supplies, as well as a justification for construction contracts, was more important than fighting terrorists?

There also was another possible outcome, however; OPEC might attempt to reassert itself. If the United States took control of Iraq, the other petroleum-rich countries might have little to lose by raising oil prices and/or reducing supplies. This possibility tied in with another scenario, one with implications that would likely occur to few people outside the world of higher international finance, yet which could tip the scales of the geopolitical balance and ultimately bring down the system the corporatocracy had worked so hard to construct. It could, in fact, turn out to be the single factor that would cause history's first truly global empire to self-destruct.

In the final analysis, the global empire depends to a large extent on the fact that the dollar acts as the standard world currency, and that the United States Mint has the right to print those dollars. Thus, we make loans to countries like Ecuador with the full knowledge that they will never repay them; in fact, we do not want them to honor their debts, since the nonpayment is what gives us our leverage, our pound of flesh. Under normal conditions, we would run the risk of eventually decimating our own funds; after all, no creditor can afford too many defaulted loans. However, ours are not normal circumstances. The United States prints currency that is not backed by gold. Indeed, it is not backed by anything other than a general worldwide confidence in our economy and our ability to marshal the forces and resources of the empire we have created to support us.

The ability to print currency gives us immense power. It means, among other things, that we can continue to make loans that will never be repaid—and that we ourselves can accumulate huge debts. By the beginning of 2003, the United States' national debt exceeded a staggering $6 trillion and was projected to reach $7 trillion before the end of the year—roughly $24,000 for each U.S. citizen. Much of this debt is owed to Asian countries, particularly to Japan and China, who purchase U.S. Treasury securities (essentially, IOUs) with funds accumulated through sales of consumer goods—including electronics, computers, automobiles, appliances, and clothing goods—to the United States and the worldwide market.[1]

As long as the world accepts the dollar as its standard currency, this excessive debt does not pose a serious obstacle to the corporatocracy. However, if another currency should come along to replace the dollar, and if some of the United States' creditors (Japan or China, for example) should decide to call in their debts, the situation would change drastically. The United States would suddenly find itself in a most precarious situation.

In fact, today the existence of such a currency is no longer hypothetical; the euro entered the international financial scene on January 1, 2002 and is growing in prestige and power with every passing month. The euro offers an unusual opportunity for OPEC, if it chooses to retaliate for the Iraq invasion, or if for any other reason it decides to flex its muscles against the United States. A decision by OPEC to substitute the euro for the dollar as its standard currency would shake the empire to its very foundations. If that were to happen, and if one or two major creditors were to demand that we repay our debts in euros, the impact would be enormous.

I had these things on my mind on the morning of Good Friday, April 18, 2003, as I walked the short distance from my house to the converted garage that serves as my office, sat down at the desk, turned on the computer, and as usual, went to the *New York Times* Web site. The headline leaped out at me; it immediately transported me from my thoughts about the new realities of international finance, the national debt, and euros back to that of my old profession: "U.S. Gives Bechtel a Major Contract in Rebuilding Iraq."

The article stated, "The Bush administration awarded the Bechtel Group of San Francisco the first major contract today in a vast reconstruction plan for Iraq." Farther down the page, the authors informed readers that "The Iraqis will then work with the World Bank and the International Monetary Fund, institutions in which the United States enjoys wide influence, to reshape the country."[2]

Wide influence! There was an understatement.

I linked to another *Times* article, "Company Has Ties in Washington, and to Iraq." I skipped through the first several paragraphs, which repeated much of the information from the previous article, and came to:

> Bechtel has longstanding ties to the national security
> establishment . . . One director is George P. Shultz,
> who was secretary of state under President Ronald
> Reagan. Before joining the Reagan administration,
> Mr. Shultz, who also serves as a senior counselor to
> Bechtel, was the company's president, working along-
> side Caspar W. Weinberger, who served as an executive
> at the San Francisco–based company before his ap-
> pointment as defense secretary. This year, President
> Bush appointed Bechtel's chief executive, Riley P.
> Bechtel, to serve on the President's Export Council.[3]

Here in these articles was the story of modern history, the drive to global empire, in a nutshell. What was going on in Iraq and described in the morning press was the result of the work Claudine had trained me to do some thirty-five years before, and of the work of other men and women who shared a lust for self-aggrandizement not unlike the one I had known. It marked the current point of the corporatocracy's progress along the road to bringing every person in the world under its influence.

These articles were about the 2003 invasion of Iraq and about the contracts now being signed, both to rebuild that country from the wreckage created by our military and to build anew in the mold of the modern, westernized model. Yet, without saying so, the news of April 18, 2003, also harked back to the early 1970s and the Saudi Arabian Money-laundering Affair. SAMA and the contracts flowing out of it had established new and irrevocable precedents that allowed—indeed mandated—U.S. engineering and construction companies and the petroleum industry to co-opt the development of a desert kingdom. In the same mighty blow, SAMA established new rules for the global management of petroleum, redefined geopolitics, and forged with the Saudi royal family an alliance that would ensure their hegemony as well as their commitment to playing by our rules.

As I read those articles, I could not help but wonder how many other people knew, as I did, that Saddam would still be in charge if he had played the game as the Saudis had. He would have his missiles and chemical plants; we would have built them for him, and our people would be in charge of upgrading and servicing them. It would be a very sweet deal—even as Saudi Arabia had been.

Until now, the mainstream media had been careful not to publicize this story. But today, here it was. True, it was a mere inkling; the articles were only the meekest ghosts of a summary, yet the story seemed to be emerging. Wondering if the *New York Times* was taking a maverick stance, I visited the CNN Web site and read, "Bechtel Wins Iraq Contract." The CNN story was very similar to the one in the *Times*, except it added,

> Several other companies have at various times been reported as possible competitors for the job, either as primary bidders or as parts of teams, including the Kellogg Brown & Root (KBR) unit of Halliburton Co.—of which Vice President Dick Cheney once was CEO . . . [Already] Halliburton has won a contract, which could be worth $7 billion and could last up to

two years, to make emergency repairs to Iraq's oil infrastructure.[4]

The story of the march to global empire did indeed appear to be leaking out. Not the details, not the fact that it was a tragic story of debt, deception, enslavement, exploitation, and the most blatant grab in history for the hearts, minds, souls, and resources of people around the world. Nothing in these articles hinted that the story of Iraq in 2003 was the continuation of a shameful story. Nor did they disclose that this story, as old as empire, has now taken on new and terrifying dimensions, both because of its magnitude during this time of globalization and because of the subtlety with which it is executed. Despite its shortfalls, however, the story did appear to be leaking out, almost reluctantly.

The idea of the reluctant story, leaking out, hit very close to home. It reminded me of my own personal story and of the many years I had postponed telling it. I had known for a very long time that I had a confession to make; still, I postponed making it. Thinking back, I see that my doubts, the whisperings of guilt, were there from the beginning. They had started in Claudine's apartment, even before I made the commitment to go to Indonesia on that first trip, and they had haunted me almost incessantly all these years.

I also knew that had the doubts, the pain, and the guilt not constantly nagged me, I would never have gotten out. Like so many others, I would have been stuck. I would not have stood on a beach in the Virgin Islands and decided to quit MAIN. Yet, I was still deferring, just as we as a culture continue to defer.

These headlines seemed to hint at the alliance between big corporations, international banks, and governments, but like my MAIN résumé, the stories barely touched the surface. It was a gloss. The real story had little to do with the fact that the major engineering and construction firms were once again receiving billions of dollars to develop a country in our image—among a people who in all likelihood had no desire to reflect that image—or that an elite band of men was repeating an age-old ritual of abusing the privileges of their high government positions.

That picture is just too simple. It implies that all we need to do, if we decide to right the wrongs of the system, is to throw these men out. It feeds into the conspiracy theories and thereby provides a convenient excuse to turn on the TV and forget about it all, comfortable in our third-grade view of history, which runs: "They" will take care of it; the ship of state is seaworthy and will get nudged back on course. We may have to wait for the next election, but all will turn out for the best.

The real story of modern empire—of the corporatocracy that exploits desperate people and is executing history's most brutal, selfish, and ultimately self-destructive resource-grab—has little to do with what was exposed in the newspapers that morning and has everything to do with us. And that, of course, explains why we have such difficulty listening to the real story. We prefer to believe the myth that thousands of years of human social evolution has finally perfected the ideal economic system, rather than to face the fact we have merely bought into a false concept and accepted it as gospel. We have convinced ourselves that all economic growth benefits humankind, and that the greater the growth, the more widespread the benefits. Finally, we have persuaded one another that the corollary to this concept is valid and morally just: that people who excel at stoking the fires of economic growth should be exalted and rewarded, while those born at the fringes are available for exploitation.

This concept and its corollary are used to justify all manner of piracy—licenses are granted to rape and pillage and murder innocent people in Iran, Panama, Colombia, Iraq, and elsewhere. EHMs, jackals, and armies flourish for as long as their activities can be shown to generate economic growth—and they almost always demonstrate such growth. Thanks to the biased "sciences" of forecasting, econometrics, and statistics, if you bomb a city and then rebuild it, the data shows a huge spike in economic growth.

The real story is that we are living a lie. Like my MAIN résumé, we have created a veneer that hides the fatal cancers beneath the surface. Those cancers are exposed by the X-rays of our statistics, which disclose the terrifying fact that history's most powerful and wealthiest empire has outrageously high rates of suicide, drug abuse, divorce, child molestation, rape, and murder, and that like a malignant cancer, these afflictions spread their tentacles in an ever-widening radius every year. In our hearts, each of us feels the pain. We cry out for change. Yet, we slam our fists to our mouths, stifling those cries, and so we go unheard.

It would be great if we could just blame it all on a conspiracy, but we cannot. The empire depends on the efficacy of big banks, corporations, and governments—the corporatocracy—but it is not a conspiracy. This corporatocracy is ourselves—we make it happen—which, of course, is why most of us find it difficult to stand up and oppose it. We would rather glimpse conspirators lurking in the shadows, because most of us work for one of those banks, corporations, or governments, or in some way are de-pendent on them for the goods and services they produce and market. We cannot bring ourselves to bite the hand of the mas-ter who feeds us.

That is the situation I was pondering as I sat staring at the headlines on the screen of my computer. And it raised a number of questions. How do you rise up against a system that appears to provide you with your home and car, food and clothes, electricity and health care—even when you know that the system also cre-ates a world where twenty-four thousand people starve to death each day and millions more hate you, or at least hate the policies made by representatives you elected? How do you muster the courage to step out of line and challenge concepts you and your neighbors have always accepted as gospel, even when you suspect that the system is ready to self-destruct? Slowly, I stood up and headed back to the house to pour myself another cup of coffee.

I took a short detour and picked up my copy of the *Palm Beach Post*, lying near the mailbox beside our driveway. It had the same Bechtel-Iraq article, copyrighted by the *New York Times*. But now I noticed the date on the masthead: April 18. It is a famous date, at least in New England, instilled in me by my Revolutionary War–minded parents and by Longfellow's poem:

> Listen, my children, and you shall hear
> Of the midnight ride of Paul Revere,
> On the eighteenth of April, in Seventy-five;
> Hardly a man is now alive
> Who remembers that famous day and year.

This year, Good Friday happened to fall on the anniversary of Paul Revere's ride. Seeing that date on the front page of the *Post* made me think of the colonial silversmith racing his horse through the dark streets of New England towns, waving his hat and shouting, "The British are coming!" Revere had risked his life to spread the word, and loyal Americans responded. They stopped the empire, back then.

I wondered what had motivated them, why those colonial Americans were willing to step out of line. Many of the ringleaders had been prosperous. What had inspired them to risk their businesses, to bite the hand that fed them, to risk their lives? Each of them undoubtedly had personal reasons, and yet there must have been some unifying force, some energy or catalyst, a spark that ignited all those individual fires at that single moment in history.

And then it came to me: words.

The telling of the real story about the British Empire and its selfish and ultimately self-destructive mercantile system had provided that spark. The exposure of the underlying meaning, through the words of men like Tom Paine and Thomas Jefferson, fired the imaginations of their countrymen, opened hearts and minds. The colonists began to question, and when they did, they discovered a new reality that cut away at the deceits. They discerned the truth behind the patina, understood the way the British Empire had manipulated, deceived, and enslaved them.

They saw that their English masters had formulated a system and then had managed to convince most people of a lie—that it was the best system mankind could offer, that the prospects for a better world depended on channeling resources through the King of England, that an imperial approach to commerce and politics was the most efficient and humane means of helping the majority of the people—when in fact the truth was that the system enriched only a very few at the expense of the many. This lie, and the resulting exploitation, endured and expanded for decades, until a handful of philosophers, businessmen, farmers, fishermen, frontiersmen, writers, and orators began to speak the truth.

Words. I thought about their power as I refilled my coffee cup, walked back to my office, and returned to the computer.

I logged off the CNN Web site and brought up the file I had been working on the night before. I read the last paragraph I had written:

> This story *must* be told. We live in a time of terrible crisis—and tremendous opportunity. The story of this particular economic hit man is the story of how we got to where we are and why we currently face crises that seem insurmountable. This story must be told because only by understanding our past mistakes will we be able to take advantage of future opportunities. . . . Most important, this story must be told because today, for the first time in history, one nation has the ability, the money, and the power to change all this. It is the

nation where I was born and the one I served as an
EHM: the United States of America.

This time I would not stop. The coincidences of my life and the choices I had made around them had brought me to this point. I would move forward.

I thought again of that other man, that lone rider galloping through the dark New England countryside, shouting out his warning. The silversmith knew that the words of pamphleteers—even before Paine—preceded him, that people had read those words in their homes and discussed them in the taverns. Paine would point out the truth about the tyranny of the British Empire. Jefferson would proclaim that our nation was dedicated to the principles of life, liberty, and the pursuit of happiness. And Revere, riding through the night, understood that men and women throughout the colonies would be empowered by words; they would rise up and fight for a better world.

Words . . .

I made my decision to stop procrastinating, to finish finally what I had started so many times over all those years, to come clean, to confess—to write the words in this book.

⊕ WHAT YOU CAN DO

We have arrived at the end of this book, and also at a beginning. You are probably wondering where to go next, what you can do to stop the corporatocracy and to end this insane and self-destructive march to global empire. You are ready to leave the book behind and pounce on the world.

You want ideas, and I could offer you some.

I could point out that the chapter you just read, about Bechtel and Halliburton in Iraq, is old news. By the time you read it, it may seem redundant. However, the significance of those newspaper articles goes far beyond the timeliness of their content. That chapter, I hope, will change the way you view the news, help you to read between the lines of every newspaper article that comes before you and to question the deeper implications of every radio and television report you tune in to.

Things are not as they appear. NBC is owned by General Electric, ABC by Disney, CBS by Viacom, and CNN is part of the huge AOL Time Warner conglomerate. Most of our newspapers, magazines, and publishing houses are owned—and manipulated—by gigantic international corporations. Our media is part of the corporatocracy. The officers and directors who control nearly all our communications outlets know their places; they are taught throughout life that one of their most important jobs is to perpetuate, strengthen, and expand the system they have inherited. They are very efficient at doing so, and when opposed, they can be ruthless. So the burden falls on you to see the truth beneath the veneer and to expose it. Speak it to your family and friends; spread the word.

I could give you a list of practical things to do. For instance, cut back on your oil consumption. In 1990, before we first invaded Iraq, we imported 8 million barrels of oil; by 2003 and the second invasion, this had increased more than 50 percent, to over 12 million barrels.[1] The next time you are tempted to go shopping, read a book instead, exercise, or meditate. Downsize your home, wardrobe, car, office, and most everything else in your life. Protest against "free" trade agreements and against companies that exploit desperate people in sweatshops or that pillage the environment.

I could tell you that there is great hope within the current system, that there is nothing inherently wrong with banks, corporations, and governments—or with the people who manage them—and that they certainly do not have to compose a corporatocracy. I could go into detail about how the problems confronting us today are not the result of malicious institutions; rather, they stem from fallacious concepts about economic development. The fault lies not in the institutions themselves, but in our perceptions of the manner in which they function and interact with one another, and of the role their managers play in that process.

In fact, those highly effective worldwide communications and distribution networks could be used to bring about positive and compassionate changes. Imagine if the Nike swoosh, MacDonald's arches, and Coca-Cola logo became symbols of companies whose primary goals were to clothe and feed the world's poor in environmentally beneficial ways. This is no more unrealistic than putting a man on the moon, breaking up the Soviet Union, or creating the infrastructure that allows those companies to reach every corner of the planet. We need a revolution in our approach to education, to empower ourselves and our children to think, to question, and to dare to act. You can set an example. Be a teacher and a student; inspire everyone around you through your example.

I could encourage you to take specific actions that will impact the institutions in your life. Speak out whenever any forum presents itself, write letters and e-mails, phone in questions and concerns, vote for enlightened school boards, county commissions, and local ordinances. When you must shop, do it consciously; get personally involved.

I could remind you of what the Shuars told me in 1990, that the world is as you dream it, and that we can trade in that old nightmare of polluting industries, clogged highways, and overcrowded cities for a new dream based on Earth-honoring and socially responsible principles of sustainability and equality. It is within our power to transform ourselves, to change the paradigm.

I could enumerate the amazing opportunities we have available to us for creating a better world, right now: enough food and water for everyone; medicines to cure diseases and to prevent epidemics that needlessly plague millions of people today; transportation systems that can deliver life's essentials to even the most remote corners of the planet; the ability to raise literacy levels and to provide Internet services that could make it possible for every person on the planet to communicate with every other person; tools for conflict resolution that could render wars obsolete; technologies that explore both the vastness of space and the most minute, subatomic energy, which could then be applied to developing more ecologic and efficient homes for everyone; sufficient resources to accomplish all of the above; and much more.

I could suggest steps for you to take immediately, to help others understand the crises and the opportunities.

- Offer study groups about *Confessions of an Economic Hit Man* at your local bookstore or library, or both (a guideline for doing this is available at www.JohnPerkins.org).

- Develop a presentation for a nearby elementary school on your favorite subject (sports, cooking, ants—almost anything), and use it to help students wake up to the true nature of the society they are inheriting.

- Send e-mails to all the addresses in your file, expressing feelings triggered by this and other books you read.

But I suspect you have already thought of most of these things. You just need to pick a couple that most appeal to you and do them, and to realize that all of these are part of a much greater commitment that you and I must make. We must commit ourselves absolutely and unequivocally to shaking ourselves and everyone around us awake. We must hear the wisdom of the prophecies, open our hearts and minds to the possibilities, become conscious, and then take action.

However, this book is not a prescription; it is a confession, pure and simple. It is the confession of a man who allowed himself to become a pawn, an economic hit man; a man who bought into a corrupt system because it offered so many perks, and because buying in was easy to justify; a man who knew better but who could always find excuses for his own greed, for exploiting desperate people and pillaging the planet; a man who took full advantage of the fact that he was born into one of the wealthiest societies history has ever known, and who also could pity himself because his parents were not at the top of the pyramid; a man who listened to his teachers, read the textbooks on economic development, and then followed the example of other men and women who legitimatize every action that promotes global empire, even if that action results in murder, genocide, and environmental destruction; a man who trained others to follow in his footsteps. It is my confession.

The fact that you have read this far indicates that you can relate on some personal level to my confession, that you and I share a lot in common. We may have traveled different roads, but we have driven similar vehicles, used the same fuels, and stopped to eat at restaurants owned by the same corporations.

For me, confessing was an essential part of my personal wake-up call. Like all confessions, it is the first step toward redemption.

Now it is your turn. You need to make your own confession. When you come clean on who you are, why you are here during this time in history, why you have done the things you have—the ones you are proud of, and those others—and where you intend to go next, you will experience an immediate sense of relief. It may be nothing less than euphoric.

Believe me when I say that writing this book has been deeply emotional, and often a painful and humiliating experience. It has been frightening in a way nothing I ever faced before has been frightening. But it has opened me to a sense of relief I have never known until now, a feeling I can only describe as ecstatic.

Ask yourself these questions. What do I need to confess? How have I deceived myself and others? Where have I deferred? Why have I allowed myself to be sucked into a system that I know is unbalanced? What will I do to make sure our children, and all children everywhere, are able to fulfill the dream of our Founding Fathers, the dream of life, liberty, and the pursuit of happiness? What course will I take to end the needless starvation, and make sure there is never again a day like September 11? How can I help our children understand that people who live gluttonous, unbalanced lives should be pitied but never, ever emulated, even if those people present themselves, through the media they control, as cultural icons and try to convince us that penthouses and yachts bring happiness? What changes will I commit to making in my attitudes and perceptions? What forums will I use to teach others and to learn more on my own?

These are the essential questions of our time. Each of us needs to answer them in our own way and to express our answers clearly, unequivocally. Paine and Jefferson and all the other patriots are watching over our shoulders. Their words continue to inspire us today. The spirits of those men and women who left their farms and fishing boats and headed out to confront the mighty British Empire, and of those who fought to emancipate the slaves during the Civil War, and of those who sacrificed their lives to protect the world from fascism, speak to us. As do the spirits of the ones who stayed at home and produced the food and clothes and gave their moral support, and of all the men and women who have defended what was won on those battlefields: the teachers, poets, artists, entrepreneurs, health workers, the manual laborers . . . you and me.

The hour is ours. It is now time for each and every one of us to step up to the battle line, to ask the important questions, to search our souls for our own answers, and to take action.

The coincidences of your life, and the choices you have made in response to them, have brought you to this point . . .

A year and a half have passed since I finished writing *Confessions of an Economic Hit Man*. The book was an immediate and unexpected grassroots success that made it to every major bestseller list and has been published in seventeen languages. During the past eighteen months, I have traveled around the United States and South America. I have talked with people from all walks of life and political persuasions and have received hundreds of emails and letters.

The most common response to *Confessions* can be paraphrased as follows: "I knew in my heart that the empire-building you describe was happening, but everyone told me I was paranoid. Your book has confirmed what I knew. Now I will take action."

A number of people have also told me that their initial reaction was anger at me. "You lived a great life as an EHM. Now you've come clean and have a bestseller. Do you expect me to forgive you?" They also told me that when they confronted their deeper feelings, they realized that much of their anger was self-directed. "I shop at Wal-Mart, buy Nike shoes, and use too much oil. It's easy to blame you, the politicians, and the corporatocracy. Now I realize that I need to do something positive. And I will."

Our nation's history is rife with examples of citizens coming together to enact change. Reflecting the spirit of this determination is an amazing call to action I recently came across in a book I was reading:

> Never was a cause more important or glorious than
> that which you are engaged in; not only your wives,
> your children, and distant posterity, but humanity at

large, the world of mankind, are interested in it; for if tyranny should prevail in this great country, we may expect liberty will expire throughout the world. Therefore, more human glory and happiness may depend upon your exertions than ever yet depended upon any of the sons of men.[1]

Signed simply "A Freeman," this message seemed very timely. Yet it first appeared in the *New England Chronicle* in 1775, at a time when Americans were terribly divided over how to deal with an oppressive empire. I was struck by the similarities between that period of history and the current one. The world's most powerful empire, Great Britain, had overstepped its bounds. Refusing to listen to the legitimate complaints of oppressed peoples, the empire responded to desperate acts of rebellion, like the Boston Massacre, with military brutality. Americans were confused. Many believed they had an obligation to support their king no matter how violent his actions. Many more thought they did not stand a chance at changing the system—a system they had been taught to believe was the most just in history. Those who opposed the empire were labeled as traitors; they were threatened with the hangman's noose.

In reading the diaries of British Revolutionary War soldiers, I discovered that they were impressed by the affluence of America. The land was bountiful. Farms prospered. The cities seemed like paradise compared to European cities in the eighteenth century. These soldiers were shocked to see that people who lived such good lives would risk all by defying a government and army that appeared invincible—and, in fact, was their own government and army.

Calls for support like the one written by "A Freeman" went a long way to helping Americans understand that they could do better, and to inspiring them to take action.

The next year, 1776, was a difficult and tumultuous one.

American soldiers, lacking clothes, food, shelter, ammunition, leadership, and pay, deserted by the thousands. General Washington and his staff made fatal blunders and lost major battles in and around New York City. A movement to fire him escalated. The Revolution was poised to collapse. Thomas Paine had already inspired American patriotism in his pamphlet *Common Sense*. Once again he took up his pen; *The American Crisis* appeared on the streets two days before Christmas 1776. Its impact was immediate and profound; its stirring opening echoes down through the ages to us today.

> These are the times that try men's souls. The summer
> soldier and the sunshine patriot will, in this crisis,
> shrink from the service of his country; but he that
> stands it now, deserves the love and thanks of man and
> woman. Tyranny, like hell, is not easily conquered; yet
> we have this consolation with us, that the harder the
> conflict, the more glorious the triumph.[2]

Today, we have arrived at a similar moment in history. Our own government, in alliance with the big corporations and banks, has created an empire that brings servitude, misery, and death to millions of people. As a result, we who reside within the walls of the empire find ourselves living in constant fear of those who claim the right to defend themselves against what they view as tyranny; we are terrified of suicide bombers, airplane hijackers, and even neighbors hailing from different ethnic backgrounds. We worry about the consequences of sending our young men and women into places like Iraq and Afghanistan where their lives are in danger and they run the risk of killing innocent civilians. We question the morality of prison camps operated by our military in far-off lands. We suspect that our soldiers are involved in torture, rape, and pillage; we fret about the impacts this war will have on their psyches, as well as on world opinion.

Many of us are guilty of being sunshine patriots. We know that service to our country is not simply a matter of joining the military or blindly supporting foreign interventions and other policies that favor the corporatocracy; we understand that true patriotism demands that we take action in defense of the principles so eloquently expressed in our most revered documents, those forged by our Founding Fathers. Loyalty requires that we stand, like American men and women during the Revolution, to oppose the tyranny of empire. Service to our country commands us to take actions that will deserve "the love and thanks of man and woman" for generations to come, actions that will lead to a more equitable, and therefore peaceful, world. Yet still we defer, we bask in the sunshine of the illusory benefits empire has brought to our shores.

As I traveled across the United States after the publication of *Confessions*, I found people who teetered on the edge of what I came to think of as a modern revolution. I heard them express outrage at our leaders. They recognized a truth that the mainstream press, politicians, and corporate executives are determined to ignore: that Iraq and Afghanistan—and Iran and Venezuela and all the other members of the "Evil Axis"—are not the real problem; the events in those and so many other countries are merely symptoms of a system that, like the British Empire in the 1770s, has run amok. People throughout the land understand that the real problem is a corporatocracy that has grown so selfish and greedy and so entrenched that it threatens the security of the United States and indeed the very survival of our species and many other life-forms.

In forum after forum and in emails and letters, I heard questions that were deeply disturbing because of what they had to say about the United States and attitudes toward her. Since I suspect that many readers have similar questions, I offer a sample of some of the most frequently asked ones and my responses below.

How come you're still alive? Aren't you afraid that a jackal will silence you?

Listen closely to this question. Nothing in *Confessions* is seditious. I am a loyal American whose forefathers fought in most of our major wars including the Revolution. I wrote this book because I believe we are a great nation and that we can do much better than to continue building an empire that is hated by millions. I hoped I would inspire us to improve ourselves and the world our children will inherit. Does that provide grounds for a jackal to come after me? If you believe it does, then you have a responsibility to do something. You must take action. While I have received a few angry letters, I try not to fear reprisal by the jackals. I know that I must focus on creating a better world for my daughter and her brothers and sisters around the planet. The fear that we will not create such a world far outweighs my occasional temptation to fear reprisals. I also hope that the jackals are smart enough to know that the book is already out, and that killing me would sell millions more copies.

Have other EHMs stepped forward?

Yes, several EHMs and jackals have contacted me since the publication of *Confessions*. They've shared their own extraordinary stories about recent events in the Middle East, Latin America, and Africa. Many of them are still connected to the EHM or jackal business—either actively employed or tied in through pensions and retirement funds, or as consultants—and are reluctant to be named. At least one appears ready to write his own book, under his own name.

What reaction, if any, have you received from your former associates at MAIN?

I've heard from quite a few. Most of these were either employees of mine or other people who, as I described in Chapters 9 and 23, were not aware of the EHM aspects of our business. They have confided that reading my story has helped them better understand things that went on at MAIN that seemed odd and inexplicable to them at the time. Some of those who were named in the book and others who were in positions to know have been hounded by journalists and—as I would expect—have refused to comment. The exception is Einar Greve, the man who recruited me. After leaving MAIN Einar became president of Tucson Electric Power Co. and since has retired. He recently granted an interview to the *Tucson Citizen*; the article states:

> "Basically his story is true," Greve said. . . . "What
> John's book says is, there was a conspiracy to put all
> these countries on the hook, and that happened. . . .
> Many of these countries are still over the barrel and
> have never been able to repay the loans."[3]

This is similar to what Einar had communicated to me in a letter. He also disclosed that he was considering writing his own book on this subject. Several journalists told me that after that article appeared Einar made statements that seemed to contradict his earlier comments about my book. This begged the question: What happened to Einar after the *Tucson Citizen* interview was published?

How about other people in high places? Are any of them speaking out about EHMs?

Yes, many insiders have written about the things I exposed in *Confessions*. In fact, every major event discussed in my book is confirmed by other sources—from Torrijos's assassination to JECOR's Saudia Arabian Money-laundering Affair. The major difference is that while most of the other authors were executives at the top of their establishments who wrote academic analyses on these subjects, I was a soldier in the trenches; mine is a personal, first-person account. Here are several examples of "confessions" published since 9/11 by people who sat at the top of the pyramid:

- Joseph Stiglitz, former Chief Economist of the World Bank and winner of the Nobel Prize in Economics: "Globalization, as it has been advocated, often seems to replace the old dictatorships of national elites with new dictatorships of international finance. . . . To make its [the IMF's] programs *seem* to work, to make the numbers 'add up,' economic forecasts have to be adjusted. . . . GDP forecasts are not based on a sophisticated statistical model, or even on the best estimates of those who know the economy well, but are merely the numbers that have been *negotiated* as part of an IMF program" (emphasis provided in the original).[4]

- James Henry, former economist for McKinsey & Co. and VP for IBM/Lotus: "The 1970s had been the heyday of the 'big project' paradigm for economic development. Officials from institutions like the World Bank, the Inter-American Development Bank (IDB), the Asian Development Bank (ADB), and the U.S. Agency for International Development (USAID) roamed the globe, making huge project loans and preaching the virtues of sophisticated development-planning techniques. . . . By 1990, developing countries had accumulated more than $1.3 trillion in foreign debt. . . . In 2000, eighty-six percent of the US EXIM Bank's $7.7 billion in new foreign export credits and guarantees went to just ten politically influential U.S. companies, including Enron, Halliburton, GE, Boeing, Bechtel, United Technologies, Schlumberger, and Raytheon."[5]

- Jeffrey D. Sachs, director of the Earth Institute at Columbia University and Special Adviser to United Nations Secretary-General Kofi Annan: "More than eight million people around the world die each year because they are too poor to stay alive. . . . The $450 billion the United States will spend this year on the military will never buy peace if it continues to spend around one thirtieth of that, just $15 billion, to address the plight of the world's poorest of the poor, whose societies are destabilized by extreme poverty and thereby become havens of unrest, violence, and even global terrorism."[6]

Why did you not discuss the Clinton Administration in Confessions?
During the 1990s I was running a nonprofit organization, taking groups into the Amazon, and being paid as a "consultant" who did very little except to keep quiet. For me it was a very different time from the 1980s when, as CEO of an energy company, I was very aware of what was going on with the first Bush Administration and George W.'s oil interests. Clinton and I had nothing to do with each other. I did watch with great interest the way the corporatocracy went after him and Hillary during his first term; it seemed like warning shots fired across the bow, and, in fact, those warning shots brought many of Clinton's promised programs to a halt. Later, I had to wonder what he had done to convince them to bring Monica out into the public—after all, they have plenty of "negatives" to expose on all leaders, but only do so when the need arises. But since I was out of the loop, had no inside information, and could only speculate like everyone else, there was nothing for me to confess—or that might enlighten others—about Clinton.

Is the current move to forgive Third World debt an indication that the EHMs are losing?
On the contrary, I'm sorry to have to say that it shows a new level of sophistication on the part of the EHMs. I certainly favor the idea of forgiving those debts—which, we must remember, were accumulated without the consent of the majority of the people in those countries and served to make the corporatocracy and a few wealthy Third World families even richer—but debt-forgiveness is not what this is all about. The G8 (the United States, the United Kingdom, Canada, France, Germany, Italy, Japan, and Russia), the World Bank, and the IMF are once again exploiting these nations and they are calling it "debt forgiveness." They are insisting

on "conditionalities" that are cloaked in phrases like "good governance," "sound economics," and "trade liberalization." While the language is enticing, it is also terribly deceptive. These policies are "good" and "sound" only if you are looking at them through corporate windows. The countries that agree to such conditionalities are called upon to privatize their health, education, electric, water, and other public services—in other words, sell them to the corporatocracy. They are forced to drop subsidies and trade restrictions that support local businesses while at the same time accepting that the U.S. and other G8 countries can continue to subsidize certain G8 businesses and erect trade barriers on imports that threaten G8 industries.

When Bolivia gave in to such "good governance" policies, it opened the door for multinationals to privatize its water supply system; prices of water skyrocketed and Bolivians claimed that service was suspended to thousands of people.[7] In Côte d'Ivoire, the French firm that bought the assets of the privatized telephone company reportedly raised prices so high that many people had to forego connections to the system, including university students who could not afford Internet access essential for their studies.[8] In Tanzania, these policies led to the appalling situation where children have to pay to go to school and many are simply too poor to do so.[9] Similar stories abound in the countries that have accepted the conditionalities that come as a prerequisite to what is being toted as debt forgiveness.

One of the shocking things about this new sham is that so many people seem willing to accept it, rather than seeing it for what it truly is—an EHM ploy and the latest and perhaps most subtle step along the road to world empire.

The Third World, however, is conscious of what is going on— and they are angry. The resistance to the July 2005 G8 meetings in Scotland was, to a large degree, an expression of anger against the deceptions. Many people believed that Blair and Bush were simply playing "good guy, bad guy" in an attempt to legitimatize a highly exploitative system that is balanced heavily in favor of multinational corporations at the expense of the poor, downtrodden, and starving around the world.

When will we in the U.S.—which is the coach and captain of the G8 corporatocracy team—demand that our leaders 'fess up to their lies? When will we admit to the deeper truth behind 9/11, the Madrid and London bombings, and so many other acts of violence—that they may be the acts of fanatical murderers but that they continue to happen only because millions of people are desperate and are silently applauding? When will someone point the finger and say "Look, the emperor isn't wearing any clothes?"

Can you please comment on Paul Wolfowitz's appointment as president of the World Bank?
Wolfowitz's appointment left no doubt—if any ever existed—that it is not a world bank. It is a U.S. bank. The president of the United States chooses its president and controls its major decisions. It really doesn't matter what I think of Wolfovitz as a person or manager. The important question should be: what do the Brazilians, Nigerians, Indonesians, and others around the world think of him? If it were a world bank, selection of its president, along with all major decisions, would be the responsibility of a board comprised of representatives from all continents.

What advice can you give me? What can I do to change this situation?
I offer a number of suggestions in the last chapter of *Confessions*. To do more than that—to tell you specifically what YOU should do—would be to follow in the corporatocracy's footsteps and say, "Here, this is my product; buy my silver bullet." That isn't an answer that will work—in fact, there is no single answer.

We each have our own interests, abilities, and skills. I'm a writer. As such, there is a great deal I can do. But it is different from what a teacher, corporate lawyer, massage therapist, or car mechanic has to offer. You must ask yourself: What am I interested in doing? Where are my strengths and weaknesses? What speaks to my heart?

One of the great strengths of the American Revolution was that it utilized the individual skills of many diverse people. Tom Paine wrote, but did not try to lead armies. George Washington led armies and did not write pamphlets. Benjamin Franklin, in his seventies, was an incredibly successful envoy to our French-speaking potential allies. Frontier hunters became sharpshooters. Fishermen sailed ships that harassed the British fleet. Women sent clothes and food to the battlefront. Children molded shot for soldiers' guns.

If you are a teacher, challenge your students to read between the lines of history and of the statements made in today's newspapers. If you are a corporate lawyer, guide your clients into becoming more environmentally and socially responsible. If you are a message therapist or a car mechanic, ask your clients how they feel about a current event in the news. Starting a dialogue is one of the easiest and most effective ways to spread the ideas of change.

One thing we each can—and must—do is to educate ourselves and those around us. Democracy is based on an educated populace—not just one that is able to read and write but also a people who constantly ask important questions. We must be skeptical of our leaders, corporate executives, and our press; we must insist that they provide us with information. We all need to read between the lines.

These questions and the exchanges that often follow during my public engagements or on call-in radio shows have convinced me that millions of people in the United States are deeply concerned about what we are doing and how our lifestyles impact the world. They are concerned and—like hundreds of millions around the planet—they are angry.

Since the original publication of *Confessions*, the role of the corporatocracy—along with its greed and its willingness to kill its own people, as well as those it calls "enemy"—has become more apparent to more people on every continent, including North America. With this changing consciousness comes a greater responsibility for us all to speak out and to take whatever actions are appropriate for each of us as an individual and a member of the world community.

These are the times that try men's souls. We will be faced with increasing acts of desperation by those who feel cheated and oppressed by the corporatocracy. Whether terrorism occurs in Manhattan, Madrid, London, Riyadh, or La Paz, it is essential that we understand that in the long-term these horrible acts will not be stopped by the military or by security guards in airports and along our borders. They will only be stopped when enough of us demand that our corporations, banks, and governments cease to exploit the majority of the world's population and resources and when we insist on dealing with the world from a place of compassion—the very place envisioned by our Founding Fathers when they wrote:

> We hold these truths to be self-evident, that all men are created equal, that they are endowed by their Creator with certain unalienable rights, that among these are life, liberty, and the pursuit of happiness . . . that whenever any form of government becomes destructive of these ends, it is the right of the people to alter or to abolish it, and to institute new government, laying its foundation on such principles and organizing its powers in such form, as to them shall seem most likely to effect their safety and happiness.

1963	Graduates prep school, enters Middlebury College.
1964	Befriends Farhad, son of an Iranian general. Drops out of Middlebury.
1965	Works for Hearst newspapers in Boston.
1966	Enters Boston University College of Business Administration.
1967	Marries former Middlebury classmate, whose "Uncle Frank" is a top-echelon executive at the National Security Agency (NSA).
1968	Profiled by the NSA as an ideal economic hit man. With Uncle Frank's blessing, joins the Peace Corps and is assigned to the Ecuadorian Amazon, where ancient indigenous tribes battle U.S. oil companies.
1969	Lives in the rain forest and the Andes. Experiences firsthand the deceitful and destructive practices employed by oil companies and government agencies, and their negative impacts on local cultures and environments.
1970	In Ecuador, meets vice president of international consulting firm MAIN, who is also an NSA liaison officer.
1971	Joins MAIN, undergoes training in Boston as an economic hit man (EHM), and is sent as part of an eleven-man team to Java, Indonesia.
1972	Due to willingness to "cooperate," is promoted to chief economist and is viewed as a "whiz kid."

Meets important leaders, including World Bank president Robert McNamara. Sent on special assignment to Panama. Befriended by Panamanian president and charismatic leader, Omar Torrijos; learns about history of U.S. imperialism and Torrijos's determination to transfer Canal ownership from the United States to Panama.

1973   Career skyrockets. Builds empire within MAIN; continues work in Panama; travels extensively and conducts studies in Asia, Latin America, and the Middle East.

1974   Instrumental in initiating a huge EHM success in Saudi Arabia. Royal family agrees to invest billions of dollars of oil income in U.S. securities and to allow the U.S. Department of the Treasury to use the interest from those investments to hire U.S. firms to build power and water systems, highways, ports, and cities in the kingdom. In exchange, the United States guarantees that the royal family will continue to rule. This will serve as a model for future EHM deals, including one that ultimately fails in Iraq.

1975   Promoted again—to youngest partner in MAIN's one hundred–year history—and named manager of Economics and Regional Planning. Publishes series of influential papers; lectures at Harvard and other institutions.

1976   Heads major projects around the world, in Africa, Asia, Latin America, North America, and the Middle East. Learns from the shah of Iran a revolutionary approach to EHM empire building.

1977   Due to personal relationships in Colombia, becomes exposed to the plight of farmers who are

branded as communist terrorists and drug traffickers, but are in fact peasants trying to protect
their families and homes.

1978   Rushed out of Iran by Farhad. Together, they fly to
the Rome home of Farhad's father, an Iranian general, who predicts the shah's imminent ouster and
blames U.S. policy, corrupt leaders, and despotic governments for the hatred sweeping the Middle East.
He warns that if the United States does not become
more compassionate, the situation will deteriorate.

1979   The shah flees his country and Iranians storm the
U.S. Embassy, taking fifty-two hostages. Realizes
that the United States is a nation laboring to deny
the truth about its imperialist role in the world.
After years of tension and frequent separations,
divorces first wife.

1980   Suffers from deep depression, guilt, and the realization that money and power have trapped him at
MAIN. Quits.

1981   Ecuador's president Jaime Roldós (who has cam-
paigned on an anti-oil platform) and Panama's
Omar Torrijos (who has incurred the wrath of
powerful Washington interests, due to his positions on the Panama Canal and U.S. military
bases) die in fiery airplane crashes that have all
the markings of CIA assassinations. Marries for
the second time, to a woman whose father is chief
architect at Bechtel Corporation and is in charge
of designing and building cities in Saudi Arabia—
work financed through the 1974 EHM deal.

1982   Creates Independent Power Systems Inc. (IPS), a
company committed to producing environmentally friendly electricity. Fathers Jessica.

1983–1989	Succeeds spectacularly as IPS CEO, with much help from "coincidences" — people in high places, tax breaks, etc. As a father, frets over world crises and former EHM role. Begins writing a tell-all book, but is offered a lucrative consultants' retainer on the condition that he not write the book.
1990–1991	Following the U.S. invasion of Panama and imprisonment of Noriega, sells IPS and retires at forty-five. Contemplates book about life as an EHM, but instead is persuaded to direct energies toward creating a nonprofit organization, an effort which, he is told, would be negatively impacted by such a book.
1992–2000	Watches the EHM failures in Iraq that result in the first Gulf War. Three times starts to write the EHM book, but instead is persuaded not to. Tries to assuage conscience by writing books about indigenous peoples, supporting nonprofit organizations, teaching at New Age forums, traveling to the Amazon and the Himalayas, meeting with the Dalai Lama, etc.
2001–2002	Leads a group of North Americans deep into the Amazon, and is there with an indigenous tribe on September 11, 2001. Spends a day at Ground Zero and commits to exposing the truth behind EHMs.
2003–2004	Returns to the Ecuadorian Amazon to meet with the indigenous tribes who have threatened war against the oil companies; writes *Confessions of an Economic Hit Man*.

⊕ NOTES

Preface

1. The United Nations World Food Programme, http://www.wfp.org/
   index.asp?section=1 (accessed December 27, 2003). In addition, the
   National Association for the Prevention of Starvation estimates that
   "Every day 34,000 children under five die of hunger or preventable diseases resulting from hunger" (http://www.napsoc.org, accessed December 27, 2003). Starvation.net estimates that "if we were to add the next
   two leading ways (after starvation) the poorest of the poor die, water-
   borne diseases and AIDS, we would be approaching a daily body count
   of 50,000 deaths" (http://www.starvation.net, accessed December 27,
   2003).

2. U.S. Department of Agriculture findings, reported by the Food Research
   and Action Center (FRAC), http://www.frac.org (accessed December 27,
   2003).

3. United Nations. *Human Development Report.* (New York: United Nations, 1999).

4. "In 1998, the United Nations Development Program estimated that it
   would cost an additional $9 billion (above current expenditures) to pro-
   vide clean water and sanitation for everyone on earth. It would cost an
   additional $12 billion, they said, to cover reproductive health services for
   all women worldwide. Another $13 billion would be enough not only to
   give every person on earth enough food to eat but also basic health care.
   An additional $6 billion could provide basic education for all . . . Com-
   bined they add up to $40 billion."—John Robbins, author of *Diet for a
   New America* and *The Food Revolution*, http://www.foodrevolution.org
   (accessed December 27, 2003).

Prologue

1. Gina Chavez et al., *Tarimiat—Firmes en Nuestro Territorio: FIPSE vs.
   ARCO*, eds. Mario Melo and Juana Sotomayor (Quito, Ecuador: CDES
   and CONAIE, 2002).

2. Sandy Tolan, "Ecuador: Lost Promises," National Public Radio, *Morning Edition,* July 9, 2003, http://www.npr.org/programs/morning/features/2003/jul/latinoil (accessed July 9, 2003).

3. Juan Forero, "Seeking Balance: Growth vs. Culture in the Amazon," *New York Times,* December 10, 2003.

4. Abby Ellin, "Suit Says ChevronTexaco Dumped Poisons in Ecuador," *New York Times,* May 8, 2003.

5. Chris Jochnick, "Perilous Prosperity," *New Internationalist,* June 2001, http://www.newint.org/issue335/perilous.htm. For more extensive information, see also Pamela Martin, *The Globalization of Contentious Politics: The Amazonian Indigenous Rights Movement* (New York: Rutledge, 2002); Kimerling, *Amazon Crude* (New York: Natural Resource Defense Council, 1991); Leslie Wirpsa, trans., *Upheaval in the Back Yard: Illegitimate Debts and Human Rights—The Case of Ecuador-Norway* (Quito, Ecuador: Centro de Derechos Económicos y Sociales, 2002); and Gregory Palast, "Inside Corporate America," *Guardian,* October 8, 2000.

6. For information about the impact of oil on national and global economies, see Michael T. Klare, *Resource Wars: The New Landscape of Global Conflict* (New York: Henry Holt and Company, 2001); Daniel Yergin, *The Prize: The Epic Quest for Oil, Money & Power* (New York: Free Press, 1993); and Daniel Yergin and Joseph Stanislaw, *The Commanding Heights: The Battle for the World Economy* (New York: Simon & Schuster, 2001).

7. James S. Henry, "Where the Money Went," *Across the Board,* March/April 2004, pp 42–45. For more information, see Henry's book *The Blood Bankers: Tales from the Global Underground Economy* (New York: Four Walls Eight Windows, 2003).

8. Gina Chavez et al., *Tarimiat—Firmes en Nuestro Territorio: FIPSE vs. ARCO,* eds. Mario Melo and Juana Sotomayor (Quito, Ecuador: CDES and CONAIE, 2002); *Petróleo, Ambiente y Derechos en la Amazonía Centro Sur,* Editión Víctor López A, Centro de Derechos Económicos y Sociales, OPIP, IACYT-A (under the auspices of Oxfam America) (Quito, Ecuador: Sergrafic, 2002).

9. Sandy Tolan, "Ecuador: Lost Promises," National Public Radio, *Morning Edition,* July 9, 2003, http://www.npr.org/programs/morning/features/2003/jul/latinoil (accessed July 9, 2003).

10. For more on the jackals and other types of hit men, see P. W. Singer, *Corporate Warriors: The Rise of the Privatized Military Industry*

(Ithaca, NY and London: Cornell University Press, 2003); James R. Davis, *Fortune's Warriors: Private Armies and the New World Order* (Vancouver and Toronto: Douglas & McIntyre, 2000); Felix I. Rodriguez and John Weisman, *Shadow Warrior: The CIA Hero of 100 Unknown Battles* (New York: Simon and Schuster, 1989).

Chapter 2. "In for Life"

1. For a detailed account of this fateful operation, see Stephen Kinzer, *All the Shah's Men: An American Coup and the Roots of Middle East Terror* (Hoboken, NJ: John Wiley & Sons, Inc., 2003).

2. Jane Mayer, "Contract Sport: What Did the Vice-President Do for Halliburton?", *New Yorker*, February 16 and 23, 2004, p 83.

Chapter 3. Indonesia: Lessons for an EHM

1. For more on Indonesia and its history, see Jean Gelman Taylor, *Indonesia: Peoples and Histories* (New Haven and London: Yale University Press, 2003); and Theodore Friend, *Indonesian Destinies* (Cambridge MA and London: The Belknap Press of Harvard University, 2003).

Chapter 6. My Role as Inquisitor

1. Theodore Friend, *Indonesian Destinies* (Cambridge, MA and London: The Belknap Press of Harvard University, 2003), p 5.

Chapter 10. Panama's President and Hero

1. See David McCullough, *The Path Between the Seas: The Creation of the Panama Canal 1870–1914* (New York: Simon and Schuster, 1999); William Friar, *Portrait of the Panama Canal: From Construction to the Twenty-First Century* (New York: Graphic Arts Publishing Company, 1999); Graham Greene, *Conversations with the General* (New York: Pocket Books, 1984).

2. See "Zapata Petroleum Corp.", *Fortune*, April 1958, p 248; Darwin Payne, *Initiative in Energy: Dresser Industries, Inc. 1880–1978* (New York: Simon and Schuster, 1979); Steve Pizzo et al., *Inside Job: The Looting of America's Savings and Loans* (New York: McGraw Hill, 1989); Gary Webb, *Dark Alliance: The CIA, The Contras, and the Crack Cocaine Explosion* (New York: Seven Stories Press, 1999); Gerard Colby and Charlotte Dennet, *Thy Will Be Done, The Conquest of the Amazon: Nelson Rockefeller and Evangelism in the Age of Oil* (New York: HarperCollins, 1995).

3. Manuel Noriega with Peter Eisner, *The Memoirs of Manuel Noriega, America's Prisoner* (New York: Random House, 1997); Omar Torrijos Herrera, *Ideario* (Editorial Universitaria Centroamericano, 1983); Graham Greene, *Conversations with the General* (New York: Pocket Books, 1984).

4. Graham Greene, *Conversations with the General* (New York: Pocket Books, 1984); Manuel Noriega with Peter Eisner, *The Memoirs of Manuel Noriega, America's Prisoner* (New York: Random House, 1997).

5. Derrick Jensen, *A Language Older than Words* (New York: Context Books, 2000), pp 86–88.

6. Graham Greene, *Conversations with the General* (New York: Pocket Books, 1984); Manuel Noriega with Peter Eisner, *The Memoirs of Manuel Noriega, America's Prisoner* (New York: Random House, 1997).

Chapter 13. Conversations with the General

1. William Shawcross: *The Shah's Last Ride: The Fate of an Ally* (New York: Simon and Schuster, 1988); Stephen Kinzer, *All the Shah's Men: An American Coup and the Roots of Middle East Terror* (Hoboken, NJ: John Wiley & Sons, Inc., 2003), p 45.

2. A great deal has been written about Arbenz, United Fruit, and the violent history of Guatemala; see for example (my Boston University political science professor) Howard Zinn, *A People's History of the United States* (New York: Harper & Row, 1980); Diane K. Stanley, *For the Record: The United Fruit Company's Sixty-Six Years in Guatemala* (Guatemala City: Centro Impresor Piedra Santa, 1994). For quick references: "The Banana Republic: The United Fruit Company," http://www.mayaparadise.com/ufc1e.html; "CIA Involved in Guatemala Coup, 1954," http://www.english.upenn.edu/~afilreis/50s/guatemala.html. For more on the Bush family's involvement: "Zapata Petroleum Corp.," *Fortune*, April 1958, p 248.

Chapter 14. Entering a New and Sinister Period in Economic History

1. "Robert S. McNamara: 8th Secretary of Defense," http://www.defenselink.mil (accessed December 23, 2003).

Chapter 15. The Saudi Arabian Money-laundering Affair

1. For more on the events leading up to the 1973 oil embargo and the impact of the embargo, see: Thomas W. Lippman, *Inside the Mirage: America's Fragile Partnership with Saudi Arabia* (Boulder, CO: Westview Press,

2004), pp 155–159; Daniel Yergin, *The Prize: The Epic Quest for Oil, Money & Power* (New York: Free Press, 1993); Stephen Schneider, *The Oil Price Revolution* (Baltimore: Johns Hopkins University Press, 1983); Ian Seymour, *OPEC: Instrument of Change* (London: McMillan, 1980).

2. Thomas W. Lippman, *Inside the Mirage: America's Fragile Partnership with Saudi Arabia* (Boulder, CO: Westview Press, 2004), p 160.

3. David Holden and Richard Johns, *The House of Saud: The Rise and Rule of the Most Powerful Dynasty in the Arab World* (New York: Holt Rinehart and Winston, 1981), p 359.

4. Thomas W. Lippman, *Inside the Mirage: America's Fragile Partnership with Saudi Arabia* (Boulder, CO: Westview Press, 2004), p 167.

Chapter 16. Pimping, and Financing Osama bin Laden

1. Robert Baer, *Sleeping with the Devil: How Washington Sold Our Soul for Saudi Oil* (New York: Crown Publishers, 2003), p 26.

2. Thomas W. Lippman, *Inside the Mirage: America's Fragile Partnership with Saudi Arabia* (Boulder, CO: Westview Press, 2004), p 162.

3. Thomas W. Lippman, *Inside the Mirage: America's Fragile Partnership with Saudi Arabia* (Boulder, CO: Westview Press, 2004), p 2.

4. Henry Wasswa, "Idi Amin, Murderous Ugandan Dictator, Dies," Associated Press, August 17, 2003.

5. "The Saudi Connection," *U.S. News & World Report*, December 15, 2003, p 21.

6. "The Saudi Connection," *U.S. News & World Report*, December 15, 2003, pp 19, 20, 26.

7. Craig Unger, "Saving the Saudis," *Vanity Fair*, October 2003. For more on the Bush family's involvement, Bechtel, etc., see: "Zapata Petroleum Corp.," *Fortune*, April 1958, p 248; Darwin Payne, *Initiative in Energy: Dresser Industries, Inc. 1880–1978* (New York: Simon and Schuster, 1979); Nathan Vardi, "Desert Storm: Bechtel Group Is Leading the Charge," and "Contacts for Contracts," both in *Forbes*, June 23, 2003, pp 63–66; Graydon Carter, "Editor's Letter: Fly the Friendly Skies . . ." *Vanity Fair*, October 2003; Richard A. Oppel with Diana B. Henriques, "A Nation at War: The Contractor. Company has ties in Washington, and to Iraq," *New York Times*, April 18, 2003.

Chapter 17. Panama Canal Negotiations and Graham Greene

1. See for example: John M. Perkins, "Colonialism in Panama Has No Place in 1975," *Boston Evening Globe*, Op-Ed page, September 19, 1975; John

M. Perkins, "U.S.–Brazil Pact Upsets Ecuador," *The Boston Globe*, Op-Ed page, May 10, 1976.

2. For examples of papers by John Perkins published in technical journals, see: John M. Perkins et al., "A Markov Process Applied to Forecasting, Part I—Economic Development" and "A Markov Process Applied to Forecasting, Part II—The Demand for Electricity," The Institute of Electrical and Electronics Engineers, Conference Papers C 73 475-1 (July 1973) and C 74 146-7 (January 1974), respectively; John M. Perkins and Nadipuram R. Prasad, "A Model for Describing Direct and Indirect Interrelationships Between the Economy and the Environment," *Consulting Engineer*, April 1973; Edwin Vennard, John M. Perkins, and Robert C. Ender, "Electric Demand from Interconnected Systems," *TAPPI Journal* (Technical Association of the Pulp and Paper Industry), 28th Conference Edition, 1974; John M. Perkins et al., "Iranian Steel: Implications for the Economy and the Demand for Electricity" and "Markov Method Applied to Planning," presented at the Fourth Iranian Conference on Engineering, Pahlavi University, Shiraz, Iran, May 12–16, 1974; and *Economic Theories and Applications: A Collection of Technical Papers* with a Foreword by John M. Perkins (Boston: Chas. T. Main, Inc., 1975).

3. John M. Perkins, "Colonialism in Panama Has No Place in 1975," *Boston Evening Globe*, Op-Ed page, September 19, 1975.

4. Graham Greene, *Getting to Know the General* (New York: Pocket Books, 1984), pp 89–90.

5. Graham Greene, *Getting to Know the General* (New York: Pocket Books, 1984).

Chapter 18. Iran's King of Kings

1. William Shawcross, *The Shah's Last Ride: The Fate of an Ally* (New York: Simon and Schuster, 1988). For more about the Shah's rise to power, see H. D. S. Greenway, "The Iran Conspiracy," *New York Review of Books*, September 23, 2003; Stephen Kinzer, *All the Shah's Men: An American Coup and the Roots of Middle East Terror* (Hoboken, NJ: John Wiley & Sons, Inc., 2003).

2. For more about Yamin, the Flowering Desert project, and Iran, see John Perkins, *Shapeshifting* (Rochester, VT: Destiny Books, 1997).

Chapter 20. The Fall of a King

1. For more about the Shah's rise to power, see H. D. S. Greenway, "The Iran Conspiracy," *New York Review of Books*, September 23, 2003;

Stephen Kinzer, *All the Shah's Men: An American Coup and the Roots of Middle East Terror* (Hoboken, NJ: John Wiley & Sons, Inc., 2003).

2. See *TIME* magazine cover articles on the Ayatollah Ruhollah Khomeini, February 12, 1979, January 7, 1980, and August 17, 1987.

Chapter 21. Colombia: Keystone of Latin America

1. Gerard Colby and Charlotte Dennet, *Thy Will Be Done, The Conquest of the Amazon: Nelson Rockefeller and Evangelism in the Age of Oil* (New York: HarperCollins, 1995), p 381.

Chapter 24. Ecuador's President Battles Big Oil

1. For extensive details on SIL, its history, activities, and association with the oil companies and the Rockefellers, see Gerard Colby and Charlotte Dennet, *Thy Will Be Done, The Conquest of the Amazon: Nelson Rockefeller and Evangelism in the Age of Oil* (New York: HarperCollins, 1995); Joe Kane, *Savages* (New York: Alfred A. Knopf, 1995) (for information on Rachel Saint, pp 85, 156, 227).

2. John D. Martz, *Politics and Petroleum in Ecuador* (New Brunswick and Oxford: Transaction Books, 1987), p 272.

3. José Carvajal Candall, "Objetivos y Políticas de CEPE" (Quito, Ecuador: Primer Seminario, 1979), p 88.

Chapter 26. Ecuador's Presidential Death

1. John D. Martz, *Politics and Petroleum in Ecuador* (New Brunswick and Oxford: Transaction Books, 1987), p 272.

2. Gerard Colby and Charlotte Dennet: *Thy Will Be Done, The Conquest of the Amazon: Nelson Rockefeller and Evangelism in the Age of Oil* (New York, HarperCollins, 1995), p 813.

3. John D. Martz, *Politics and Petroleum in Ecuador* (New Brunswick and Oxford: Transaction Books, 1987), p 303.

4. John D. Martz, *Politics and Petroleum in Ecuador* (New Brunswick and Oxford: Transaction Books, 1987), pp 381, 400.

Chapter 27. Panama: Another Presidential Death

1. Graham Greene, *Getting to Know the General* (New York: Pocket Books, 1984), p 11.

2. George Shultz was secretary of the Treasury and chairman of the Council on Economic Policy under Nixon-Ford, 1972–1974, executive president or president of Bechtel, 1974–1982, secretary of state under

Reagan-Bush, 1982–1989; Caspar Weinberger was director of the Office of Management and Budget and secretary of Health, Education, and Welfare under Nixon-Ford, 1973–1975, vice president and general counsel of Bechtel Group, 1975–1980, secretary of defense under Reagan-Bush, 1980–1987.

3. During the 1973 Watergate hearings, in his testimony before the U.S. Senate, John Dean was the first to disclose U.S. plots to assassinate Torrijos; in 1975, at Senate inquiries into the CIA, chaired by Senator Frank Church, additional testimony and documentation of plans to kill both Torrijos and Noriega were presented. See, for example, Manuel Noriega with Peter Eisner, *The Memoirs of Manuel Noriega, America's Prisoner* (New York: Random House, 1997), p 107.

Chapter 28. My Energy Company, Enron, and George W. Bush

1. For additional information on IPS, its wholly-owned subsidiary Archbald Power Corporation, and former CEO John Perkins, see Jack M. Daly and Thomas J. Duffy, "Burning Coal's Waste at Archbald," *Civil Engineering*, July 1988; Vince Coveleskie, "Co-Generation Plant Attributes Cited," *The Scranton Times*, October 17, 1987; Robert Curran, "Archbald Facility Dedicated," *Scranton Tribune*, October 17, 1987; "Archbald Plant Will Turn Coal Waste into Power," *Citizen's Voice*, Wilkes-Barre, PA, June 6, 1988; "Liabilities to Assets: Culm to Light, Food," editorial, *Citizen's Voice*, Wilkes-Barre, PA, June 7, 1988.

2. Joe Conason, "The George W. Bush Success Story," *Harpers Magazine*, February 2000; Craig Unger, "Saving the Saudis," *Vanity Fair*, October 2003, p 165.

3. Craig Unger, "Saving the Saudis," *Vanity Fair*, October 2003, p 178.

4. See George Lardner Jr. and Lois Romano, "The Turning Point After Coming Up Dry," *Washington Post*, July 30, 1999; Joe Conason, "The George W. Bush Success Story," *Harpers Magazine*, February 2000; and Sam Parry, "The Bush Family Oiligarchy—Part Two: The Third Generation," http://www.newnetizen.com/presidential/bushoiligarchy.htm (accessed April 19, 2002).

5. This theory took on new significance and seemed ready to fall under the spotlight of public scrutiny when, years later, it became clear that the highly respected accounting firm of Arthur Andersen had conspired with Enron executives to cheat energy consumers, Enron employees, and the American public out of billions of dollars. The impending 2003 Iraq war pushed the spotlight away. During the war, Bahrain played a critical role in President George W. Bush's strategy.

Chapter 29. I Take a Bribe

1. Jim Garrison, *American Empire: Global Leader or Rogue Power?* (San Francisco: Berrett-Koehler Publishers, Inc., 2004), p 38.

Chapter 30. The United States Invades Panama

1. Manuel Noriega with Peter Eisner, *The Memoirs of Manuel Noriega, America's Prisoner* (New York: Random House, 1997), p 56.

2. David Harris, *Shooting the Moon: The True Story of an American Manhunt Unlike Any Other, Ever* (Boston: Little, Brown and Company, 2001), p 31–34.

3. David Harris, *Shooting the Moon: The True Story of an American Manhunt Unlike Any Other, Ever* (Boston: Little, Brown and Company, 2001), p 43.

4. Manuel Noriega with Peter Eisner, *The Memoirs of Manuel Noriega, America's Prisoner* (New York: Random House, 1997), p 212; see also Craig Unger, "Saving the Saudis," *Vanity Fair*, October 2003, p 165.

5. Manuel Noriega with Peter Eisner, *The Memoirs of Manuel Noriega, America's Prisoner* (New York: Random House, 1997), p 114.

6. See www.famoustexans.com/georgebush.htm, p 2.

7. Manuel Noriega with Peter Eisner, *The Memoirs of Manuel Noriega, America's Prisoner* (New York: Random House, 1997), p 56–57.

8. David Harris, *Shooting the Moon: The True Story of an American Manhunt Unlike Any Other, Ever* (Boston: Little, Brown and Company, 2001), p 6.

9. www.famoustexans.com/georgebush.htm, p 3.

10. David Harris, *Shooting the Moon: The True Story of an American Manhunt Unlike Any Other, Ever* (Boston: Little, Brown and Company, 2001), p 4.

11. Manuel Noriega with Peter Eisner, *The Memoirs of Manuel Noriega, America's Prisoner* (New York: Random House, 1997), p 248.

12. Manuel Noriega with Peter Eisner, *The Memoirs of Manuel Noriega, America's Prisoner* (New York: Random House, 1997), p 211.

13. Manuel Noriega with Peter Eisner, *The Memoirs of Manuel Noriega, America's Prisoner* (New York: Random House, 1997), p xxi.

Chapter 31. An EHM Failure in Iraq

1. Morris Barrett, "The Web's Wild World," *TIME*, April 26, 1999, p 62.

Chapter 32. September 11 and Its Aftermath for Me, Personally

1. For more about the Huaoranis, see Joe Kane, *Savages* (New York: Alfred A. Knopf, 1995).

Chapter 33. Venezuela: Saved by Saddam

1. "Venezuela on the Brink," editorial, *New York Times*, December 18, 2002.

2. *The Revolution Will Not Be Televised*, directed by Kim Bartley and Donnacha O'Briain (in association with the Irish Film Board, 2003). See www.chavezthefilm.com.

3. "Venezuelan President Forced to Resign," Associated Press, April 12, 2002.

4. Simon Romero, "Tenuous Truce in Venezuela for the State and Its Oil Company," *New York Times*, April 24, 2002.

5. Bob Edwards, "What Went Wrong with the Oil Dream in Venezuela," National Public Radio, *Morning Edition*, July 8, 2003.

6. Ginger Thompson, "Venezuela Strikers Keep Pressure on Chávez and Oil Exports," *New York Times*, December 30, 2002.

7. For more on the jackals and other types of hit men, see: P. W. Singer, *Corporate Warriors: The Rise of the Privatized Military Industry* (Ithaca, NY and London: Cornell University Press, 2003); James R. Davis, *Fortune's Warriors: Private Armies and the New World Order* (Vancouver and Toronto: Douglas & McIntyre, 2000); Felix I. Rodriguez and John Weisman, *Shadow Warrior: The CIA Hero of 100 Unknown Battles* (New York: Simon and Schuster, 1989).

8. Tim Weiner, "A Coup by Any Other Name," *New York Times*, April 14, 2002.

9. "Venezuela Leader Urges 20 Years for Strike Chiefs," *Associated Press*, February 22, 2003.

10. Paul Richter, "U.S. Had Talks on Chávez Ouster," *Los Angeles Times*, April 17, 2002.

Chapter 34. Ecuador Revisited

1. Chris Jochnick, "Perilous Prosperity," *New Internationalist*, June 2001, http://www.newint.org/issue335/perilous.htm.

2. United Nations. *Human Development Report* (New York: United Nations, 1999).

3. For additional information on the hostage situation, see Alan Zibel, "Natives Seek Redress for Pollution," *Oakland Tribune,* December 10, 2002; *Hoy* (Quito, Ecuador, daily newspaper) articles of December 10–28, 2003; "Achuar Free Eight Oil Hostages," *El Commercio* (Quito daily newspaper), December 16, 2002 (also carried by Reuters); "Ecuador: Oil Firm Stops Work because Staff Seized, Demands Government Action," and "Sarayacu—Indigenous Groups to Discuss Release of Kidnapped Oil Men," *El Universo* (Guayaquil, Ecuador, daily newspaper), http://www.eluniverso.com, December 24, 2002; and Juan Forero, "Seeking Balance: Growth vs. Culture in the Amazon," *New York Times*, December 10, 2003. Current, updated information about Ecuador's Amazonian people is available at the Pachamama Alliance Web site: http://www.pachamama.org.

Chapter 35. Piercing the Veneer

1. National debt statistics from the Bureau of the Public Debt, reported at www.publicdebt.treas.gov/opd/opdpenny.htm; national income statistics from the World Bank at www.worldbank.org/data/databytopic/GNIPC.pdf.

2. Elizabeth Becker and Richard A. Oppel, "A Nation at War: Reconstruction. U.S. Gives Bechtel a Major Contract in Rebuilding Iraq," *New York Times*, April 18, 2003, http://www.nytimes.com/2003/04/18/ international/worldspecial/18REBU.html.

3. Richard A. Oppel with Diana B. Henriques, "A Nation at War: The Contractor. Company Has Ties in Washington, and to Iraq," *New York Times*, April 18, 2003, http://www.nytimes.com/2003/04/18/ international/ worldspecial/18CONT.html.

4. http://money.cnn.com/2003/04/17/news/companies/war-bechtel/ index.htm.

What You Can Do

1. Energy Information Administration, reported in *USA Today*, March 1, 2004, p 1.

Epilogue

1. Frank Moore, *Diary of the American Revolution, I* (New York: Scribner, 1860), p 172.

2. David McCullouch, *1776* (New York: Simon & Schuster, 2005), p 41.

3. C. T. Revere, "Author: Tsunami aid may line U.S. pockets," *Tucson Citizen*, January 17, 2005, pp 1–3A.

4. Joseph E. Stiglitz, *Globalization and Its Discontents* (New York: WW Norton & Company, 2002), pp 232, 247, 248.

5. James S. Henry, *The Blood Bankers: Tales from the Global Underground Economy* (New York: Four Walls Eight Windows, 2003), pp xiii, xiv, 40.

6. Jeffrey D. Sachs, *The End of Poverty: Economic Possibilities for Our Time* (New York: The Penguin Press, 2005), p 1.

7. See "Bolivia President's Resignation Rejected," http://cnn.worldnews.com, 3/10/2005.

8. See Joseph E. Stiglitz, *Globalization and Its Discontents* (New York: WW Norton & Company, 2003), p. 56.

9. See "Nelson Mandela on G8 Summit: Overcoming Poverty Is Not a Gesture of Charity, It Is an Act of Justice," www.democracynow.org, 7/6/2005.

⊕ INDEX

Department of the Treasury and, 96

effects of Saudi Arabian deal, 108–13

electrical forecasting, 127

electrification project in Southeast Asia, 25

energy industry, position on, 194

firing of Bruno Zambotti, 170–72

folding of, 193–94

gender biases, 16

losses in Iran, 140

Manifest Destiny, 69–70, 85–86, 181–82

Markov method for econometric modeling, 118

"Martin, Claudine," xiii–xiv, 16–21, 23, 60–62

Martínez, José de Jesús (Sergeant Chuchu), 186

"Mary," 172–76

McNamara, Robert, 32, 62–63, 90–91, 196

media, 261

Memoirs of Manuel Noriega: America's Prisoner (Eisner), 209

military-industrial complex, 90–91

military support to Saudi Arabia, conditions of, 103–4

missionary groups, Summer Institute of Linguistics (SIL), 166–67

Monroe, James, 69

Monroe Doctrine, 69–70

Montesinos, Vladimiro L., 236

Mormino, Paul, 61

Mossadegh, Mohammad, 21, 82, 105, 134

Muslims, 51–52, 138–40

N

national budget/debt, Ecuador's, 239–40

National Security Agency (NSA), 7–9

nation-building programs, 142

natural resources, xxii, 216, 241–42, 244–45

New Deal policies, 90

New Hampshire Public Service Commission, 191

New York City, 223–30

Nicaragua, 236

Nixon, Richard, 49–50, 88

Noriega, Manuel, 188, 203–9, 236

nuclear power, 180, 191

O

October War, 93

off-shore drilling rights (Bahrain), 195

oil income, 95

oil industry

devastation of rain forests, 241, 244–45

George W. Bush and, 194–95

global management of petroleum, 253

guarantee of oil supplies to U.S. by Saudi Arabia, 102–3

hydrocarbons law, 182–83, 231

Indonesia, 30–31

off-shore drilling rights (Bahrain), 195

Oil Boom, xxii

oil concessions, xxiii–xxiv

oil embargos, 87–88, 93–95, 102–3, 232

oil spills, xxi

OPEC, 87–88, 127, 232, 249–50

ABOUT THE AUTHOR

R. Darrow Bernick

The author of five previous books, John Perkins currently writes and teaches about achieving peace and prosperity by expanding our personal awareness and transforming our institutions. He founded the nonprofit organization Dream Change. He lives with his wife and daughter in Florida.

For additional information, visit:

www.JohnPerkins.org
www.dreamchange.org

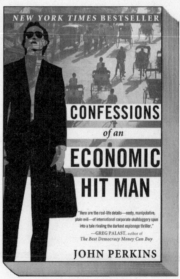